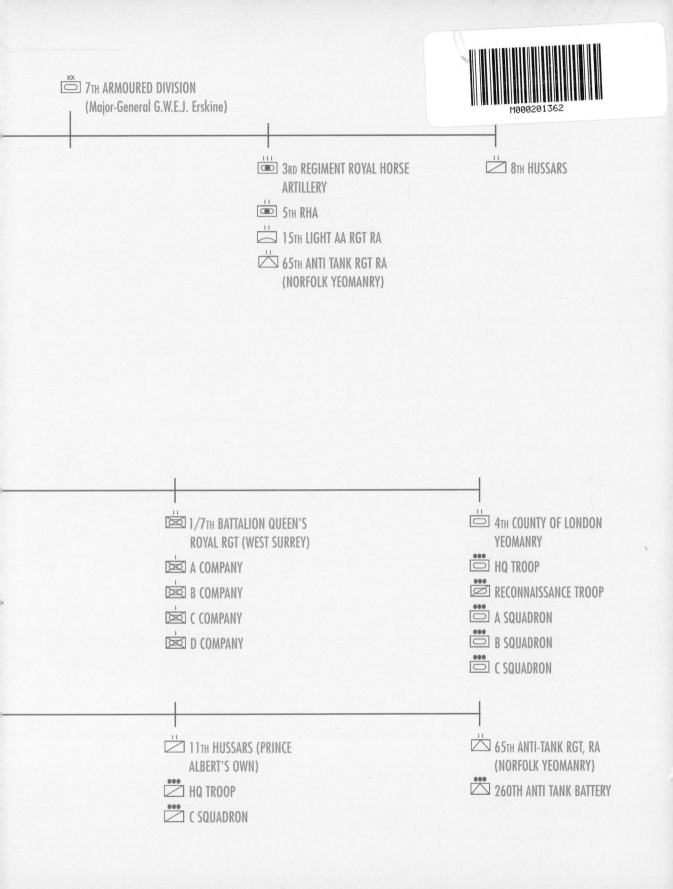

XX
7TH ARMOURED DIVISION
(Major-General G.W.E.J. Erskine)

3RD REGIMENT ROYAL HORSE ARTILLERY

5TH RHA

15TH LIGHT AA RGT RA

65TH ANTI TANK RGT RA (NORFOLK YEOMANRY)

8TH HUSSARS

1/7TH BATTALION QUEEN'S ROYAL RGT (WEST SURREY)

A COMPANY

B COMPANY

C COMPANY

D COMPANY

4TH COUNTY OF LONDON YEOMANRY

HQ TROOP

RECONNAISSANCE TROOP

A SQUADRON

B SQUADRON

C SQUADRON

11TH HUSSARS (PRINCE ALBERT'S OWN)

HQ TROOP

C SQUADRON

65TH ANTI-TANK RGT, RA (NORFOLK YEOMANRY)

260TH ANTI TANK BATTERY

VISUAL BATTLE GUIDE

7TH ARMOURED DIVISION AT VILLERS-BOCAGE

7TH ARMOURED DIVISION AT VILLERS-BOCAGE
13 JUNE 1944

DAVID PORTER

amber
BOOKS

This edition first published in 2012

Published by
Amber Books Ltd
Bradley's Close
74–77 White Lion Street
London N1 9PF
United Kingdom
www.amberbooks.co.uk

ISBN: 978-1-908273-77-2

Project Editor: Michael Spilling
Design: Hawes Design
Picture Research: Terry Forshaw

Printed in China

CONTENTS

Chapter 1
The Normandy Campaign: Plans and Reality

During summer 1944, the Allies intended to mount Operation 'Overlord', the amphibious assault on the German-occupied coast of Normandy. This was a colossal task in that it involved assaulting a heavily defended enemy coastline and then defeating in battle some of the best German divisions from one of the finest military machines the world has ever seen, battle hardened from over four years of war.

To achieve success in this undertaking the Allies had, amongst other things, to: formulate an excellent multifaceted invasion plan; undertake vast amounts of incredibly detailed staff-work to realize this plan; create a coherent Allied integrated coalition command hierarchy; and soften up the enemy with preliminary aerial bombing. It is these plans and preparations that this chapter examines.

OPPOSITE: British infantry practise assault tactics in the preparations for the invasion of France sometime in 1943. Nearly 160,000 troops crossed the English Channel on D-Day, while more than three million troops were in France by the end of August 1944.

Allied Plans

One of the most challenging aspects of mounting successfully the D-Day landings was developing appropriate plans and enacting all the preparations required to realize them.

The Allied plans for the D-Day landings were code-named Operation 'Neptune' (for the naval aspects) and Operation 'Overlord' (for the ground/air aspects). Detailed Allied planning began in 1943 but did not obtain final gear until January 1944. On 1 February, the Allies published the '"Neptune" Initial Joint Plan', the cornerstone planning framework for the landings. This document stated that the Allied intention was to launch a simultaneous amphibious and airborne assault on the Normandy coast as the

Allied air attacks on German coastal positions were carefully orchestrated so that they would not give any indication of where the main landings were taking place. For every one attack on Normandy there were two others on coastal positions elsewhere. This photograph shows wrecked defences near the port of Cherbourg.

first step to securing, in the area between the Rivers Loire and Seine, a large lodgement area as a base for future operations.

The plan for D-Day itself envisaged that under the cover of darkness a vast armada of Allied warships and troop transports, with 130,000 soldiers embarked, would cross the English Channel. Once these forces had approached the coastline, these fleets would drop anchor opposite the five designated invasion beaches and commence their preliminary bombardments; from west to east, these beaches were code-named 'Utah', 'Omaha', 'Gold', 'Juno' and 'Sword'. By the time that the five Allied amphibious assaults had begun shortly after dawn, the bulk of three Allied airborne divisions would already have been landed behind enemy lines and begun to secure the invasion sector's flanks.

After the initial Allied amphibious assault forces had successfully established their five beachheads during that first morning, follow-up forces would land and thrust deeper inland, aiming to begin the process of linking up the beachheads. The plans stated that by the end of D-Day, the Allied advance would have captured the key towns of Caen and Bayeux, and consolidated the four eastern beachheads and the British airborne zone into a single 62.8km (39-mile) wide salient. To facilitate these efforts, three armoured brigades would simultaneously race 24.14km (15 miles) inland and seize three key road junctions, including Villers-Bocage; these risky advances were designed to block any German armoured reserves from pushing forward towards the coast to launch counter-attacks against the still-vulnerable Allied beachheads.

ATTACKING THE INFRASTRUCTURE

Before the Allies could execute these plans, however, a number of preparatory efforts had to be addressed. One prerequisite for the successful execution of 'Overlord' was an effective bombing campaign of Normandy and the rest of France. It was essential that the Allies hamper the Germans' capacity both to redeploy reserve forces and reinforcements to the invasion zone and to resupply those already there with the ammunition, petrol and rations they required to resist Allied operations.

The Allies achieved this aim during the first half of 1944 by undertaking an intensive aerial interdiction effort against the railway and road networks in France. By targeting marshalling yards, signalling infrastructure, junctions, railway bridges, track, locomotives and rolling stock, Allied bombing comprehensively destroyed the French railway system. At the same time, Allied bombers attacked the road network, military supply depots and their associated infrastructure, as well as ports and military units deployed in barracks or in the field. The result achieved by this mammoth Allied effort was considerable.

As a result of this bombing, during the six days following the D-Day landings, not a single German military resupply train reached the Normandy area, while 5000 German military trains remained trapped somewhere along their journeys due to the damage caused by aerial bombing, as well as by sabotage undertaken by the French Resistance. Indeed, throughout the Normandy battle, the Germans were never able to deliver sufficient supplies and reinforcements to the front; this helped facilitate Allied victory. The scale of this Allied interdiction campaign had to be immense: so as not to identify Normandy as the intended landing zone, the Allies were compelled to attack targets through all of France, as well as in Belgium and Holland.

COMMAND AND CONTROL

Another prerequisite for the successful execution of the D-Day landings was the creation of an appropriate integrated coalition senior command hierarchy that could effectively wield the various American, Canadian, British, French, Polish and other national contingents in a combined multinational campaign effort. The Supreme Headquarters Allied Expeditionary Force (SHAEF), established on 12 February 1944, was a multinational inter-service military headquarters. The Supreme Allied Commander, the American General Dwight Eisenhower, led SHAEF. Eisenhower's British deputy, Air Chief Marshal Sir Arthur Tedder, coordinated the heavy bombing campaign slated to support 'Overlord'.

Below Tedder came the three theatre service commanders, all of whom were British: Admiral Bertram Ramsay, Air Chief Marshal Trafford Leigh-Mallory and General Bernard Montgomery ('Monty'), who commanded the 21st Army Group. In addition to controlling all the British and Canadian ground forces involved in 'Overlord', Montgomery temporarily acted as the theatre land commander, thus also controlling Lieutenant-General Omar Bradley's First US Army (FUSA). Under Montgomery's direction, the forces of Lieutenant-General Miles Dempsey's Second (British) Army and Bradley's FUSA would assault the German coastal defences in the eastern and western invasion sectors, respectively. In the west, Lieutenant-General Collins' US VII Corps would assault Utah Beach while Lieutenant-General Gerow's US V Corps would land on Omaha Beach. In the east, meanwhile, Lieutenant-General John Crocker's I (British) Corps would land on Sword and Juno Beaches, while Lieutenant-General Gerard Bucknall's XXX Corps would assault Gold Beach.

On 8 May 1944, Eisenhower decided to schedule the D-Day landings for 5 June, one of the few days in that month with both acceptable tidal conditions (for avoiding beach obstacles) and good moonlight (for the airborne drops). One factor that could not be predicted, however, was the weather on the 5th. During 2–3 June the naval bombardment flotillas headed south from the Scottish ports, but on 4 June deteriorating weather forced Eisenhower to postpone the attack to the 6th. Those soldiers already embarked thus had to spend an unpleasant night aboard rolling transport vessels. If continuing bad weather had forced the Allies to postpone the

invasion beyond 7 June, however, they would have had to wait two more weeks before the conditions required for a landing recurred. This was a dangerous delay given that the Germans were then rapidly strengthening their defences in Normandy. The storm grew worse during the night of 4–5 June, but Allied meteorologists then predicted somewhat less bad conditions for 6 June. At 04:00 hours on 5 June Eisenhower courageously decided to initiate the invasion on 6 June despite the poor weather. Within minutes, Allied shipping began to move into its pre-designated assembly areas off the southern coast of England. The D-Day landings had begun.

Interdiction Bombing of Northern France, May–August 1944

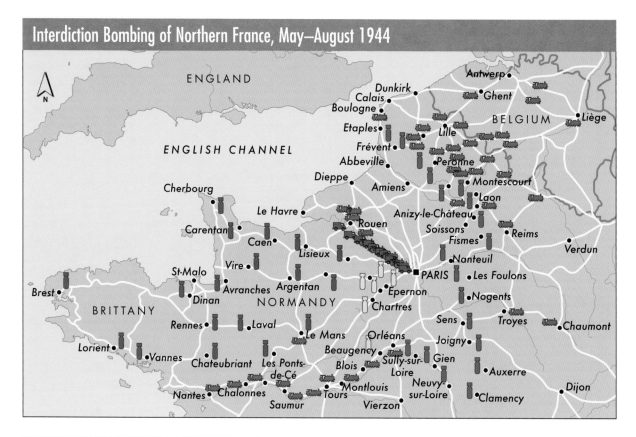

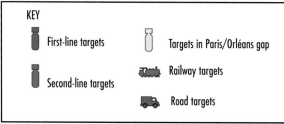

KEY

🔲 First-line targets

🔲 Targets in Paris/Orléans gap

🔲 Second-line targets

🚂 Railway targets

🚚 Road targets

The heavy Allied bombing of the infrastructure of northern France and the Low Countries meant that during the week following the D-Day landings, not a single German military resupply train reached the Normandy area, while 5000 German military trains were trapped on the rail lines due to the damage caused by aerial bombing. Throughout the Normandy battle, the Germans were never able to deliver sufficient supplies and reinforcements to the front, which helped facilitate the Allied victory.

German Dispositions

Facing the five slated Allied D-Day amphibious assault beach sectors along the Normandy coast were the defending forces from General Erich Marcks' LXXXIV Corps.

In spring 1944, all of the German military forces located in France and the Low Countries nominally came under the tri-service authority of the Supreme Command West, which was led by the elderly Field Marshal Gerd von Rundstedt. In theory, von Rundstedt exercised command authority over both the German naval and air force commands in the theatre as well as the ground troops, although in reality the former two services enjoyed considerable autonomy. Admiral Kranke's Naval High Command West controlled numerous small surface vessels and

German gunners backfill sand and soil around the concrete gun pit of a 15cm (5.9in) K18 gun in a coastal artillery position. The position is camouflaged with turf around the base and a netting frame suspended over the gun.

40 U-boats, but no capital ships, as well as many dozen naval coastal artillery batteries. General Sperrle's beleaguered III Air Fleet meanwhile had only a few hundred planes to defend French airspace against thousands of Allied aircraft.

Gerd von Rundstedt's ground forces came under the authority of three separate principal subordinate commands. Army Group B, commanded by Field Marshal Erwin Rommel – the 'Desert Fox' – controlled Belgium and all of northern France. Army Group G was led by Colonel-General Johannes Blaskowitz and controlled all of southern France. Finally, the independent German LXXXVIII Corps controlled most of the Netherlands, reporting directly to von Rundstedt's

headquarters. These three commands between them controlled 58 formations, including six Army and three SS armoured (Panzer) divisions, plus a further SS mechanized division. Many of these mobile formations were re-fitting after being mauled in the east and would only be partially combat ready by mid-June. Apart from two parachute divisions, most of the remaining formations were infantry divisions.

ARMY COMMANDS

Rommel's army group headquarters controlled two subordinate army commands and an independent armoured corps. Colonel-General Friedrich Dollmann's Seventh Army controlled the area of Brittany and Normandy, while Colonel-General Hans von Salmuth's Fifteenth Army controlled all of northern France, from Le Havre along the Pas-de-Calais to the Scheldt estuary in the southwestern Netherlands. Last, XLVIII Panzer Corps controlled the three Panzer divisions that constituted the army group's armoured reserves. Dollmann's Seventh Army controlled four subordinate commands: General of Artillery Wilhelm Fahmbacher's XXV Corps, with three infantry divisions; General of Infantry Erich Straube's LXXIV Corps, which controlled three infantry divisions; General of Artillery Erich Marcks' LXXXIV Corps, with six infantry divisions; and General of Paratroopers Eugen Meindl's II Parachute Corps, which fielded two parachute divisions. Including the army reserve, Dollmann's command fielded 16 divisions. Guarding the Pas-de-Calais, where the Germans thought an Allied invasion was most likely to occur, Colonel-General von Salmuth's powerful Fifteenth Army controlled 18 infantry divisions.

Blaskowitz's headquarters, meanwhile, controlled the First Army, deployed along the western Atlantic coast, and the Nineteenth Army, which defended the southern French Mediterranean coast from the Spanish to the Italian borders. Finally, there was Panzer Group West, another independent command that reported directly back to von Rundstedt. Led by General of Armoured Troops Leo von Schweppenburg and located near Paris, this headquarters controlled some of the armoured reserves tasked with driving the invaders back into the sea. Yet if these command arrangements were not complex enough, some of von Schweppenburg's

armoured divisions had been designated as German Armed Forces High Command (OKW) strategic reserves – formations that could only be committed to combat with Hitler's explicit permission. The complex command arrangements concerning the German armoured forces reflected an intense series of disagreements known as the 'Panzer debate'. A veteran of the Eastern Front, von Schweppenburg wished to hold all the Panzer divisions in a depth reserve ready to mount a strategic counter-offensive long after the invasion had been initiated. Rommel, who had experienced the full power of Allied aerial superiority in North Africa, fundamentally disagreed: the Panzers needed to be held close to the coast, ready to mount immediate local counter-attacks against the still-vulnerable Allied beachheads that would wipe them out in the first two days of the invasion. In the end, Hitler imposed the clumsy and complex compromise outlined above, which satisfied none of the major protagonists in this dispute.

NORMANDY COMMAND

General Marcks' LXXXIV Corps controlled the sector that ran along the Normandy coastline from northeast of Caen in the east, along the Bay of the Seine and the Cotentin Peninsula right down to northeastern Brittany in the southwest. Given the size and importance of its sector, Marcks' corps headquarters controlled an unusally large number of subordinate formations. The corps' eastern boundary ran broadly north–south from the coast to down near Chambois. In Marcks' northeastern sector, the 716th Infantry Division held the coast from near Ouistreham west through to Port-en-Bessin (which covered the Sword, Juno and Gold Beach sectors). The 716th was a static occupation division, staffed to some degree by lower-calibre personnel, including *Ost Truppen* – Soviet prisoners of war who had 'volunteered' to fight for the Germans rather than face death through prolonged forced labour.

Further west, the 352nd Infantry Division held the sector that stretched through to the Vire estuary near Isigny, which included Omaha Beach. This formation had only recently arrived in the area, and had not been detected by Allied intelligence, in a rare failure amid an amazingly comprehensive Allied understanding of their opponents. Further west still, the 709th (Static) Infantry Division held the eastern coast of the Cotentin Peninsula, against which the Americans would mount their Utah Beach assault. Also deployed in the Cotentin Peninsula were the 91st and 243rd Infantry Divisions, which covered the approaches to the key port of Cherbourg at the north of the peninsula, while the 77th Division was just arriving in this sector. Another recent arrival in the area was the 6th Parachute Regiment, which deployed around the key town of Carentan, located just southwest of the estuary of the Dives and Vire Rivers. The corps' crucial armoured reserve was formed by the 21st Panzer Division, which was located in the vicinity of Caen. In addition to these formations, Marcks' corps controlled a significant number of independent units, such as rocket-launcher regiments and artillery battalions.

Normandy: German Deployments, April–June 1944

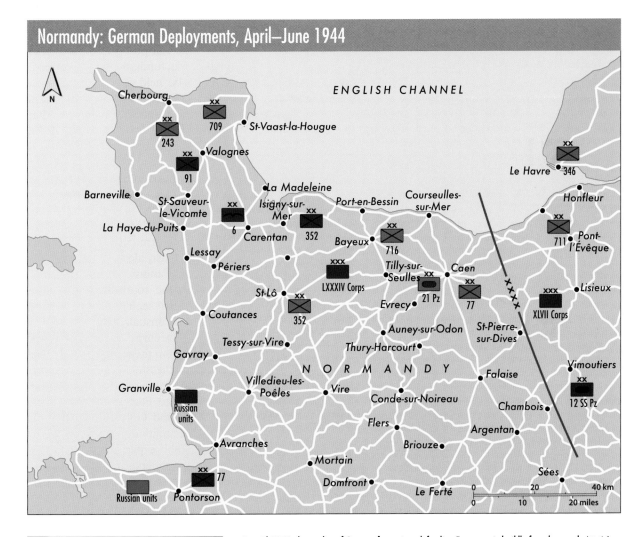

KEY

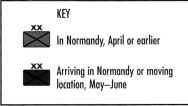

In Normandy, April or earlier

Arriving in Normandy or moving location, May–June

By mid-1944, the quality of German formations defending France varied wildly from low-grade 'static' infantry divisions with minimal artillery and support weapons to elite *Waffen-SS* formations such as 12th SS Panzergrenadier Division. Fortunately for the Allies, the majority of the most formidable German divisions were too far from the coast to intervene effectively during the first few hours of the landings when the beachheads were at their most vulnerable. (The dangers of this period were bloodily demonstrated at Omaha Beach, where the undetected deployment of the tough German 352nd Infantry Division was instrumental in inflicting 3000 US casualties on D-Day.)

Deception – Operation 'Fortitude'

Allied planners recognized that the invasion could easily be a bloody failure if German intelligence could identify even the approximate landing area.

The Allied Operation 'Fortitude' deception schemes formed a crucial part of the overall D-Day plan. The success of the landings would be rendered significantly more likely if the Allies could prevent the enemy from identifying the precise location of the intended assault before it was initiated; this would prevent the enemy from strengthening their Normandy defences.

Once the landings had commenced, the Allies also needed to convince the enemy that the landings that had taken place were in fact only a deception feint, and that the 'real' invasion had not yet taken place. The latter deception would retard the movement of German reserves and reinforcements to the Normandy area after the D-Day landings had taken place – this was crucial because the Germans could reinforce the Normandy front more quickly by land than the Allies could do by sea across the Channel.

'FORTITUDE NORTH'

These plans involved two principal schemes: Operations 'Fortitude North' and 'Fortitude South'. 'Fortitude North' involved the creation of a fake field army: the British Fourth Army. The eight divisions it apparently controlled were based primarily in Scotland, and appeared to exist for the mission of launching an invasion of the southwestern region of German-occupied Norway. Fourth Army actually controlled two fictitious British corps, the II and VII, as well as the genuine US XV Corps, located in Northern Ireland. 'Fortitude North' was successful in that the Germans did not withdraw any divisions from Norway to France prior to the initiation of the D-Day landings.

US Army half-ton 4x4 Ford GPA amphibians, widely called 'Amphijeeps', sit in a vehicle park somewhere in Britain. Similar to the larger DUKW, more than 12,000 were produced between 1942 and 1943. Although used during the Normandy campaign, the Amphijeeps proved to be much less robust than the truck-based DUKW, and did not perform well.

'FORTITUDE SOUTH'

The aim of 'Fortitude South' was to convince the Germans, after the D-Day landings had been initiated, that these landings were a feint designed to draw German forces away from the genuine landings that would soon occur at the Pas-de-Calais. The latter was the obvious sector of German-controlled Northwestern Europe to attack, as it was geographically closest to Britain, thus minimizing the distance of the sea crossing; it was also the area from where the Germans had planned to launch their 1940 invasion of Britain. To fool the Germans into believing this, the Allies established many genuine and fictitious units in Kent, controlled by General George Patton's First US Army Group (FUSAG), which had its headquarters near Sunningdale in Surrey. FUSAG controlled two genuine subordinate commands, the First Canadian Army and the Third US Army. Some of their subordinate divisions, however, were either just skeleton or entirely fictitious formations designed to fool the enemy. German intelligence was taken in by 'Fortitude South', concluding that FUSAG alone controlled more than one million troops.

To realize these attempted deception schemes, the Allies employed a complex combination of different activities. First, they physically created the

impression that substantial numbers of Allied units were deployed in Scotland and Kent. This involved deploying fake equipment, such as tanks made from inflatable rubber and artillery guns made out of plywood. Allied media announced the presence of famous commanders and their staffs in these areas; most famously, it publicized Patton's presence as FUSAG commander. These fictitious commands and units had genuine signals units attached to them. These units generated a regular flow of messages, orders and reports, some of which would be intercepted by the enemy. Through these means, the enemy formed the impression that these were real headquarters, generating the normal sorts of messages that one would expect to hear. Furthermore, Allied diplomats abroad would let slip to diplomats of neutral countries little tit-bits of information about these fake armies; inevitably,

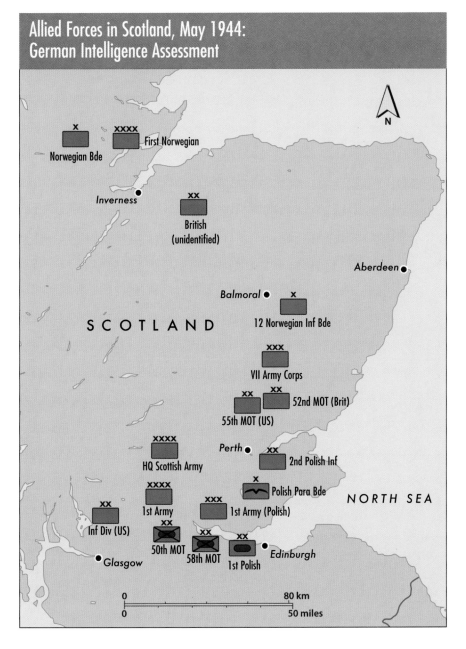

Allied Forces in Scotland, May 1944: German Intelligence Assessment

The 'Fortitude North' deception plan was based on the Fourth Army, comprising the British VII Corps (fictitious) at Dundee, the British II Corps (fictitious) at Stirling and the US XV Corps (real) in Northern Ireland. The US XV Corps consisted of the 2nd, 5th and 8th Infantry Divisions and was training for its role as a follow-on force for the Normandy invasion, but its wireless traffic would reflect preparations for participation in an attack on Stavanger. The British II Corps was to lead the Stavanger assault and consisted of the real British 55th Division, 113th Infantry Brigade and the fictitious 58th Infantry Division, which would make the initial assault. The British VII Corps would assault Narvik and comprised the fictitious US 55th Division with three US Ranger battalions from Iceland and the real British 52nd Lowland Division with a real Norwegian Brigade.

15

a proportion of these would be relayed on to German leaders both from identifying Normandy as the intended landing zone, and after 6 June from identifying the landings as the real ones, rather than merely feint attacks; this substantially slowed the rate of German reinforcement to the Normandy front.

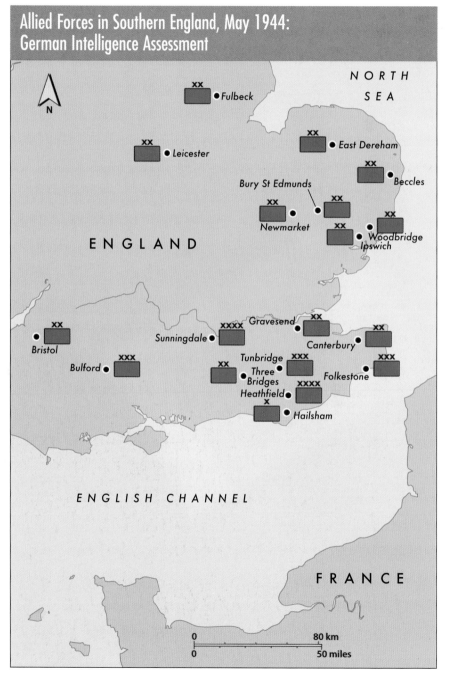

Allied Forces in Southern England, May 1944: German Intelligence Assessment

The main element of the 'Fortitude South' deception plan was the entirely fictitious First US Army Group (FUSAG) supposedly commanded by Lieutenant-General George Patton with his HQ in Surrey. By May 1944, the Germans were convinced that FUSAG comprised two armies, the First Canadian Army and the Third US Army, with a total strength of over a million men. The First Canadian Army consisted of the Canadian II Corps (2nd Infantry and 4th Armoured Divisions) and the US VIII Corps (28th, 79th and 83rd Infantry Divisions). The Third US Army consisted of the XX Armored Corps (4th, 5th and 6th US Armored Divisions) and XII Corps (35th and 80th US Infantry Divisions and the 7th US Armored Division). As late as 8 July, German intelligence still believed that FUSAG was about to launch a major amphibious assault on the Pas-de-Calais.

The Landings

Early on 6 June 1944, after all the plans, preparations, deception schemes and aerial interdiction efforts had been implemented and a vast armada of thousands of Allied ships had crossed the Channel, thousands of Allied troops assaulted the five invasion beaches. 'The Longest Day' had begun.

On 5 June the Allies decided to initiate the D-Day landings early on 6 June, despite the appalling weather; this gamble caught the Germans by surprise, and the latter's ensuing slow reactions let slip their best chance to drive the invaders back into the sea. During 5 June, therefore, a vast naval armada of 6937 vessels assembled off the coast of southern England. As the armada headed south towards Normandy, the first Allied bombers passed overhead en route to strike the German defences. Next, from 23:30 hours, 1120 Allied transport planes flew south across the Channel to transport some 17,200 airborne troops to Normandy.

Next, from 00:16 hours, the British 6th Airborne Division landed northeast of Caen to seize 'Pegasus Bridge' over the Caen Canal and the adjacent River Orne crossing, which they held until relieved later that day by forces that had landed on Sword Beach. Meanwhile, other 6th Airborne units also secured the Ranville–Hérouvillette area east of the river, as well as the dangerous enemy Merville coastal artillery battery.

Meanwhile, from 01:00 hours, two American airborne divisions landed in the marshes behind Utah Beach to seize key bridges and road junctions and thus delay German counter-attacks. As these airborne assaults unfolded, the Allied naval armada approached the Normandy coastline, being detected by the enemy at 03:25 hours, and then dropped anchor opposite the five invasion beaches.

British Commandos disembark amongst the surf of Juno Beach on 6 June 1944, as the D-Day landings begin.

After 1890 Allied bombers had attacked the enemy coastal defences, the invasion fleet then opened fire on the German positions. Next, from between 06:30 hours at Utah Beach and 07:45 hours at Juno Beach, the Allied amphibious assaults on the five invasion beaches commenced.

BEACH LANDINGS

The most westerly of the five invasion beaches, the American Utah Beach, was the only one located on the Cotentin Peninsula, in this case along its southeastern corner. Utah was the also the first beach of the five to be attacked. At 06:30 hours, the 4th US Infantry Division's assault began after accurate naval gunfire had inflicted serious damage on the enemy's coastal defences. Here, the American assault troops, backed by tanks and other specialized armoured vehicles, encountered only moderate resistance, and within a few hours had managed to advance off the beach and across the inundated hinterland marshes towards the American airborne forces that had dropped a few hours previously.

Separated by the wide estuary of the Douvre and Vire Rivers, some 11.3km (7 miles) further east came the other American assault beach, code-named Omaha. Events here panned out very differently than at Utah. The 1st US Infantry Division's assault was hampered by inaccurate fire support, the sinking of many amphibious DD tanks in the rough seas, the area's difficult terrain and the unexpected presence of recent German reinforcements. For hours, the waves of incoming American assault forces encountered murderous enemy fire that inflicted many hundreds of casualties. Indeed, it was not until the afternoon that the first American soldiers managed to fight their way into the draws that bisected the coastal ridge; yet, even by midnight, Omaha Beach remained the only place where the Allied foothold on enemy-occupied soil still remained precarious.

Although the Allies were firmly ashore as D-Day ended, fierce German resistance had prevented them from taking all their objectives. The failure to capture Caen was particularly serious, as the Germans heavily reinforced the position and managed to hold the city for a further two months. During this period they defeated 7th Armoured Division's attempt to outflank the city at Villers-Bocage and severely delayed the entire Allied breakout from Normandy.

Some 6.4km (4 miles) east of Omaha came the most westerly Anglo-Canadian beach sector, Gold Beach. This stretched for 14.48km (9 miles) from Port-en-Bessin in the west through to La Rivière in the east. The British 50th (Northumbrian) Infantry Division – part of XXX Corps – undertook the assault on Gold Beach. At 07:30 hours, the 69th Brigade Group assaulted 'King' sector while the 231st Brigade Group, plus an additional Royal Marine (RM) Commando, landed on 'Jig' sector. At Mont Fleury, behind King Beach, the 6th Green Howards successfully fought their way off the beach. Further west, the German strongpoint of Le Hamel remained largely undamaged, despite the

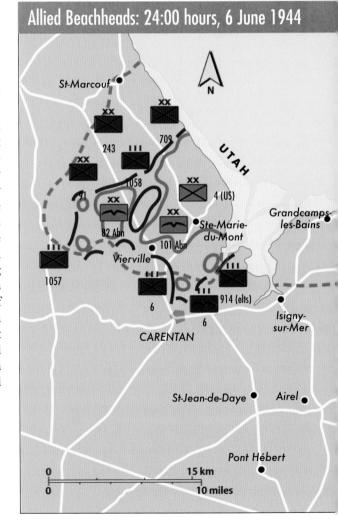

Allied Beachheads: 24:00 hours, 6 June 1944

recent strikes mounted by Allied Typhoon fighter-bombers. The limited amount of available Allied armoured support proved insufficient to prevent the infantry from becoming halted by heavy enemy fire opposite Le Hamel. Despite suffering heavy losses, the British forces nevertheless managed to fight their way doggedly forward. By around 09:30 hours they had secured the beach against determined enemy resistance. The battle for Le Hamel itself, however, raged on until the afternoon.

Subsequently, during the rest of the morning, the forces of the 50th Division pushed inland 6.4km (4 miles) towards Creully, while 47 Commando struck west 6.4km (4 miles) to seize Port-en-Bessin

and close the gap with the Americans at Omaha Beach. That afternoon, the 50th Division's 69th Brigade successfully captured Creully, where it linked up with the Canadians' advance from Juno Beach. Further west, the 50th Division's other two brigades advanced 8km (5 miles) southwest to close on the key town of Bayeux.

Meanwhile, the 3rd Canadian Infantry Division, part of I Corps, assaulted Juno Beach, the central British–Canadian beach. The Allies had divided this beach, which stretched 9.6km (6 miles) from St-Aubin-sur-Mer in the west through to La Rivière, into three sectors – Nan, Mike and Love. On Nan Beach, the 8th Canadian Brigade Group assaulted

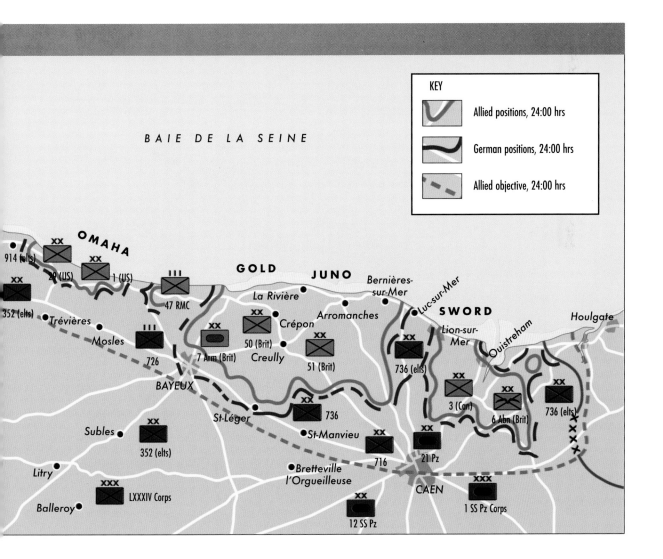

with two infantry battalions plus 48 Royal Marine (RM) Commando, supported by specialized armour; further west, the 7th Canadian Brigade Group landed on Mike Beach. At 07:45 hours, the assault forces approached the beach, only to encounter determined enemy resistance. Thus, it was not until 09:00 hours that they managed to secure the first exits from the beach. Subsequently, during the rest of the morning, Canadian and British forces advanced through St-Aubin and Courseulles, before pushing up to 6.4km (4 miles) inland; pockets of enemy forces, however, continued to hold out in the coastal villages until early evening. In the meantime, the 3rd Canadian Division had advanced that afternoon up to 8km (5 miles) inland across an 8km (5-mile) front that ran from Anisy in the east through to Creully; at the latter location they linked up with British forces that had pushed inland from Gold Beach.

The most easterly of the five invasion sites – the British Sword Beach – stretched west to east for 12.8km (8 miles) from St-Aubin-sur-Mer to the Orne River estuary at Ouistreham. From 07:15 hours, the 3rd Infantry Division's 8th Brigade Group assaulted the 'Queen' sector, which included the strongpoint at La Brèche. During the next two hours, the British forces doggedly overcame intense enemy resistance to capture the coastal strongpoint of La Brèche and the eastern fringes of Ouistreham. During the rest of the morning, follow-up forces from the 185th and 9th Infantry Brigades, together with the Commandos of the 1st Special Service Brigade, landed on the beach. Despite encountering substantial traffic jams as hundreds of vehicles struggled to move inland, the spearheads of the forces landed earlier at Sword Beach managed to secure Hermannville early that afternoon.

Subsequently, elements from 185th Brigade advanced south further inland to capture Biéville, while 45 Commando thrust southeast to reach Pegasus Bridge, where it linked up with the airborne forces; the Commandos then continued northeast to link up with the Paras in the Merville area. That afternoon, the 8th and 9th Infantry Brigades simultaneously thrust southwest, but the determined resistance offered by the 'Hillman' strongpoint halted their attempt to seize the vital Périers ridge. In the

A Churchill AVRE tank and an M10 tank destroyer sit on Sword Beach as wounded men are tended to following the D-Day landings.

meantime, elements of the German 21st Panzer Division had advanced north towards the coast through the 4.8km (3-mile) gap that still existed between the Sword and Gold beachheads. Over the ensuing days, the next phase of 'Overlord' would be an Allied advance deeper inland to create a much larger lodgement area in Normandy.

BEACHHEAD

By midnight on 6 June 1944, an incredible 159,000 Allied troops were ashore in enemy-occupied Normandy, with the vast majority having been landed on the beaches. During the day the five assaults had successfully established individual beachheads, two of which (Gold and Juno) were linked up so that there were, by midnight, four sizeable beachheads. The forces that had assaulted Sword had linked up with the 6th Airborne to create a 64.8km^2 (25-square-mile) salient, while the forces landed at Juno and Gold had joined up to create a 19km (12-mile) wide beachhead; further west came the two American beachheads. Although the invasion front remained vulnerable to German counter-attack, the stunning success achieved on D-Day now made it extraordinarily difficult, if not impossible, for the enemy to throw the invaders back into the sea.

General Sir Miles Dempsey
(15 December 1896 – 5 June 1969)

After graduating from Sandhurst in 1915, Dempsey joined the Royal Berkshire Regiment and won the MC while serving on the Western Front during World War I. He continued to serve throughout the interwar years, when promotion was extremely slow even for the ablest officers. In November 1939, he was appointed to command the BEF's 13th Infantry Brigade whilst still only a lieutenant-colonel. His brigade formed part of the rearguard covering the Dunkirk evacuation – his ability was finally recognized with his promotion to brigadier and the award of the DSO.

After Dunkirk, Dempsey served on the staff of VII Corps and I Canadian Corps before commanding 42nd Armoured Division in England. In December 1942, he was promoted to lieutenant-general and commanded the Eighth Army's XIII Corps during the North African campaign. He played a key role in planning the invasion of Sicily and led XIII Corps in the campaign on the island in July/August 1943. Dempsey remained in command of XIII Corps in the initial stages of the invasion of Italy, in which his troops advanced more than 480km (300 miles) to the north to link up with US troops at Salerno.

Montgomery was impressed with Dempsey's ability (particularly his expertise in combined operations) and appointed him as commander of the Second Army in January 1944. Dempsey handled his British and Canadian divisions with considerable skill in the D-Day landings and the fierce fighting of the Normandy campaign. Although his quiet modesty prevented him from becoming a public hero in the mould of Montgomery or Patton, he had a firm grasp of the practicalities of the campaign.

After the breakout from Normandy, Second Army made a spectacular advance across northern France into Belgium, liberating Brussels and Antwerp in September 1944. On 15 October 1944, King George VI knighted Dempsey on the battlefield, the first such ceremony to be conducted by a monarch since Henry V at Agincourt in 1415.

Dempsey continued to command Second Army for the remainder of the war in Europe, planning the Rhine crossings of March 1945 and the subsequent advance on Bremen, Hamburg and Kiel.

Shortly after VE Day, he was transferred to the Far East as commander of Fourteenth Army and subsequently Commander-in-Chief Allied Land Forces Far East. In 1946, he was promoted to full general and appointed Commander-in-Chief Middle East Land Forces. Dempsey retired in July 1947 and died at Yattendon, Berkshire, in 1969, almost 25 years to the day after the D-Day landings.

Chapter 2

7th Armoured Division: From the Western Desert to Normandy

During 1940–43, the 7th Armoured Division honed its tactics during a prolonged campaign in North Africa. During the 1940–41 Western Desert campaign, the 'Desert Rats' spearheaded the Allied victory over the Italians in Operation 'Compass'. Subsequently, the division fought in the June 1941 'Battleaxe' offensive, the November 1941 'Crusader' attacks and the January 1942 Battle of Gazala.

The 7th Armoured Division also participated in Operation 'Supercharge', the finale to the victorious Second Battle of El Alamein, before making a staunch defensive stand during the March 1943 Battle of Medenine.

After the successful end of the North African campaign, in September 1943 the division landed at Salerno in southern Italy and fought its way north to the River Volturno before being withdrawn to the UK.

OPPOSITE: British tankmen sit atop a Vickers Light Tank Mark VI, somewhere near the Egyptian–Libyan border. This tank probably served with the 1st Royal Tank Regiment as part of the 7th Armoured Brigade in June 1940.

Western Desert Campaign

The origins of the 7th Armoured Division are to be found back in the Mobile Division created in Egypt during the late 1930s under the command of Major-General Percy Hobart.

This formation had been raised from motorized cavalry units to defend Egypt from any invasion launched from Italian forces located in Libya. By February 1940, this formation had been reorganized and redesignated as the 7th Armoured Division; by then, Major-General Michael O'Moore Creagh had succeeded Hobart as its commander. On 10 June 1940, after the successful German conquest of France, Italy declared war on Britain. On the Libyan–Egyptian border, however, there was no fighting other than some minor raiding. Then, on 9 September 1940, three Italian divisions attacked from northeastern Libya across the border into northwestern Egypt. By 16 September the Italian forces had advanced 93km (58 miles) along the coast to capture Sollum and Sidi Barrani; here, the

Italians paused to reorganize their logistical system and dug in, intending to mount a further offensive in December.

In the ensuing brief tactical pause, the 7th Armoured Division hurriedly completed its lengthy ongoing reorganization and re-equipping process. By November 1940, the division now fielded two full armoured brigades, the 4th and 7th; each of these brigades deployed three armoured regiments plus an additional armoured squadron, as well as a battery of Royal Horse Artillery. In addition, the division fielded a support group (which comprised two motor battalions and an artillery regiment), and the usual range of ancillary units (including engineers, light field ambulances and vehicle repair workshops). The division fielded a mix of light tanks (such as the Mark VIB), Cruiser

Light Tank Mark VIB

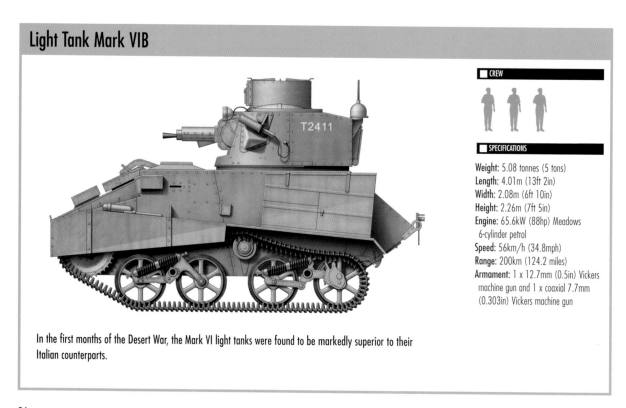

CREW

SPECIFICATIONS

Weight: 5.08 tonnes (5 tons)
Length: 4.01m (13ft 2in)
Width: 2.08m (6ft 10in)
Height: 2.26m (7ft 5in)
Engine: 65.6kW (88hp) Meadows
6-cylinder petrol
Speed: 56km/h (34.8mph)
Range: 200km (124.2 miles)
Armament: 1 x 12.7mm (0.5in) Vickers
machine gun and 1 x coaxial 7.7mm
(0.303in) Vickers machine gun

In the first months of the Desert War, the Mark VI light tanks were found to be markedly superior to their Italian counterparts.

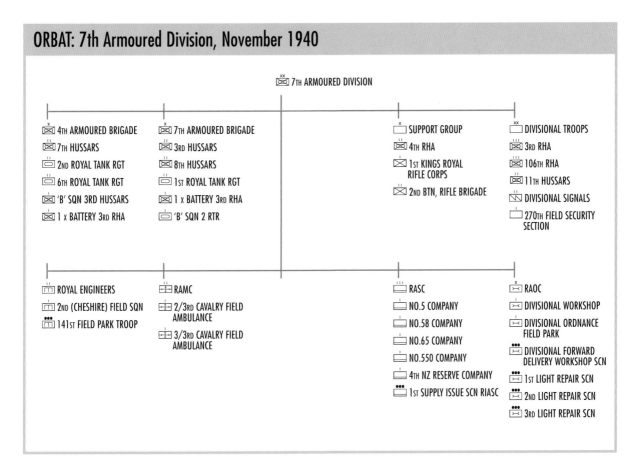

ORBAT: 7th Armoured Division, November 1940

7TH ARMOURED DIVISION

4TH ARMOURED BRIGADE
- 7TH HUSSARS
- 2ND ROYAL TANK RGT
- 6TH ROYAL TANK RGT
- 'B' SQN 3RD HUSSARS
- 1 x BATTERY 3RD RHA

7TH ARMOURED BRIGADE
- 3RD HUSSARS
- 8TH HUSSARS
- 1ST ROYAL TANK RGT
- 1 x BATTERY 3RD RHA
- 'B' SQN 2 RTR

SUPPORT GROUP
- 4TH RHA
- 1ST KINGS ROYAL RIFLE CORPS
- 2ND BTN, RIFLE BRIGADE

DIVISIONAL TROOPS
- 3RD RHA
- 106TH RHA
- 11TH HUSSARS
- DIVISIONAL SIGNALS
- 270TH FIELD SECURITY SECTION

ROYAL ENGINEERS
- 2ND (CHESHIRE) FIELD SQN
- 141ST FIELD PARK TROOP

RAMC
- 2/3RD CAVALRY FIELD AMBULANCE
- 3/3RD CAVALRY FIELD AMBULANCE

RASC
- NO.5 COMPANY
- NO.58 COMPANY
- NO.65 COMPANY
- NO.550 COMPANY
- 4TH NZ RESERVE COMPANY
- 1ST SUPPLY ISSUE SCN RIASC

RAOC
- DIVISIONAL WORKSHOP
- DIVISIONAL ORDNANCE FIELD PARK
- DIVISIONAL FORWARD DELIVERY WORKSHOP SCN
- 1ST LIGHT REPAIR SCN
- 2ND LIGHT REPAIR SCN
- 3RD LIGHT REPAIR SCN

tanks (such as the A9 and the A10), and a few heavy infantry support tanks, (such as the Matilda II).

OPERATION 'COMPASS'

On 9 December 1940, General Richard O'Connor's Western Desert Force, spearheaded by the 7th Armoured Division and elements of 4th Indian Division, initiated a counter-offensive, which took the Italians completely by surprise. Within a week, the British forces had recaptured Sollum and Sidi Barrani. O'Connor's forces then advanced west along the coast road into Libyan territory. By 5 January 1941, they had captured Bardia, and subsequently pushed further west to capture Tobruk on 22 January.

With the Italians in disorganized retreat west along the coast road back to Benghazi, O'Connor ordered the 7th Armoured Division to enact a daring 290km (180-mile) dash inland via Mechili and Msus to reach the Mediterranean coast at the village of Beda Fomm, south of Benghazi, thus cutting the enemy's line of retreat. General Creagh formed a small mobile forward detachment, named Combe Force, which charged off in front of the rest of the division in a mad race to get to Beda Fomm before the retreating Italians reached it. On 6 February, Combe Force reached the village and established a road block, just as the retreating enemy reached the area. In a bitter struggle, Combe Force fought off the desperate Italian attacks; with the enemy believing that they had been surrounded by powerful enemy forces, they now surrendered en masse.

Operation 'Compass' had been a tremendous triumph, with 130,000 Italian troops captured for the cost of just 2100 British Commonwealth casualties. In the wake of this fighting, the 7th Armoured Division was then withdrawn to Cairo for a much needed period of rest, reorganization and lengthy re-equipment, although two of its regiments – the 3rd Hussars and 6th Royal Tank Regiment (6 RTR) – remained at the front.

Following this defeat, the Italian forces retreated to the western part of the eastern Libyan province of Cyrenaica and re-established themselves in a strong defensive position that protected the western province of Tripolitania. On 12 February 1941, moreover, Hitler sent a small mobile force, led by Panzer General Erwin Rommel, to North Africa to assist the Italian forces. Hitler did not expect the Africa Corps to make significant advances, however, as the North African theatre was but a minor sideshow to the main German effort, the impending

Operation *Barbarossa* invasion of the Soviet Union. Rommel's Africa Corps arrived in western Cyrenaica during February and initially consisted of just the 5th Light Division (which later became the 21st Panzer Division). In the meantime, much of O'Connor's British Commonwealth forces had been redirected to Greece to fend off the German invasion there, itself a preliminary to the initiation of *Barbarossa*.

However, Rommel, ever the daring armoured commander, seized the opportunity presented by this Allied weakness to initiate an immediate offensive. On 20 March 1941, the 5th Light Division, backed by Italian troops, attacked and during the ensuing three weeks the Axis offensive drove the British forces back east, recapturing Benghazi and encircling an Allied garrison at Tobruk. By 25 April, Rommel's advance had reached Egyptian soil, and his 160,000 troops – now with grossly overextended lines of supply – had to dig in along a front between Sollum and the Halfaya Pass.

9 DECEMBER 1940–FEBRUARY 1941

The bold stroke of the British XIII Corps (formerly the Western Desert Force), dubbed Operation 'Compass', succeeded well beyond the expectations of its planners. Not only did the Commonwealth forces eject the Italians from Egypt, they destroyed Mussolini's Tenth Army, capturing 130,000 prisoners. In the process, they won victories at Sidi Barrani, Bardia, the great port of Tobruk and Beda Fomm. During two months of fighting, the Italians had been driven back 800km (500 miles), their morale shattered. Hitler was later required to send German troops to support the Italians in North Africa. On 12 February 1941, two German divisions under General Erwin Rommel arrived in Tripoli.

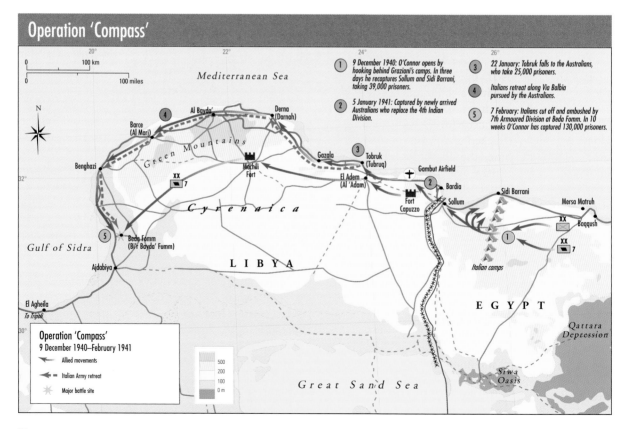

Operation 'Compass'

1. 9 December 1940: O'Connor opens by hooking behind Graziani's camps. In three days he recaptures Sollum and Sidi Barrani, taking 39,000 prisoners.

2. 5 January 1941: Captured by newly arrived Australians who replace the 4th Indian Division.

3. 22 January: Tobruk falls to the Australians, who take 25,000 prisoners.

4. Italians retreat along Via Balbia pursued by the Australians.

5. 7 February: Italians cut off and ambushed by 7th Armoured Division at Beda Fomm. In 10 weeks O'Connor has captured 130,000 prisoners.

Operation 'Compass'
9 December 1940–February 1941
→ Allied movements
◄— Italian Army retreat
✳ Major battle site

On 15 May 1941 the British Commonwealth forces responded with a counter-attack against Rommel's defensive front, code-named Operation 'Brevity'. After a successful British push west, Rommel counter-attacked and recaptured all the lost ground. On 15 June, the British forces launched another counter-offensive against Rommel's defences, code-named Operation 'Battleaxe'. For this attack, the British forces were reinforced by the arrival of the quickly reconstituted 7th Armoured Division from Cairo; with its planned fundamental reorganization merely part completed, the division only fielded four armoured regiments, with its third brigade (4th Armoured), which was equipped with infantry tanks, detached to operate with the 4th Indian Division.

The 7th Armoured Division was now equipped with a mix of Stuart light tanks, together with the new A15 Crusader and the old A10 Cruiser tanks. Operation 'Brevity' intended that the 4th Division would break the Axis line at Sollum and then the 7th Armoured Division would exploit this success with an advance west to Mechili.

An A15 Crusader tank halts during operations in the Western Desert, June 1941. Some A15s were dogged by mechanical problems.

During 15–16 June, 7th Armoured's advance, however, became bogged down by the fluid German defensive actions; subsequently, Rommel initiated a series of armoured counter-attacks on 17 June that restored the original frontline. By then the 'Desert Rats' had lost more than 70 tanks and discovered that some of their new A15 Crusader tanks were dogged by serious problems with their mechanical reliability.

OPERATION 'CRUSADER'

In the wake of these actions, a lengthy pause descended over the front, during which the 7th Armoured Division absorbed a third armoured brigade, the 22nd. On 18 November 1941, the British Commonwealth forces – now designated the (British) Eighth Army – initiated a powerful new offensive – code-named Operation 'Crusader'. By then, the balance of forces had shifted in favour of the Allies. The Axis forces fielded 172 German and 141 Italian tanks, plus 320 aircraft, whereas the Allies deployed 710 tanks backed by 697 aircraft.

The British XIII Corps assaulted Rommel's main defences, while simultaneously XXX Corps, including the 'Desert Rats', outflanked the Axis line to the south, thus sucking in and fixing Rommel's armoured reserves on ground of their choosing. Over two days of bitter fighting, in which 7th Armoured suffered badly, XXX Corps pushed northwest to threaten Sidi Rezegh, while inflicting heavy losses on the Africa Corps.

However, Rommel's armour counter–attacked at Sidi Azeiz during 20–22 November. Seizing the ensuing opportunity, on the 24th Rommel then audaciously launched his depleted 21st Panzer Division in a mad raid, described as a 'dash for the frontier wire'; racing east over the Egyptian frontier, his armoured spearheads cut the lines of communications of the British Commonwealth forces now deployed many kilometres behind him to the west. However, holding its nerve, the New Zealand Division nonetheless advanced rapidly west along the coast from Bardia toward Tobruk, thus threatening Rommel's lines of supply. The failure of this raid now forced Rommel's forces back onto the defensive as they attempted to fend off repeated British Commonwealth attacks. By early December, however, the Africa Corps' successful parrying of these 'Crusader' attacks had left it decimated, with just 58 tanks still operational.

Consequently, on 7 December, Rommel was compelled to order a strategic retreat west through the province of Cyrenaica; the Allies followed up this retreat, relieving the encircled garrison at Tobruk after a 242-day siege. During 7–25 December, Rommel's forces successfully retreated west 245km (152 miles) to Cyrenaica's western border. Here, Rommel's forces established new defensive positions – along the very line on which the two sides had first clashed some nine months previously.

NEW-LOOK DIVISION

'Crusader' had been the 7th Armoured Division's most complex and sustained offensive action to date, but the ensuing severe losses it suffered again compelled the formation to be withdrawn for a major reorganization. The new-look division had two self-contained brigade groups, the 4th Armoured and the 7th Motor, each with their own integral supporting arms. The former had three armoured regiments plus a motor battalion and artillery regiment, while the latter had three motor battalions plus an artillery regiment. The division's Stuart light tanks were now also replaced with Grants.

After a brief tactical pause, Rommel, daring as ever, attacked the now overextended Commonwealth forces on 21 January 1942. Over the ensuing 16 days, the Axis forces advanced east until they reached the powerful Eighth Army defensive line established between Gazala in the north and Bir Hakeim in the south. Next, a four-month tactical pause ensued during which both sides built up their forces, with the Allies receiving reinforcement during April in the shape of the arrival of the re-fitted 7th Armoured Division.

On 26 May, the Axis forces – now renamed Panzer Army Africa and fielding 561 tanks – assaulted the Gazala Line. For 17 days, the Commonwealth forces fought bitterly to fend off these assaults, with epic struggles ensuing for the 'Knightsbridge' Box and the 'Cauldron'. During

A Matilda Mk II undergoing repairs during the early years of the Western Desert campaign.

Matilda II Infantry Tank

■ CREW

■ SPECIFICATIONS

Weight: 26.9 tonnes (26.5 tons)
Length: 5.61m (18ft 5in)
Width: 2.59m (8ft 6in)
Height: 2.52m (8ft 3in)
Engine: 2 x 64.8kW (87hp) AEC
   6-cylinder diesel
Speed: 13km/h (8mph)
Range: 258km (160 miles)
Armament: 1 x 40mm (1.57in)
   2-pdr OQF gun and a coaxial
   7.92mm (0.31in) Besa MG

During Operation 'Compass', Matildas of the 7th Armoured Division wreaked havoc among the Italian forces in Egypt. The Italians were equipped with L3 tankettes and M11/39 medium tanks, neither of which was able to penetrate the thicker armour of the Matildas.

Cruiser Tank Mark IIA, A10 Mark IA

■ CREW

■ SPECIFICATIONS

Weight: 13.97 tonnes (13.75 tons)
Length: 5.51m (18ft 1in)
Width: 2.54m (8ft 4in)
Height: 2.59m (8ft 6in)
Engine: 111.9kW (150hp) AEC Type
   A179 6-cylinder petrol
Speed: 26km/h (16.16mph)
Range: 161km (100 miles)
Armament: 1 x 40mm (1.57in)
   2-pdr OQF gun and 2 x 7.92mm
   (0.31in) Besa machine guns
   (1 coaxial and 1 ball-mounted
   in hull front)

The A10's 30mm (1.18in) frontal armour was immune to most Italian tank and anti-tank guns, while its 40mm (1.57in) 2-pdr main armament could destroy any Italian AFV at normal combat ranges.

these see-saw encounters elements of the 7th Armoured Division were all but overrun in the bitter struggles for the brigade box positions located to the rear (east) of Bir Hakeim and around 'Knightsbridge'; the division HQ was even overrun and its staff captured, albeit briefly, before they made good their escape.

Finally, during 11–14 June, Rommel's spearheads achieved a decisive breakthrough. Exploiting this ruthlessly, over the ensuing month, the Panzers charged east, eventually crossing the Egyptian border. By 4 July, the Axis forces' forward momentum had been halted by the Commonwealth defence of the line that protected the railway station at El Alamein; the battered remnants of the 'Desert Rats' again played a key part in this desperate defensive stand. The El Alamein line was just 98km (61 miles) short of the key town of Alexandria in central Egypt, and 975km (606 miles) east of Cyrenaica's western border, from where Rommel had initiated his offensive back in January; another brief tactical pause ensued.

During August 1942, as the Axis forces readied themselves for a renewed attack on El Alamein, large amounts of American-supplied equipment reached Egypt to reinforce the British Commonwealth forces, including 250 new Sherman tanks. On 30 August 1942, Rommel initiated his attack on the powerful defences that the Eighth Army's new commander, Bernard Montgomery, had established at Alam Halfa. Some of Rommel's forces launched a feint in the north, while others outflanked the line to the south, smashing into the depth reserve position held by the 7th Armoured Division's Motor Brigade.

Skirting north of this bastion, the 15th Panzer Division turned north to advance onto the Alam Halfa Ridge by 2 September, thus threatening the Allied lines of communications. During 3–6 September, however, bitter Allied resistance spearheaded along the ridge's western fringes by 22nd Armoured Brigade, and augmented by incessant tactical air strikes, fought the German attacks to a standstill and then drove them back to their starting positions. The defensive success cost the Eighth Army 67 tanks, noticeably fewer than in previous encounters. In the aftermath of the struggle at Alam Halfa, Montgomery's forces undertook extensive preparations for the slated imminent great offensive, soon to be known as the Second Battle of El Alamein. The future of the North African theatre lay in the balance.

Cruiser Tank Mark IV, A13 Mark II

CREW

SPECIFICATIONS

Weight: 15.04 tonnes (14.8 tons)
Length: 6m (19ft 9in)
Width: 2.59m (8ft 6in)
Height: 2.59m (8ft 6in)
Engine: 253.64kW (340hp) Nuffield Liberty V-12 petrol
Speed: 48km/h (30mph)
Range: 145km (90 miles)
Armament: 1 x 40mm (1.57in) 2-pdr OQF gun and 1 x coaxial 7.92mm (0.31in) Besa machine gun

The A13's high speed and good cross-country performance proved invaluable during Operation 'Compass'.

El Alamein to Italy

While General Bernard Montgomery's forces finalized their preparations for this new major offensive – the Second Battle of El Alamein – during early October 1942, the Axis forces meanwhile worked feverishly to establish unprecedentedly deep minefields to protect their main defensive positions.

During this period, the 7th Armoured Division, now commanded by Major-General John Harding, again undertook a major reorganization process. After this had been completed, the division fielded three brigades. Firstly, 'Pip' Roberts' 22nd Armoured Brigade, with three armoured regiments (the 1 RTR, 5 RTR and 4th CLY) equipped with Crusader and Grant tanks, as well as two field artillery regiments. Secondly, Mark Roddick's 4th (Light) Armoured Brigade, with three armoured regiments (the 4/8th Hussars, the Royal Scots Greys and the 2nd

Derbyshire Yeomanry), together with a motor battalion and one field artillery regiment.

Finally, the division included the newly arrived 131st (Queen's) Infantry Brigade, with three infantry battalions – the 1/5th, 1/6th, and 1/7th Battalions, the Queen's Royal Regiment. This formation had been a standard infantry brigade rather than a lorried infantry brigade, and was duly motorized before and during the Second Battle of El Alamein. For part of the forthcoming battle, the 4th (Light) Armoured Brigade was detached to operate as an independent formation.

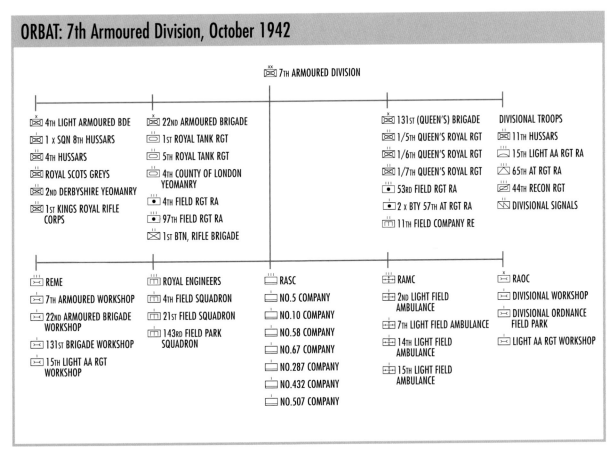

ORBAT: 7th Armoured Division, October 1942

7TH ARMOURED DIVISION

4TH LIGHT ARMOURED BDE	22ND ARMOURED BRIGADE	131ST (QUEEN'S) BRIGADE	DIVISIONAL TROOPS
1 x SQN 8TH HUSSARS	1ST ROYAL TANK RGT	1/5TH QUEEN'S ROYAL RGT	11TH HUSSARS
4TH HUSSARS	5TH ROYAL TANK RGT	1/6TH QUEEN'S ROYAL RGT	15TH LIGHT AA RGT RA
ROYAL SCOTS GREYS	4TH COUNTY OF LONDON YEOMANRY	1/7TH QUEEN'S ROYAL RGT	65TH AT RGT RA
2ND DERBYSHIRE YEOMANRY	4TH FIELD RGT RA	53RD FIELD RGT RA	44TH RECON RGT
1ST KINGS ROYAL RIFLE CORPS	97TH FIELD RGT RA	2 x BTY 57TH AT RGT RA	DIVISIONAL SIGNALS
	1ST BTN, RIFLE BRIGADE	11TH FIELD COMPANY RE	

REME	ROYAL ENGINEERS	RASC	RAMC	RAOC
7TH ARMOURED WORKSHOP	4TH FIELD SQUADRON	NO.5 COMPANY	2ND LIGHT FIELD AMBULANCE	DIVISIONAL WORKSHOP
22ND ARMOURED BRIGADE WORKSHOP	21ST FIELD SQUADRON	NO.10 COMPANY	7TH LIGHT FIELD AMBULANCE	DIVISIONAL ORDNANCE FIELD PARK
131ST BRIGADE WORKSHOP	143RD FIELD PARK SQUADRON	NO.58 COMPANY	14TH LIGHT FIELD AMBULANCE	LIGHT AA RGT WORKSHOP
15TH LIGHT AA RGT WORKSHOP		NO.67 COMPANY	15TH LIGHT FIELD AMBULANCE	
		NO.287 COMPANY		
		NO.432 COMPANY		
		NO.507 COMPANY		

OPERATION 'LIGHTFOOT'

Finally, on 23 October 1942, Montgomery's Eighth Army initiated its long-anticipated Operation 'Lightfoot' with an intense 1040-gun artillery bombardment that was augmented by heavy bomber attacks. Following up on this intense fire-plan, the largest British bombardment of the war to date, Montgomery's forces commenced a large-scale armoured and infantry assault into the deep German defensive positions, cocooned behind the minefields.

For perhaps the first time in the theatre, the Allies now enjoyed a significant numerical superiority. The Eighth Army deployed 1028 tanks, including 252 new Shermans, while the Germans fielded just 213 Panzers plus 278 largely obsolete Italian tanks. The Allied ground forces amounted to 193,000 troops, while Rommel's forces fielded just 104,000 troops. Some 532 aircraft supported Montgomery's offensive, whereas just 340 planes assisted Rommel's ground forces.

Montgomery's plan of attack involved two main elements. XIII Corps' three divisions, which included the 7th Armoured Division, were to mount a diversionary assault in the south to draw in the Axis reserves. Meanwhile, to the north, XXX Corps launched the main British break-in thrust to open up two corridors through the enemy minefields, through which the reserve armour of X Corps would subsequently advance.

During 23–29 October, XXX Corps' units determinedly fought their way through the

OPPOSITE: 2–4 NOVEMBER 1942

Operation 'Supercharge', an even more powerful offensive than its predecessor, began with the 7th Battalion, Argyll and Sutherland Highlanders, rapidly advancing on 2 November, while more than 200 tanks and armoured vehicles of the 1st Armoured Division spearheaded a drive towards Tel el Aqqaqir. Finally, XXX Corps had driven more than 3km (2 miles) into the German lines.

The 7th and 10th Armoured Divisions, along with the 9th Armoured Brigade and New Zealand infantry units, rapidly exploited the breakthrough. Sledgehammer attacks the following day finally succeeded in clearing German positions between Kidney Ridge and the Mediterranean Sea. During the fighting at El Alamein, German armoured strength was reduced to only 35 tanks, while casualties were estimated at 50,000. The British lost about 14,000 dead and wounded.

extensive Axis minefields. By then Rommel had rushed back from his recent convalescence in Germany to deal with the crisis. On 28 October, having moved two mobile divisions north, Rommel used them to mount a counter–attack against the threatening Australian thrust that was being developed along the coast.

In the face of bitter resistance, the Allied forces continued their unrelenting fight forward, gradually grinding down Rommel's forces; by 1 November, for example, Montgomery's continued attacks had so weakened Rommel's two key armoured divisions that they now fielded between them just 32 operational tanks.

OPERATION 'SUPERCHARGE'

On the next day, 2 November, Montgomery rightly concluded that the Axis forces were on the point of collapse, and thus he decided to initiate his final breakthrough attack, Operation 'Supercharge'. This aimed to complete the breakthrough of the entire enemy position by advancing west to reach the Rahman Track north of the so-called Kidney Ridge feature.

Montgomery committed the 7th Armoured Division, led by the 11th Hussars, to 'Supercharge' on the morning of 4 November near Tel el Aqqaqir. Here its armoured squadrons

Mobile and durable in desert conditions, the Universal Carrier proved highly effective for reconnaissance missions and armoured support during the Western Desert campaign.

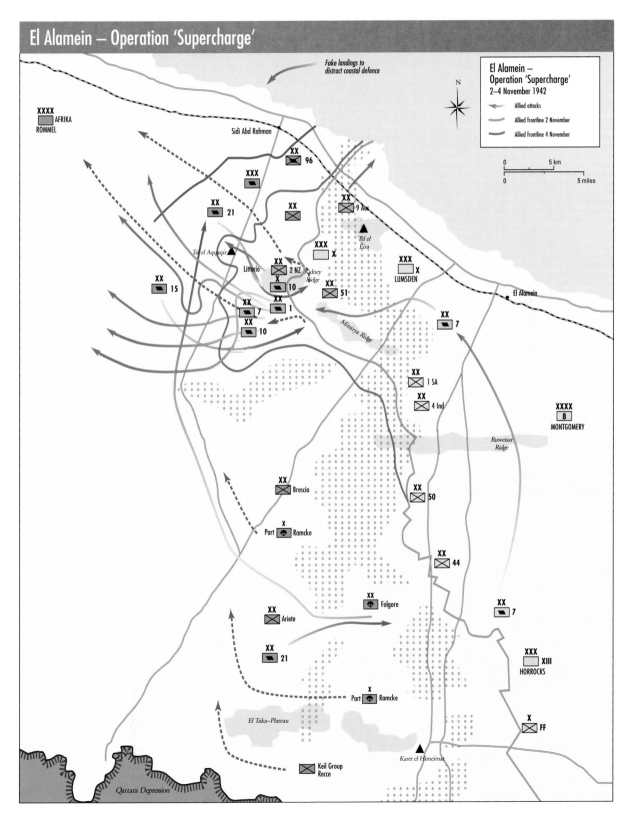

El Alamein – Operation 'Supercharge'

Fake landings to
distract coastal defence

El Alamein –
Operation 'Supercharge'
2–4 November 1942

Allied attacks
Allied frontline 2 November
Allied frontline 4 November

N

0   5 km
0   5 miles

XXXX
AFRIKA
ROMMEL

XX
96

XXX

Sidi Abd Rahman

XX
21

XX

XX
9 Aus

Tel el Aqqaqir

Littorio

XXX
X

Tel el
Eisa

XX
2 NZ Ridney
Ridge

XXX
X
LUMSDEN

XX
15

X
10

XX
51

El Alamein

XX
7

XX
1

XX
7

XX
10

Miteirya Ridge

XX
1 SA

XX
4 Ind

XXXX
8
MONTGOMERY

Ruweisat
Ridge

XX
Brescia

XX
50

X
Part Ramcke

XX
44

XX
Folgore

XX
7

XX
Ariete

XX
21

XXX
XIII
HORROCKS

X
Part Ramcke

X
FF

El Taka–Plateau

Karet el Himeimat

Keil Group
Recce

Qattara Depression

33

quickly swept aside weak combat teams of the Italian *Ariete* mobile division and subsequently advanced quickly across the open desert ground.

By then, Rommel had conceded that the Panzer Army Africa had become so weakened that it could no longer hold the El Alamein position. Admitting defeat, he thus he ordered his forces to conduct a strategic withdrawal west. During this brutally hard-fought encounter, the Allies had suffered 14,000 casualties against the Germans' 49,000; the 'Desert Rats' incurred around 500 casualties during the actions they fought on 4–7 November. The Allied victory achieved during the Second Battle of El Alamein proved to be the decisive turning point of the war in North Africa.

During November 1942, the surviving Axis troops then conducted a series of ably executed withdrawals 1118km (695 miles) west back through Cyrenaica to the Mersa-el-Brega position. The British Commonwealth forces, often spearheaded by the 7th Armoured Division, avidly followed up Rommel's retreating forces. By then, the formerly detached 4th (Light) Armoured Brigade had rejoined the division. Then, on 11 December, Rommel's forces abandoned the Mersa-el-Brega line when the Allies reached

it and retreated further west through Tripolitania to the Buerat line. Here, on 18 January 1943, the Axis forces again initiated a strategic retreat after Montgomery's forces had outflanked them to the south.

Finally, on 26 January 1943, the Axis forces established themselves along the old French Mareth Line frontier defences on the Libyan–Tunisian border, an incredible 2976km (1290 miles) west of their point of furthest easterly advance at El Alamein. In the process, the Axis abandoned the key city of Tripoli, which the 'Desert Rats' liberated on 23 January 1943.

LANDINGS

Meanwhile, as the Second Battle of El Alamein raged, on 8 November 1942, Anglo–American forces initiated a series of amphibious assaults along the coast of Vichy-controlled Algeria and Morocco. After securing beachheads, the British First Army aimed to advance east into northwestern Tunisia to threaten the rear of Rommel's forces as they retreated west back though Libya to the Mareth Line defences in southeastern Tunisia. By mid-December, however, the Axis forces had established a cohesive defensive position that covered western

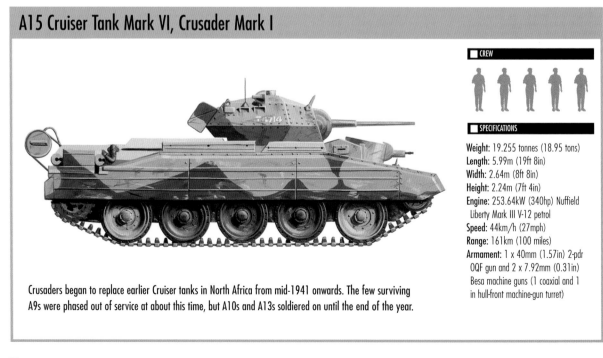

A15 Cruiser Tank Mark VI, Crusader Mark I

CREW

SPECIFICATIONS

Weight: 19.255 tonnes (18.95 tons)
Length: 5.99m (19ft 8in)
Width: 2.64m (8ft 8in)
Height: 2.24m (7ft 4in)
Engine: 253.64kW (340hp) Nuffield Liberty Mark III V-12 petrol
Speed: 44km/h (27mph)
Range: 161km (100 miles)
Armament: 1 x 40mm (1.57in) 2-pdr OQF gun and 2 x 7.92mm (0.31in) Besa machine guns (1 coaxial and 1 in hull-front machine-gun turret)

Crusaders began to replace earlier Cruiser tanks in North Africa from mid-1941 onwards. The few surviving A9s were phased out of service at about this time, but A10s and A13s soldiered on until the end of the year.

Tunisia, running from Sedjenane through Kasserine and Gafsa, where they linked up with the positions held by the former Panzer Army Africa in southeastern Tunisia, now redesignated the German–Italian Panzer Army and commanded by the Italian General Giovanni Messe. On 23 February 1943, moreover, Rommel took command of all Axis forces in North Africa, and was later replaced by Colonel-General Hans–Jürgen von Arnim.

During February 1943, back in eastern Tunisia, the 22nd Armoured Brigade, now led by Brigadier 'Looney' Hinde, advanced up to the German–Italian Panzer Army's Mareth Line defences, capturing the village of Medenine on the 19th. During 6–7 March 1943, the Axis forces then initiated an unexpected two-division spoiling attack at Medenine. Part of this riposte fell on the defensive line held by the 7th Armoured Division's 131st Brigade, which beat back the enemy onslaught with heavy losses.

During late March, Montgomery launched Operation 'Pugilist'. While XXX Corps attacked the main Axis Mareth Line defences close to the coast, X Corps outflanked the enemy to the south. The 7th Armoured Division supported XXX Corps' assaulting infantry divisions as they struck the enemy's main defences. The outflanking attack was successful, and the Axis forces withdrew northeast back to the Wadi Akarit. During the ensuing battle to break the enemy defence of the Wadi Akarit line, one of the 7th Armoured Division's armoured regiments, the 4th CLY, supported the initial infantry division strike. After successfully breaking the enemy line on 9 April, the armoured spearheads of the 'Desert Rats' advanced north towards Sfax on the coast.

PUSH INTO TUNISIA

By mid-April, therefore, the combination of the Anglo–American assaults launched from the west into northwestern Tunisia, and Montgomery's advance north from southeastern Tunisia, had forced the remaining Axis forces into a small perimeter that protected the key ports of Tunis and

M3 Stuart I Light Tank

CREW

SPECIFICATIONS

Weight: 12.9 tonnes (12.7 tons)
Length: 4.52m (14ft 10in)
Width: 2.24m (7ft 4in)
Height: 2.31m (7ft 7in)
Engine: 186.4kW (250hp) Continental W-670 7-cylinder radial petrol
Speed: 58km/h (36mph)
Range: 113km (70 miles)
Armament: 1 x 37mm (1.5in) M6 gun and 3 x 7.62mm (0.3in) Browning machine guns (1 AA, 1 coaxial, 1 ball-mounted in hull front)

An initial shipment of 84 Stuarts arrived in North Africa in July 1941 and by November a total of 280 had been received, which equipped all three tank regiments of 4th Armoured Brigade. The Stuart was highly popular with its crews for its speed and reliability. It was widely referred to as the 'Honey', supposedly after a driver remarked 'She's a honey!' on returning from his first test drive.

Bizerte in northern Tunisia. During late April and into early May, Allied offensives drove the defending Axis forces inexorably towards the coast. On 7 May 1943, the Allies captured the key ports of Bizerte and Tunis, sealing the doom of the battered Axis remnants in Tunisia.

By 12 May, the remaining Axis forces in North Africa – some 275,000 troops – surrendered. In the aftermath of this triumph the 7th Armoured Division again undertook a reorganization and re-equipment process. The 22nd Armoured Brigade moved to Bou Arada and had their old Crusader tanks replaced with new Shermans, while the three battalions of 131st Brigade underwent refresher training at Homs.

In the aftermath of this triumph, Allied forces successfully liberated the island of Sicily, located to the southwest of the Italian 'toe', between 9 July and 17 August 1943. Major-General Erskine's 7th Armoured Division was rested during these operations, but its Tactical Divisional Headquarters

was deployed to the island to observe the fighting and draw appropriate lessons to incorporate into the training regimen.

During this period, the division's organization was consolidated around the 22nd Armoured Brigade and the 131st (Queen's) Infantry Brigade. During 3–9 September, British forces from Montgomery's Eighth Army invaded the 'toe' and 'heel' of southern Italy. In the meantime, on the 8th, the Italians had surrendered and the German forces located in Italy raced to take full control of the entire country.

SALERNO LANDINGS

On 9 September 1943, some 55,000 British and American troops of the US Fifth Army landed at Salerno on Italy's western coast just south of Naples. During 10–13 September, the Allies consolidated the beachhead as German reserves raced to seal off the area. The German counter-attacks mounted during 14–17 September sorely

M3 Grant Medium Tank

CREW

SPECIFICATIONS

Weight: 27.22 tonnes (26.7 tons)
Length: 5.64m (18ft 6in)
Width: 2.72m (8ft 11in)
Height: 3.12m (10ft 3in)
Engine: 253.5kW (340hp) Continental R-975-EC2 radial petrol
Speed: 42km/h (26mph)
Range: 193km (120 miles)
Armament: 1 x 75mm (2.9in) M2 gun; 1 x 37mm (1.5in) M4 gun (turret); plus 4 x 7.62mm (0.3in) MGs (1 in commander's cupola, 1 coaxial and 2 forward-firing)

The Grant M3s, modified to meet British specifications by the adoption of a new low turret without a cupola, were first used in action at Gazala in May 1942 when a total of 167 equipped three armoured brigades. Standard M3s, designated Lees in British service, were also sent to North Africa to replace combat losses, and a total of 210 Grants/Lees were in service by October 1942.

pressed the Allied line, which ultimately held, but it was a close-run thing.

Then, during 16–19 September, the 7th Armoured Division was landed at Salerno, a vital reinforcement intended to help repel these heavy German counter-attacks. These reinforcements brought the number of Allied troops in the beachhead to 160,000 and, with this strength, the Allies attacked north towards Naples on 19 September. By 1 October the advance north–west along the coast mounted by the 'Desert Rats' had reached Naples itself, with its units participating in the city's capture.

The 7th Armoured Division continued its thrust northwest along the coast until, by 6 October, its spearheads had reached the eastwards-running line of the River Volturno, 50km (31 miles) to the north, in the proximity of Cancello. Here, the 7th Division assaulted across the river. In the meantime, the British Eighth Army had advanced up Italy's Adriatic coast to the River Biferno, thus linking up with the Fifth Army.

HOME TRANSFER

During 5–10 November, having been earmarked for the future Allied Operation 'Overlord' amphibious assault on Normandy, the 7th Armoured Division was withdrawn from the bitter fighting on the Italian front. Having handed over their armoured vehicles and equipment, by now well battered in battle, to the newly arrived 5th Canadian Armoured Division, the 'Desert Rats' moved to the Naples area for a much needed period of rest and recuperation.

On 20 December, the division began its long journey by ship back to the United Kingdom. Finally, on 7 January 1944, the division docked at Glasgow. After another period of UK leave, in the ensuing weeks the division undertook extensive training to ready itself for the forthcoming D-Day amphibious landings, in which it was to play such a crucial role.

A Daimler Mk I armoured car provides fire support to a British infantry unit during the battle of El Alamein, November 1942.

Chapter 3
Preparing for Battle: 1944

After years of service in North Africa and the Mediterranean theatre, XXX Corps
returned to Britain in January 1944 to prepare for the Normandy landings.
The corps had already experienced the frustrations of having to adjust from operating
in the vast open spaces of North Africa to the broken terrain of Sicily and Italy.
Now it had to prepare for the challenge of a campaign in Northwest Europe, where
it was likely to face a far higher concentration of elite German units equipped
with some of the most formidable armoured fighting vehicles of the era.

Arguably the greatest challenge lay in devising effective methods of armour/infantry
co-operation at a time when it was struggling to ensure that its formations were up
to strength and fully equipped for the forthcoming campaign. The flood of official
tactical publications had to be translated into practical 'standard operating procedures'
(SOPs) that could readily be followed in the heat of combat.

OPPOSITE: Watched by French civilians, a Sherman OP tank leads a British armoured column through a Norman village
shortly after the D-Day landings.

XXX Corps

In addition to devising solutions to the tactical problems likely to be encountered in Normandy, the corps had to adapt to its new role as part of 21st Army Group.

Many of the problems of command and control that became bloodily apparent at Villers-Bocage had their origins in the fact that between 1815 and 1939 the British Army had been essentially a small colonial defence force. World War I had given it its first taste of large-scale continental warfare since the Napoleonic Wars, but this was widely regarded as a 'one-off', after which the bulk of the British Army's hierarchy heaved a sigh of relief and returned to what it regarded as 'real soldiering' – the familiar colonial wars of Africa and Asia.

The casualties of World War I included many potential future generals and had a considerable impact on the command of the British Army in 1939–45. Four of the field marshals of World War II (Montgomery, Alexander, Wavell and Gort) were lucky to survive serious wounds sustained in 1914–18. Well before the Normandy campaign, Field Marshal Alan Brooke, the Chief of the Imperial General Staff (CIGS), had written that: 'Half our corps and divisional commanders are totally unfit for their appointments. If I were to sack them, I could find no better! They lack character, drive and the power of leadership. The reason for this state of affairs is to be found in the losses we sustained in the last war of all our best officers who should now be our senior officers.'

The first two years of the North African campaign did nothing to help matters – a succession

A column of British Cromwell tanks wait by the roadside during the push for Caen, July 1944. The Cromwell was used to fully equip only one armoured division in the Normandy campaign – the 7th.

of unsuccessful British commanders attempted to counter Rommel's operational superiority by 'decentralization', forming a variety of special forces. Some of these, such as the Special Air Service (SAS) and the Long Range Desert Group

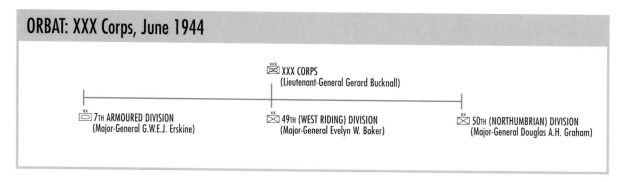

ORBAT: XXX Corps, June 1944

XXX CORPS
(Lieutenant-General Gerard Bucknall)

7TH ARMOURED DIVISION
(Major-General G.W.E.J. Erskine)

49TH (WEST RIDING) DIVISION
(Major-General Evelyn W. Baker)

50TH (NORTHUMBRIAN) DIVISION
(Major-General Douglas A.H. Graham)

(LRDG), were highly skilled and inflicted damage out of all proportion to their numerical strength. However, others, notably the improvised raiding 'Jock Columns', simply absorbed a high proportion of the more able and enterprising unit commanders, besides dispersing armour and artillery to a point where their effectiveness was seriously compromised.

MONTY TAKES OVER

When Montgomery took command of the Eighth Army in August 1942, he was determined to reimpose a proper chain of command through the existing corps and divisional structures. Both in the Eighth Army, and on the larger canvas of 21st Army Group, Montgomery developed a style of command that owed much to the administrative excellence of Haig's GHQ in the latter stages of World War I, but which sought to eradicate its operational errors.

He was determined to 'maintain a firm grip' on operations at corps and divisional level, chiefly by daily reports from Liaison Officers (LOs). These were handpicked young officers whom Montgomery would send out on a punishing schedule of daily visits to corps and divisional HQs to 'keep his finger on the pulse' of what was actually going on. (Sometimes, similar visits would be made to frontline units – it was not uncommon for an LO to arrive at a battalion HQ to see just how the battle was progressing.)

On 17 June, one LO, Johnny Henderson, recorded a typical day's activities: 'Gen. Montgomery sent me off to see General Bucknall, commanding XXX Corps, to find out his plan for the part XXX Corps was going to play in the breakthrough. I then went on to visit 49th and 50th Divs. XXX Corps' plan was to strike south to Aunay with 49th Div. and then do a wide right hook with 7th Armoured directed on the same place.' He noted that he was then: 'Sent off after dinner to 11th Armoured Div. to fix Monty's visit for tomorrow… Whiskey and plenty of it.'

On their return to Montgomery's Tactical HQ each evening, the LOs were debriefed by Major Paul Odgers, dictating their notes to 'very fast typists'. Even after such long and arduous days, they were never allowed a break 'until they had unburdened themselves, and we got it straight from

Lieutenant-General Gerard Bucknall (1894–1980)

Educated at West Downs School, Gerard Bucknall was commissioned into the Middlesex Regiment in 1914.
He served with his regiment in France throughout World War I with distinction. Between the wars he was seconded to the Egyptian Army before attending the Staff College, Camberley. At the beginning of World War II he commanded the Middlesex Regiment's 2nd Battalion, relinquishing command to Brian Horrocks in May 1940. He was then promoted to brigadier and took over 138th Infantry Brigade before being appointed as General Officer Commanding (GOC) 53rd (Welsh) Division in 1941 before eventually seeing action in 1943, commanding 5th Division in Sicily and Italy.

Montgomery was impressed by Bucknall's performance as a divisional commander and in early 1944 arranged for his promotion to command XXX Corps in the forthcoming Normandy campaign. Other senior officers had severe doubts – two months before D-Day, the Chief of the Imperial General Staff (CIGS), Field Marshal Alan Brooke, noted in his diary that 'Bucknall was very weak, and I am certain quite unfit to command a corps'. Events at Villers-Bocage and later in the campaign were to show that Brooke's opinion was all too accurate – Bucknall had been a capable divisional commander, but was out of his depth commanding a full corps.

In August 1944, Dempsey finally relieved Bucknall of command after XXX Corps had again performed poorly during Operations 'Goodwood' and 'Bluecoat', replacing him with Sir Brian Horrocks. Bucknall was sent home and appointed to command Northern Ireland, a post that he held until his retirement in 1948.

the horse's mouth'. Later that evening, each LO would report to Montgomery in person with his typed notes.

LIMITED COMMANDERS

Given the limited ability of so many of his corps and divisional commanders, Montgomery had little choice but to exercise such close control of operations. Some of his senior colleagues, especially the CIGS, had a poor opinion of XXX Corps' commander, Lieutenant-General Bucknall, well before D-Day. Matters came to a head during Exercise 'Thunderclap', a high-level briefing

attended by Churchill, Brooke, Eisenhower and Montgomery covering all aspects of the invasion, at which Bucknall had been allocated seven minutes for his presentation on XXX Corps' role. On the day, he rambled on for 17 minutes before being ordered to 'sit down'. Brooke's scathing assessment was that he was 'very weak … unfit to command a corps'.

He certainly fell short of the combat role of a corps commander as defined by the dynamic Lieutenant-General Brian Horrocks, who was to take over command of XXX Corps in August 1944: 'The main – perhaps the sole – function of a corps commander in battle is ruthlessly to ensure that the aim of the operation is maintained.'

However, Montgomery retained confidence in Bucknall until the fiasco of Villers-Bocage and only agreed to his removal from command after the corps' poor performance in Operations 'Goodwood' and 'Bluecoat'.

British Churchills and Shermans on a road 'somewhere in Normandy'. The 75mm (2.9in) guns of the vast majority of Churchills, Cromwells and Shermans proved to be ineffective against heavier German AFVs such as the Tiger and Panther. Even the relatively heavily armoured Churchills were vulnerable to the German 88mm (3.5in) and 75mm (2.9in) tank and anti-tank guns, which led crews to festoon their tanks with spare track links as rudimentary appliqué armour.

7th Armoured Division

When the 7th Armoured Division returned to Britain in January 1944, it found a very different country to that which many veterans of the Desert War had last seen four or five years earlier.

The bleakness of the fifth winter of the war was accentuated by the draughty Nissen huts in Norfolk in which so many units were billeted, whilst the rain and bitter cold were in marked contrast to the baking heat of the North African desert.

There was a degree of resentment that the 7th Armoured Division were going to spearhead yet another major campaign. The division's commander, Major-General Erskine, noted that: 'There was undoubtedly a feeling amongst a few that it was time somebody else had a go ... With 7th Armoured Division it was no use trying to pull the wool over their eyes. They knew war too well to take it light-heartedly or carelessly.'

Most elements of the division were stationed in and around the Mundford, Thetford Forest and Swaffham areas of Norfolk, but the 11th Hussars had left the division as part of Montgomery's reorganization that brought all armoured car reconnaissance regiments under corps, rather than divisional, command. Although based at Ashridge Park, near Berkhamsted, 11th Hussars exercised with the division in April 1944. In practice, Montgomery's reorganization had little effect, as the 11th Hussars continued to work closely with the division in Normandy before officially brought under its command once more.

NEW TANKS

The 22nd Armoured Brigade spent an uncomfortable few months in Nissen huts at High Ash Camp north of Mundford with its HQ at Cockley Cley, while 3rd Royal Horse Artillery (RHA) were based near Swaffham, 5th RHA at Cranwich Camp and 1st Rifle Brigade close by at Dixon's West Camp, Ickburgh. The 15th (Isle of Man) Light Anti-Aircraft (LAA) Regiment was spread out with their Regimental HQ (RHQ) at Morley Hall, Wymondham. The regiment's 1st LAA Battery was at Hargam Hall, Attleborough, 41st LAA Battery at Uplands House, Diss, and 42nd LAA Battery at Moss Manor, Gissing, near Diss.

7th Armoured Division: the 'Desert Rats'

Following a visit to Cairo Zoo, the wife of General Creagh (the divisional commander) produced a drawing of a jerboa (desert rat) that provided the inspiration for the formation's badge. The 'Desert Rat' insignia was applied to all 7th Armoured Division vehicles from the spring of 1940 onwards for the duration of the war. The formation sign was also worn as a cloth patch at the top of the sleeve of all personnel. By the time of the Normandy campaign, the original 'Desert Rat' symbol had been superseded by a slightly revised artwork. However, the 22nd Armoured Brigade retained the original (illustrated above) for all its vehicles.

8th Hussars Tactical Markings

All AFVs of 8th King's Royal Irish Hussars bore the 'Desert Rat' insignia of the 7th Armoured Division, together with the green over blue arm-of-service patch of divisional armoured reconnaissance regiments superimposed with a white 45, which identified the individual unit.

As part of the divisional reorganization, all its tank regiments were issued with the new Cromwell tank. This was far from universally popular – Peter Roach of 1st Royal Tank Regiment (RTR) wrote:

'I will always remember a vehicle recognition class taken by our OC in which we questioned him about the thickness of armour, weight of projectile and muzzle velocities of the respective tanks, ours and the Germans. He was an honest man and when he had finished there was silence. Each man sat brooding. Again we were to be hopelessly out-gunned and after our period of equality, this was a bitter blow.'

He was unimpressed by the Cromwells, recalling that he 'knew that many of us would die because the tanks lacked a proper gun ... The experts who brought the Cromwells were no help, for they insisted that all was well and that we knew nothing.' Despite the inadequacies of their tanks, there was a grim determination to 'finish the job', albeit one tinged with resentment.

Peter Roach again: 'We were sure of ourselves, with an inner calm that was often taken as conceit, but was a very different thing. We had come to terms with our life and the many faces of death ... There seemed no need for enthusiasm and histrionics. We took unkindly to learning new techniques for we all knew that death was the lot of every one of us whether in the near future or in our old age ... There was a feeling that because we had done well in the past this was no reason that we should be expected to carry the burden now. There were too many men who had done enough to warrant an easier passage.' He concluded that: 'The regiment was tired, yet like an old war horse at the smell of powder, it raised its head and would not be left behind.'

FIREFLY SUPPORT

In a tacit acknowledgement of the Cromwell's inadequacies, each troop had a Sherman Firefly to provide anti-tank support for its three Cromwells. The division was unique in that it was fully equipped with the Cromwell, in contrast to all other armoured divisions, which had either all Shermans or a mixture of both types.

The Cromwell was undergunned, but was a fast, mechanically reliable tank that had the advantage of not 'brewing up' as easily as the Sherman. The Crusader Anti-Aircraft tank (Crusader AA) armed with twin 20mm (0.79in) Oerlikon cannon also entered service, with a six-vehicle AA Troop being allocated to each tank regiment.

The 8th Hussars based at West Tofts were designated as the divisional armoured reconnaissance

7th Armoured Division: AFV Strength, June 1944

EQUIPMENT	STRENGTH
Stuart Mk V	44
Cromwell IV, V, VII	201
Cromwell OP	8
Cromwell VI CS	24
Cromwell ARV	14
Sherman VC Firefly	36
Valentine B/L (bridge layer)	3
Crusader Mk II AA	28

ORBAT: 7th Armoured Division, 6 June 1944

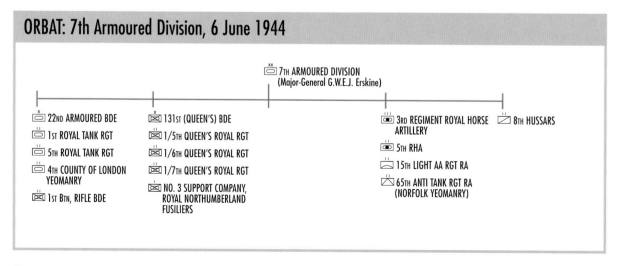

7TH ARMOURED DIVISION
(Major-General G.W.E.J. Erskine)

22ND ARMOURED BDE
1ST ROYAL TANK RGT
5TH ROYAL TANK RGT
4TH COUNTY OF LONDON YEOMANRY
1ST BTN, RIFLE BDE

131ST (QUEEN'S) BDE
1/5TH QUEEN'S ROYAL RGT
1/6TH QUEEN'S ROYAL RGT
1/7TH QUEEN'S ROYAL RGT
NO. 3 SUPPORT COMPANY, ROYAL NORTHUMBERLAND FUSILIERS

3RD REGIMENT ROYAL HORSE ARTILLERY
5TH RHA
15TH LIGHT AA RGT RA
65TH ANTI TANK RGT RA (NORFOLK YEOMANRY)

8TH HUSSARS

regiment, equipped with Cromwells, Stuarts and the Crusader AA.

ARTILLERY SUPPORT

The divisional artillery regiments were also re-equipped, with 5th RHA receiving the Sexton self-propelled gun, to provide fire support for the tank regiments. 3rd RHA and 15th LAA Regiment received new 25-pdr and 40mm (1.57in) Bofors guns respectively, with the latter also including 18 lorry-mounted versions for 41st LAA Battery. The Norfolk Yeomanry's RHQ, and 257th and 260th Batteries were based at Kimberly Hall near Wymondham, with 258th Battery billeted in Attleborough and 259th Battery in Wymondham itself. They received 'Achilles' (17-pdr-armed M10 tank destroyers) and 'Wolverine' (unmodified M10) tank destroyers armed with the less effective US 76mm/3in gun. These equipped 260th and 258th Batteries, respectively, together with towed 17-pdr anti-tank guns for 257th and 259th Batteries.

The Queen's Brigade and 1st Batalion, Rifle Brigade were supplied with US halftracks for their infantry, to provide more protection from small arms fire, while the 11th Hussars were issued with the large Staghound armoured car. The latter was not really suited to the narrow lanes of Northern Europe, so whenever possible they still used their Humber armoured cars instead.

SPECIALIZED ROLE

The training that took place in preparation for the Normandy landings was rarely realistic – Ken Tout of the Northants Yeomanry remembered that: 'Because of the requirements of British farmers every battle seemed to be an eyes-to-the-front, straight back and forward situation.' His subsequent experience in Normandy convinced him that 'war is geographically messy'. It also emphasized the price of training restrictions – he recalled that 'German Mark IV tanks cheated and did not approach from up-range'. His unit lost an entire

A Cromwell IV stands in a muddy field. The 7th Armoured Division was the only armoured division to be equipped with Cromwells as the main battle tank, and had a complement of almost 250 Cromwells of all types.

troop to a single Panzer IV that worked its way into position for a rear attack near Caen.

After a few weeks in Normandy there was a far greater sense of realism about what were the essential requirements of training. Many units produced briefing notes for newly arrived junior officers – a typical example read:

'The job of an armoured division is a highly specialized one. The point is three regiments of tanks and in close support of each of them is a company of the 1st Rifle Brigade in halftracks (and carriers). The blade is you, riding in Troop Carrying Vehicles (TCVs) – three battalions of infantry. You now belong to the 1st/6th Queens Royal Regiment. You also belong to 131 Lorried Infantry Brigade of the 7th Armoured Division. An armoured division probes and pushes its way through or around opposition. It does not bash blindly ahead. It does not stop to 'mop up'. It moves on and hopes to God that its supplies last out, or catch up. The limit of the advance is the limit of those supplies. An armoured division is basically restricted to main roads, but it can use good firm tank-country. Tanks make their way ahead. If they meet machine guns they deal with them.

'If they bump into anti-tank guns or anti-tank ditches – it's the infantry's job to deal with those.

Anti-tank guns are cleared by infantry flank attacks. Infantry also clear and hold anti-tank ditches until AVREs (Armoured Vehicles Royal Engineers) bring up tank bridges or "fascines" to fill in the ditch. At night the tanks laager on some prominent feature such as a hill or river. Round them in all-round defence are the infantry. During the night supply columns battle their way to you – we hope! By next day your TCVs have brought up an ordinary infantry division to relieve you and on you go again! From dawn to dusk you have rocket-firing "Tiffies" (Typhoons) constantly circling round – and all the division's artillery to play with. We don't have to worry much about wood or street clearing. That's not our job. That's for ordinary infantry divisions – very costly in men. If our tanks go and play with someone else, we're taken out of the line because we're not strong enough to hold anything.'

ASSEMBLY AND EMBARKATION

In early May 1944, the division moved to its assembly areas near the embarkation ports. The 22nd Armoured Brigade moved to the grounds of Orwell Park School, near Ipswich, Suffolk, where waterproofing of the tanks and other final preparations were completed in readiness for embarkation at nearby Felixstowe, while the rest of the division moved to Tilbury, Essex, in preparation for embarkation at Tilbury Docks. 11th Hussars and 5th RHA found themselves in the West Ham Dog Stadium. Meanwhile, 8th Hussars had moved to the south coast, ready to embark at Gosport.

On 3 June 1944, the tanks of 22nd Armoured Brigade moved by road to Felixstowe Docks, where they were loaded on to LCTs (Landing Craft Tank). By 4 June the whole division had embarked and set sail for Normandy the next day.

A British soldier examines a knocked-out Panther of the 130th *Panzer Lehr* Regiment destroyed during the night of 15–16 June 1944. The Panther's frontal armour was virtually immune to British and US 75mm (2.9in) tank guns.

General Sir George Erskine
(23 August 1899 – 29 August 1965)

Erskine was commissioned into the King's Royal Rifle Corps and served on the Western Front during World War I. After service in India, he returned to Britain in 1937 to become Deputy Adjutant & Quartermaster-General Eastern Command. In 1939, he was appointed as General Staff Officer 1, 1st London Division (Territorial Army). In 1941, he commanded 2nd Battalion King's Royal Rifle Corps, which was then in North Africa as part of 69th Infantry Brigade. He was awarded the DSO in 1942 and then commanded 7th Armoured Division in North Africa, Italy and Normandy between January 1943 and August 1944.

The action at Villers-Bocage raised doubts about Erskine's ability further up the chain of command. Lieutenant-General Dempsey was restrained in his criticism at the time, but was understandably unimpressed with 7th Armoured Division's performance. Erskine's handling of the division during Operations 'Goodwood' and 'Bluecoat' was equally uninspired and he was relieved of command on 4 August 1944. Later that year, he became head of the Supreme Headquarters Allied Expeditionary Force Mission to Belgium.

After the war Erskine was Commander of British Forces in Hong Kong in 1946, Director-General of the Territorial Army in 1948–49 and GOC British Troops, Egypt and Mediterranean Command, 1949–52, when he returned to Britain to become GOC-in-Chief, Eastern Command. The following year, he was appointed GOC-in-Chief, East Africa Command, where he was responsible for combating the Mau Mau Uprising in Kenya. His final post was GOC-in-Chief, Southern Command, 1955–58, when he retired.

22nd Armoured Brigade

The main combat strength of 7th Armoured Division was divided between 22nd Armoured Brigade and 131st (Lorried) Infantry Brigade.

British armoured divisions of 1940–42 had been 'tank-heavy' formations, each of which was based on two armoured brigades. These brigades had only a single infantry battalion apiece – a totally inadequate level of infantry support that was formally recognized in 1942 when armoured divisions were reorganized on the basis of one armoured and one infantry brigade.

COMBINED OPERATIONS

This improved the balance between infantry and armour within each division, but did not solve the problem of how to integrate the two arms in action. The official view was that they should be kept separate to prevent the armoured brigade's mobility from being compromised by the slower infantry. In practice, this relegated the infantry to acting as a shield for the armour, often occupying defensive 'boxes', while the tanks operated in the offensive role. The introduction of the 75mm (2.9in) gun in the Grant and Sherman from mid-1942 allowed the armoured brigade to generate a substantial amount of high explosive (HE) firepower to counter enemy infantry and dug-in anti-tank guns without having to rely on the infantry brigade or the divisional artillery. In theory, this capability would enable the armoured brigade (and its integral motor infantry battalion) to tackle all but the most powerful enemy defences, leaving the infantry brigade to mop up and secure the division's flanks.

When the ex-cavalryman Brigadier 'Looney' Hinde took command of 22nd Armoured Brigade in 1943, he seems to have taken the 1942 reorganization as a vindication of his view that the proper role of the tank was to act as mechanized cavalry. This had been formed in the mid-1930s, when as a captain in the 15th/19th Hussars he wrote that mechanization was acceptable, as 'the duties of the Divisional Cavalry Regiment remain constant and only a modification of tactics is necessary to fit a mechanized regiment to carry out the duties of a horsed regiment.'

22nd Armoured Brigade Badge

This is one of several variations of 22nd Armoured Brigade's badge of a red stag's head on a white background. The badge is said to have been based on that of the Carr family – Brigadier Carr commanded the brigade in 1942.

Trooper, 5th Royal Tank Regiment

This trooper from the 5 RTR wears the black beret, standard regimental dress for all tank crew from the RTR. His clothing consists of a one-piece canvas overall, made from water-repellant material and fitted with numerous pouches and pockets for carrying items he might need to retrieve quickly within the enclosed confines of a tank interior. Around his waist hangs an Enfield .38 (9.6mm/ 0.38in) service revolver in a canvas web holster.

Hinde saw 22nd Armoured Brigade's role primarily as that of light cavalry – long-range reconnaissance, raiding and pursuit. His experience of armoured warfare in North Africa reinforced this opinion, but he inexplicably failed to modify his views following the brigade's operations in Sicily and Italy, where the broken terrain largely confined tanks to the infantry support role. He later wrote that these places had been 'infantryman's country, far from comfortable for us and we shall be glad to see something a bit more open'.

In early 1944, 22nd Armoured Brigade's motor battalion, 1st Rifle Brigade (1st RB), was re-equipped with US-made M5 armoured halftracks. This at last made it possible for the battalion (the brigade's only integral infantry unit) to keep up with the tanks over all but the worst terrain. However, the potential for developing closely integrated armour/infantry tactics seems to have been largely ignored by the 'Desert War orientated' 22nd Armoured Brigade, and this failing would be a factor in the action at Villers-Bocage.

It was thus hardly surprising that both Hinde and the brigade were unprepared for the challenges of the Normandy bocage – he quickly realized that the terrain made it impossible for armoured divisions to operate in the free and easy way of the Desert War, but was unable to devise a solution to the problem. He observed that 'the need for more infantry was felt at once. However, the fact that infantry can only

22nd Armoured Brigade: Personnel			
UNIT	OFFICERS	MEN	TOTAL
Brigade HQ	21	200	221
4th CLY	37	655	692
5 RTR	37	655	692
8th (KRI) Hussars	28	506	534
11th Hussars (PAO)	15	185	200
1st RB	38	816	854
1/5th QRR	38	816	854
1/7th QRR	38	816	854
5th RHA	39	674	713

see to the next hedge and tanks possibly to the next hedge but one, makes maintenance of direction and keeping touch of exceptional difficulty.'

Furthermore, the difficulty experienced in locating the well-camouflaged German anti-tank guns and other defences meant that the country 'was unquestionably one for infantry supported by a few tanks and not for tanks with a small supporting component of infantry'.

ORBAT: 22nd Armoured Brigade, 12 June 1944

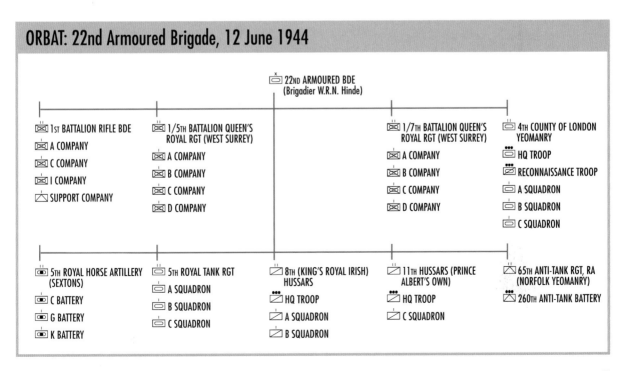

49

Major-General Sir William Hinde
(1901–81)

Hinde commanded 15th/19th Hussars between 1940 and 1942 before being promoted to command 20th Armoured Brigade. In 1943, he took over 22nd Armoured Brigade, which he led in the final stages of the North African campaign and in Italy, earning a reputation for eccentricity and recklessness. Unsurprisingly, he soon acquired the nickname 'Looney'.

He carried a belief in 'leading from the front' to ridiculous extremes – his staff officers had to issue repeated warnings to all forward units not to automatically open fire on vehicles in advance of their positions, as the brigadier was somewhere ahead of them. His command of the brigade during Operation 'Perch' (Villers-Bocage) was controversial, with suggestions that his failure to ensure adequate reconnaissance was a major factor in the failure of the operation. When organizing the brigade's withdrawal at the end of the action, he suddenly broke off from issuing orders and peered intently at the ground. 'Anyone got a matchbox?' he asked excitedly. Lieutenant-Colonel Carver of 1 RTR (a future field marshal) understandably suggested that this might not be a good moment to worry about nature. 'Don't be such a bloody fool, Mike!' exploded Hinde. 'You can fight a battle every day of your life, but you might not see a caterpillar like that in fifteen years!' Hinde's command of the brigade in Operations 'Goodwood' and 'Bluecoat' was also considered unsatisfactory and he was relieved of command in August 1944.

After the war, he was promoted to major-general, serving as Deputy Military Governor of the British sector of Berlin (1945–48) and as Deputy Commander of British forces in Lower Saxony (1949–51). He held his final post as Director of Operations in Kenya during the early stages of the Mau Mau Uprising (1953–56) and retired in 1957.

4th County of London Yeomanry

In common with other veteran armoured units that had fought in North Africa, 4th County of London Yeomanry had the difficult task of retraining for the very different conditions of Normandy.

In the wide open spaces of North Africa, armoured formations had very much been the decisive weapon, with infantry largely relegated to a supporting role. While it was recognized that armour, infantry and artillery would have to operate in a far more closely integrated way in Normandy, there was little appreciation of just how complex this would be.

The situation was worsened by the fact that virtually no one had anticipated prolonged combat in the terrain known as 'bocage'. There was certainly awareness of the nature of the terrain. An analysis completed for 21st Army Group in May 1944 described bocage, which is general throughout almost all of Normandy, observing that it 'may have

a considerable influence on the speed with which operations may progress'. The analysis concluded: 'The tactics to be employed in fighting through bocage country should be given considerable study by formations to be employed therein.' This was sound advice, but was clearly never implemented.

Those planning Operation 'Overlord' were more concerned with getting ashore: the assault formations' training focused on disembarkation and waterproofing procedures; and on fighting their way across the Normandy beaches rather than worrying about the terrain to be found inland. In fact, the bocage was generally regarded as terrain to be crossed rather than fought through – it was widely assumed that after the Allies had broken through the coastal defences, German forces would pull back to readily defensible lines beyond the range of naval gunfire support and that the decisive actions would be fought on the 'far side' of the bocage.

INFANTRY SHORTAGES

The problem of integrating armour and infantry was complicated by the fact that from 1942 onwards the British Army was suffering from a steadily worsening shortage of infantry. As early as December 1942, two infantry divisions had to be disbanded to replace losses in other formations. Operational methods that were likely to incur heavy infantry casualties simply could not be risked, no matter how effective they might be – it was considered imperative to focus on the use of equipment rather than manpower to win battles. As 21st Army Group's chief intelligence officer, Brigadier Williams, put it: 'Let metal do it rather than flesh.'

In this context, Montgomery's determination to keep tight control of operations is understandable. He had seen the disastrous effects of armour, infantry and artillery fighting what were virtually separate battles in North Africa and was determined to avoid any repetition in Normandy. He accordingly developed an operational technique that centred on highly concentrated air and artillery bombardments in preparation for the delivery of a well-prepared and carefully organized armoured offensive. While this made maximum use of 21st Army Group's firepower, it could go badly wrong – the massive bombardment of narrow fronted assault sectors could destroy or block the very roads along which armoured units were supposed to advance.

4th County of London Yeomanry Cap Badge

In 1901, 4th County of London Imperial Yeomanry (King's Colonials) was formed as a regiment from overseas volunteers resident in England, with 'colonial' squadrons:

- *'A' Squadron (British Asian)*
- *'B' Squadron (British American) [i.e. Canadian]*
- *'C' Squadron (Australasian)*
- *'D' Squadron (British African) [i.e. South African]*

In 1905, it was renamed The King's Colonials, Imperial Yeomanry and in 1909 the colonial squadrons lost their regional identities.

In 1910, the regiment was again renamed, becoming King Edward's Horse (The King's Overseas Dominions Regiment), before being transferred to Special Reserve and losing its yeomanry status in 1913.

The regiment was disbanded in 1924, but was re-formed in 1939 as 4th County of London Yeomanry (Sharpshooters). It served throughout the war until the heavy casualties suffered in Normandy led to its amalgamation with 3rd County of London Yeomanry (Sharpshooters) to become 3rd/4th County of London Yeomanry (Sharpshooters) on 31 July 1944.

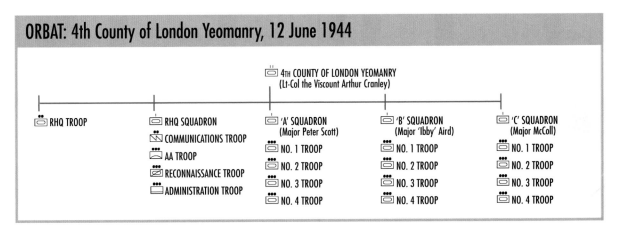

ORBAT: 4th County of London Yeomanry, 12 June 1944

4TH COUNTY OF LONDON YEOMANRY
(Lt-Col the Viscount Arthur Cranley)

RHQ TROOP	RHQ SQUADRON	'A' SQUADRON (Major Peter Scott)	'B' SQUADRON (Major 'Ibby' Aird)	'C' SQUADRON (Major McColl)
	COMMUNICATIONS TROOP	NO. 1 TROOP	NO. 1 TROOP	NO. 1 TROOP
	AA TROOP	NO. 2 TROOP	NO. 2 TROOP	NO. 2 TROOP
	RECONNAISSANCE TROOP	NO. 3 TROOP	NO. 3 TROOP	NO. 3 TROOP
	ADMINISTRATION TROOP	NO. 4 TROOP	NO. 4 TROOP	NO. 4 TROOP

4th County of London Yeomanry (AFVs, Trucks and Guns)

Humber Scout Car: 9	Cromwell IV: 40	M3A3 Stuart: 11	CMP 15cwt: 6
Universal Carrier MkII: 1	Cromwell VI CS: 9	Crusader AA MkII: 6	Ford WOT 3-ton: 15
M5A1 halftrack: 2	M4A4 Sherman Firefly: 12	Jeep: 6	

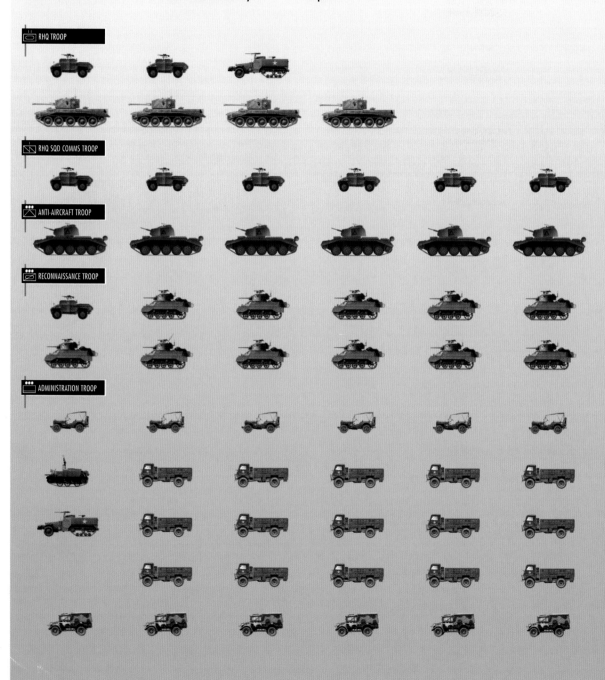

'A' SQUADRON HQ TROOP
NO 1 TROOP
NO 2 TROOP
NO 3 TROOP
NO 4 TROOP
'B' SQUADRON HQ TROOP
NO 1 TROOP
NO 2 TROOP
NO 3 TROOP
NO 4 TROOP
'C' SQUADRON HQ TROOP
NO 1 TROOP
NO 2 TROOP
NO 3 TROOP
NO 4 TROOP

Ultimately, it was down to 4th County of London Yeomanry (4th CLY) and the other armoured regiments to put the theory into practice. The advance to Villers-Bocage suffered from the problems noted by Major Bill Close of 3 RTR: 'We had to travel on roads ... instead of being able simply to deploy and open up your squadron or regiment. In fact, many times we operated on the divisional centre line and squadrons were put out on parallel roads, perhaps two or three miles to the right or left flanks.' The bocage terrain largely prevented the use of the tactical formations such as 'diamond' and 'arrowhead' developed in North Africa, in which a troop of tanks might be spread out over a frontage of perhaps 275m (300 yards).

Ideally, in an advance to contact such as that in Operation 'Perch', the armour would lead with artillery and air support employed as necessary to suppress enemy strongpoints. The Stuarts of the reconnaissance troop would normally lead the advance, falling back into flanking positions as soon as they came under fire, allowing the rest of the unit to engage the enemy.

In the attack, each squadron would generally lead with two troops while the other two followed, ready to give supporting fire. The regiment's three squadrons were often deployed on the principle of 'two up, one in support', while self-propelled artillery would form an important part of the follow-on force, ready to deploy rapidly to provide fire support whenever required.

COMBINED OPERATIONS

So far, so good, but the problem of ensuring that the infantry could keep up with the tanks remained. The Universal Carrier was too small to act as an armoured personnel carrier (APC) but the introduction of US halftracks in early 1944 went a long way towards solving the problem,

4th County of London Yeomanry: Personnel		
UNIT	OFFICERS	MEN
Headquarter Squadron (composed of):	8	193
Squadron HQ	2	4
Anti-Aircraft Troop	1	23
Reconnaissance Troop	1	43
Communications Troop	1	17
Administration Troop	3	106
3 x Armoured Squadrons (each composed of):	24	149
Squadron HQ	3	22
Administrative Troop	–	57
5 x Troops (each composed of):	1	14
Total Strength of 692 all ranks	32	640

although these lacked the cross-country capability of the tanks that they were supposed to support. It also became relatively common for tank units to carry infantry as tank riders – this worked reasonably well in the bocage, as tank riders helped to spot camouflaged enemy positions and were instantly available for action.

In such close terrain, their vulnerability while on the tanks was not appreciably greater than when they were actually fighting dismounted. (The ultimate wartime solution to the problem was the conversion of Ram tanks and Priest self-propelled guns to fully tracked Kangaroo APCs from July 1944 onwards.)

A knocked-out Cromwell stands abandoned near a Norman farmhouse during the Normandy campaign.

In theory, it was the infantry's responsibility to deal with German anti-tank guns and *Panzerschreck/Panzerfaust* teams, but all too often, the tanks were 'on their own' at the critical moment. In such cases, it was calculated that a troop of tanks firing 75mm (2.9in) HE stood a good chance of destroying an anti-tank gun without loss to themselves, if they could engage at ranges below 732m (800 yards), but if the range was 1829m (2000 yards), the gun might well destroy four or five tanks before being knocked out.

Tank machine-gun fire could be highly effective against *Panzerschreck/Panzerfaust* teams, but these teams were invariably heavily camouflaged and very difficult to spot before they opened fire.

In Normandy, 4th CLY's experience was reflected in 22nd Armoured Brigade's 'Notes on Operations 6th – 15th June', which commented

4th County of London Yeomanry: AFV Strength	
EQUIPMENT	STRENGTH
Jeeps	6
CMP 15cwt truck	6
Ford WOT 3-ton truck	15
Humber Scout Cars	9
Crusader Mk II AA tanks	6
M3A3 Stuart light tanks	11
Cromwell Mk IV	40
Cromwell Mk VI CS	9
Sherman Firefly	12

that: 'The need for more infantry was felt at once and the country … was unquestionably one for infantry supported by a few tanks and not for tanks with a small supporting component of infantry.'

RHQ and RHQ Squadron

The RHQ Troop was essentially the unit's small command staff, and the RHQ Squadron, officially comprising all the regiment's 'non-tank' elements, was an administrative rather than a tactical unit.

At regimental level, command was largely based on radio (wireless in 1940s terminology) supplemented by Orders Groups (O Groups) of officers (and sometimes senior NCOs) to plan the day's operations. In rapidly changing tactical situations there might well be more than one O Group each day, but the radio (especially the No. 19 set) remained the primary means of command for armoured regiments.

WIRELESS SET NO. 19

This was developed specifically for use in AFVs by the War Office Signals Research and Development Establishment (SRDE) during 1940. The initial Mark I set was quickly replaced by an improved Mark II. This in turn was superseded in 1942 by the Mark III, which had lower power consumption and a wider frequency range.

The Mark III was a remarkably successful design that was robust and easy to maintain and to operate – in action the operator could rapidly change

between two pre-selected frequencies by flicking a single switch. Tuning the receiver automatically tuned the transmitter, further reducing the operator's workload. The set also had clarity of voice transmission when using the Very High Frequency (VHF) B set.

The set's versatility was largely due to the fact that it was essentially three sets in one:
■ A set. A High Frequency (HF) voice (range 16km/10 miles) and Morse (range 24km/15 miles) transmitter for command use down to troop level. Each squadron would have a net including all troop leaders. Other tanks within each troop would not need this set but would normally have it tuned to the squadron net in case the troop commander or his tank became a casualty.
■ B set. A Very High Frequency (VHF) voice transceiver, which was deliberately designed to have a short range of no more than 914m (1000 yards). This restricted range allowed the same frequency to be used by several units within a given sector,

though these were not usually in the same regiment or even brigade.

■ C set. An intercom set for each vehicle's crew.

Each crewman's position was fitted with a connection point to the intercom and a headset (usually stowed in a small satchel when not in use.) In action the commander could switch between sets from his position, but could not speak to individual crew members, so always had to clearly identify to whom he was speaking. The radio operator/loader was responsible for keeping the wireless netted, and for keeping a listening watch.

Control tanks frequently carried a Wireless No. 19 High Powered set, which had an amplifier that gave considerably increased range. The B set was

RHQ Squadron: Personnel

UNIT	OFFICERS	MEN
Squadron HQ	2	4
Anti-Aircraft Troop	1	23
Reconnaissance Troop	1	43
Communications Troop	1	17
Administration Troop	3	106
Total Strength of 201 all ranks	8	193

RHQ Squadron: AFV Strength

UNIT	STRENGTH
RHQ Troop	
Cromwell IV	4
M5A1 halftrack	1
Humber Scout Cars	2
Communications Troop	
Humber Scout Cars	6
Anti-Aircraft Troop	
Crusader AA Mk II tanks	6
Reconnaissance Troop	
M3A3 Stuart light tanks	11
Humber Scout Cars	1
Administration Troop	
Jeeps	6
CMP 15cwt truck	6
Ford WOT 3-ton truck	15
Universal Carrier	1
M5A1 halftrack	1

disconnected in this role, as it was used in conjunction with a second No. 19 set.

INTERCEPT PROBLEMS

Good as the No. 19 was, it was susceptible to the expert German signal intercept companies. Major John Foley recalled how 153 Regiment Royal Armoured Corps (RAC) was targeted by them in Normandy: 'We had a reserve squadron standing by, and Alan ... sent out a call for reinforcements. "Hello Baker," he said. Would you send up another shilling?"

'Shilling was the simple code-name for a squadron; individual tanks were known as pennies and troops as sixpences.

'We thought that these code-names were pretty darned clever; fox the enemy every time. We learned.

'People were now being understandably cautious about driving up over the skyline so Alan got out of his tank ... walked calmly up to the top of the hill and studied the scene below through his binoculars ... he walked firmly back to my tank and climbed up on to it.

'"There's just one tank I can see, John," he said. "And it's got with it a sort of staff car with a long radio aerial. If you go out to the left and creep gently along the top you may be able to get a shot in his flank."

'I opened my mouth to answer but before I could say a word I was interrupted by Alan's voice coming out of the headphones slung around my neck.

'"Hello Baker," said Alan's voice. "You needn't bother about that shilling now. It won't be needed."

'"Roger, out," replied the voice of the operator at RHQ.

'Alan and I stared at one another in incredulous amazement for a couple of seconds, and then he grabbed my microphone and said: "Hello Baker. Ignore that last message. It wasn't me – it was the enemy."

'That explained the radio car, of course and as soon as Alan had jumped off my tank I took the troop round to where he had indicated. But the birds had flown ...

'"Hello Baker Five," called Alan over the "A" set. "Any luck?"

'"No," I replied. "I think they have withdrawn."

'"Of course they have," said a smug voice in my earphones.'

4th County of London Yeomanry RHQ Squadron

Humber Scout Car: 9
Universal Carrier MkII: 1
M5A1 halftrack: 2

Cromwell IV: 4
Crusader AA Mk II: 6
M3A3 Stuart: 11

CMP 15cwt: 6
Ford WOT 3-ton: 15
Jeep: 6

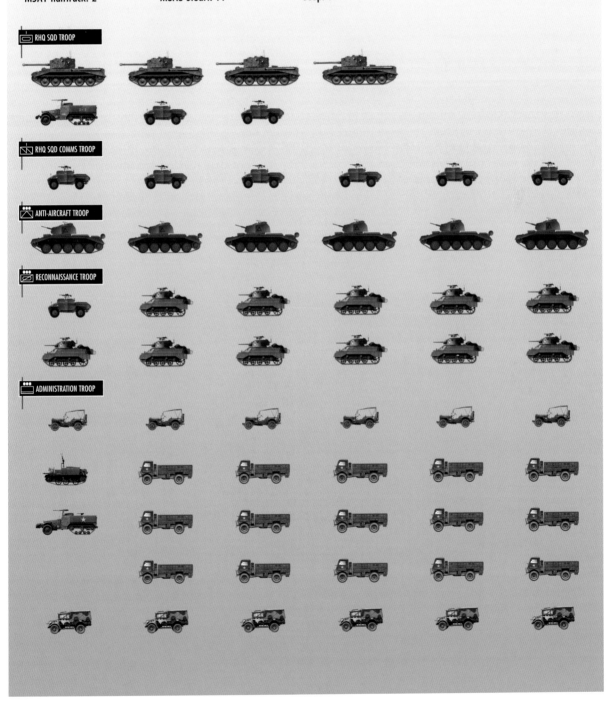

Communications Troop

Consisting of a handful of armoured scout cars, elements of the communications troop unit were frequently deployed throughout the regiment for maintaining communication links in a variety of ways, from acting as radio relay vehicles to general liaison duties.

The troop was equipped with the Humber Scout Car, which had been developed in 1942 in response to a shortage of the highly popular Daimler Dingo Scout Car. The preferred solution would have been simply to add new factories to the Dingo production programme, but the design was too sophisticated for some manufacturers and others believed that they could do better. This seems to have been the case with the Rootes Group, which developed the Humber Scout Car based on its experience with the earlier Humber Armoured and Light Reconnaissance Cars.

The prototype, which incorporated components of the Humber Armoured Car, was completed in 1942. It was far simpler than the Daimler, with a conventional chassis and a rear-mounted Super Snipe engine. While this simplicity undoubtedly made production easier, it did nothing for the vehicle's reputation in comparison to the Daimler, which had a far better automotive performance and thicker armour.

LIMITATIONS

The Humber was also disliked for its enclosed fighting compartment, accessed by two small sliding roof hatches. To make matters worse, it was horribly vulnerable to mines, as the floor of the fighting compartment was unarmoured. Units routinely

Humber Scout Car

CREW

SPECIFICATIONS

Weight: 2.4 tonnes (2.36 tons)
Length: 3.83m (12ft 7in)
Width: 1.87m (6ft 2in)
Height: 2.13m (7ft)
Engine: 65kW (87hp) 6-cylinder petrol
Speed: 100km/h (62mph)
Range: 320km (200 miles)
Armament: 1 x 7.7mm (0.303in) Bren gun

Production of the excellent Daimler Dingo Scout Car never kept pace with demand and in 1941 orders for a similar scout car were placed with Humber, which was already producing armoured cars and the Humber Light Reconnaissance Car. The vehicle had a crew of two, with an emergency seat for a third and was fitted with a No. 19 radio set. The armament consisted of one or two Bren guns (usually fitted with 100-round drum magazines), which were mounted above the roof and could be operated from inside the vehicle using a system resembling bicycle handlebars, in which the 'brake' levers fired the guns. Production of the type continued until 1945, by which time at least 4100 had been completed. Although it was effective as a reconnaissance and liaison vehicle, the Humber was generally considered less capable and reliable than the Dingo.

lined the floor with sandbags in an attempt to give some degree of protection from mines. The type's only real advantage over the Daimler lay in its larger fighting compartment which gave room for up to three men. The earliest vehicles had armoured observation ports in the rear of the fighting compartment, but these were soon deleted. In an attempt to rectify the worst of the problems, the Mark II was fitted with a different gearbox and a bulged plate above the steering wheel which gave welcome extra space for the driver. Later examples of the Mark II finally introduced a degree of armoured protection for the floor of the fighting compartment.

Anti-Aircraft Troop

Having been on the receiving end of devastating air attacks from the *Luftwaffe* in France in 1940 and the early stages of the North Africa campaign, the British Army stepped up its development of anti-aircraft protection for armoured formations.

At its most basic, this was simply a matter of fitting each tank with a Bren light machine gun on a suitable anti-aircraft (AA) mount. However, this was at best a partial solution as the Bren was not an ideal AA weapon due to its magazine feed and relatively low rate of fire. These drawbacks were compounded by its rifle-calibre ammunition, which lacked both range and penetrative power against the increasingly well-armoured Axis fighter-bombers and ground-attack aircraft.

The first proper AA AFVs had been under development as early as 1939 – prototypes based on the Light Tank Mark V underwent trials with turrets mounting twin 15mm (0.59in) Besa machine guns or quadruple 7.7mm (.303in) Brownings. These trials led to the decision to standardize on a newly designed turret armed with quadruple 7.92mm (0.31in) Besa machine guns, which went into limited production for both the Light Tank Mark VI and Humber Armoured Car. The quadruple Besas delivered a fairly high rate of fire, but their range and effectiveness were still relatively poor.

EARLY AA TANKS

The first AA tank based on the hull of the Crusader was the Crusader III AAI, which carried the 40mm (1.57in) Bofors gun in an open-topped turret. This version carried a crew of four – commander, gun layer, loader and driver – and was issued to some Royal Artillery AA units in 1943–44. Armoured units were equipped with the Crusader III AAII or III,

both of which were armed with twin 20mm (0.79in) Oerlikon cannon. (In wartime manuals, this weapon was referred to as the 20mm Oerlikon machine gun.) Both these versions of the Crusader were very similar and were covered by the same instruction manual, which gave the following general description:

'The Crusader III, A.A.II & A.A.III have both been designed and built for defence against low flying aircraft and, due to the high power to weight ratio, the acceleration and general performance is of a high order. These facts combined with the firepower of the twin Oerlikon machine guns place an important weapon in the hands of the crew.

'The difference between the two vehicles is mainly in the turret, and in the case of the Crusader III, A.A.II the W/T set is fitted in the rear of the turret, but in the A.A.III this space is utilized by the commander/gunner, thus providing more room in the fighting compartment. The W/T set in this case is fitted in the left-hand forward compartment.'

All the differences between the two versions are noted. Under the heading of 'Crew', the 'Vehicle Instruction Book' noted that:

'... the A.A.II has a four-man complement of commander/gunner, two loaders and a driver, though on the A.A.III the driver operates the W/T set. On both types, the turret is a welded structure, with the exception of the front plate, which is bolted in place.

'Suspended from the turret by tubular supports is the turntable on which is carried the commander/gunner's and loaders' seats. The whole turret assembly is carried on a caged hull race and rotated through 360° by means of a hydraulic traversing gear, or manually by gear engagement on a fixed rack-ring.

'Twin Oerlikon guns are fitted and high angle elevation is provided by a special rotating mantlet pivoting on trunnion bearings formed by "hanger brackets" suspended from the turret roof. A handlebar type of hydraulic valve box, the head of which moves in two directions, controls the operation of traversing, gun elevation and depression. The rotary movement of the valve box head controls the turret traverse, while the movement from the vertical controls the gun elevation, etc.

'The ring sight is mounted in an inverted "U" shaped bar, pivoted at either end to the turret side plates, and connected to the gun cradle by means of a link bar, so that the sights alter in correct relationship to the gun elevation or depression.

'On Crusader III A.A.II a hinged cover of armour plate affords protection in action by reducing the sighting aperture to a minimum. This cover is operated by a lever inside the turret, and secured in the upright position by a spring-loaded catch. The turret roof is open, but a folding hinged metal cover is provided as a waterproof covering, arranged so that it can be drawn over the roof, folding against the turret rear sloping plate when out of use. Two periscopes are fitted to provide vision facilities for the loaders.

'On Crusader III A.A.III the turret differs from the Crusader III A.A.II, the rear plate having been extended to permit the commander/gunner to sit further back, this providing a greater range of view and allowing more room in the fighting compartment. An armoured shield is provided for additional protection for the commander/gunner.'

ARMAMENT

The guns were carried in a 'Mounting, Twin A.A. Oerlikon 20mm M.G. Mark I'. Some sources indicate that the AAIII was also fitted with a coaxial 7.7mm (.303in) Vickers K machine gun, but it is not listed in

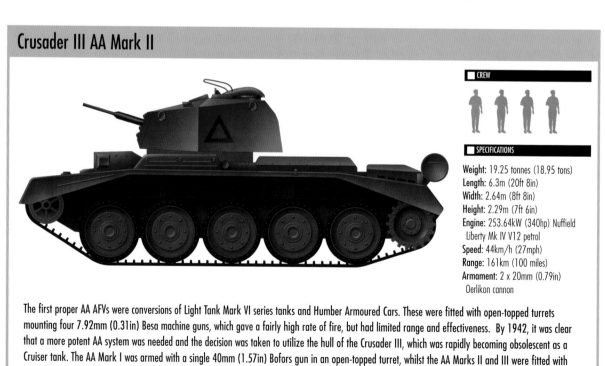

Crusader III AA Mark II

CREW

SPECIFICATIONS

Weight: 19.25 tonnes (18.95 tons)
Length: 6.3m (20ft 8in)
Width: 2.64m (8ft 8in)
Height: 2.29m (7ft 6in)
Engine: 253.64kW (340hp) Nuffield Liberty Mk IV V12 petrol
Speed: 44km/h (27mph)
Range: 161km (100 miles)
Armament: 2 x 20mm (0.79in) Oerlikon cannon

The first proper AA AFVs were conversions of Light Tank Mark VI series tanks and Humber Armoured Cars. These were fitted with open-topped turrets mounting four 7.92mm (0.31in) Besa machine guns, which gave a fairly high rate of fire, but had limited range and effectiveness. By 1942, it was clear that a more potent AA system was needed and the decision was taken to utilize the hull of the Crusader III, which was rapidly becoming obsolescent as a Cruiser tank. The AA Mark I was armed with a single 40mm (1.57in) Bofors gun in an open-topped turret, whilst the AA Marks II and III were fitted with twin 20mm (0.79in) Oerlikon cannon. A total of over 250 tanks (mainly Mark IIIs) were attached to armoured divisions in the opening stages of the Normandy campaign, but were phased out of service as it became apparent that there was little threat from Luftwaffe ground-attack aircraft.

the 'Vehicle Instruction Book' or the 'Illustrated Parts List'. These sources show a counterweight on the outside of the mantlet consisting of a large metal cylinder mounted on a threaded rod with large nuts at either end of the cylinder to allow for adjustment back and forth. This mounting allowed for almost vertical fire at up to 87° elevation and a maximum depression of -5°.

An official requirement for 400 AAII and III tanks was confirmed in 1942, the vehicles to be issued on a scale of two per divisional HQ and eight to each armoured regiment and tank battalion.

In the 'Half Yearly Report on the Progress of the Royal Armoured Corps' for 31 December 1943, Crusader AA tanks were listed as being in service: Crusader AAI – two in training units, three in establishments, 205 in ordnance depots; Crusader AAII – four in Guards Armoured Division, 25 in training units, 44 in establishments, 90 in ordnance depots. Further details were given in the section on vehicle development and production, which noted that the turrets of early vehicles were seriously out of balance, and stated:

'100 out of the 400 vehicles will be issued for training purposes only. At present they are unmodified and training units have been warned of the cramped position of the loaders; their legs are liable to be badly damaged when the gun is in extreme elevation. Modifications will be introduced retrospectively whereby the loaders seat will be lowered by 4.5in to give more clearance. The remaining 300 vehicles will be issued to Armoured Regts, Tank Bns and Div HQ on the scale –
■ Each Divisional HQ – 2
■ Each Armoured Regiment, and Tank Battalion – 6
■ Each Brigade HQ – 2
■ Each Armd Recce Regt – 5'

UNBATTLEWORTHY

By June 1944, a total of 300 Crusader III AAIIIs had been ordered, and the type was officially recorded as being 'in service'. A detailed listing for 21st Army Group AFVs dated 30 June showed a total of 252 in service with units. The AAII was also listed, but production was limited to 100 vehicles, as the type was categorized as 'unbattleworthy' – it had the coaxial Vickers machine gun, which was replaced by a counterweight in the AAIII, as it was found that spent cartridge cases tended to jam the cannon.

A December 1944 report only includes the Crusader III AAIII, stating that 299 had been ordered and that these had all been built.

Units seem to have begun receiving the new vehicles in early 1944 – 8th Armoured Brigade collected nine Crusader AAs from Cowley, Oxford, on 22 February. The AFV State for 7 March shows one at Brigade HQ, two in 4th/7th Dragoon Guards and three each with 24th Lancers and Nottinghamshire Sherwood Rangers Yeomanry.

Courses were run in March, including range firing, with brigade HQ allocated 300 rounds and each regiment 400 rounds. By 20 March, each regiment had five vehicles with none in brigade HQ and by 3 April they were at full strength. According to their landing plans, the regimental AA tanks would not be landed until D+5, whilst those assigned to brigade HQ would arrive three weeks after D-Day. Whilst there are regular records of tank strengths, there is no mention of AA vehicles.

SWAMPED WHILE LANDING

The 13th/18th Hussars 'War Diary' records a general reorganization on 10 July as new tanks were issued, three in Squadron HQ and four troops each of four tanks, with Fireflies spread equally between all squadrons, but there was no mention of AA tanks until 17 August when it was recorded that 'AA Tp is being done away with'.

The 22nd Armoured Brigade's 'War Diary' does not go into great detail on the subject of AA tanks; however, it does note that on 15 March 1944: 'It was stated that the Bde may have to accept its full quota of AA tanks, the balance not already included in the loading tables may therefore have to proceed overseas with the residue.'

This refers to the landing of vehicles in France, and suggests that not all vehicles would land in the first wave. However, when they landed on D+1 the 'Diary' records that 130 Cromwell 75mm, 15 Cromwell CS, 15 Sherman VC and 31 Stuart tanks had been landed successfully without any mention of the AA tanks, but under the heading 'Tks temporarily drowned' (awaiting recovery and repair after being swamped while landing) were:
■ Bde HQ – 1 Cromwell IV, 1 AA Tk
■ 5RTR – 1 Sherman VC, 1 Stuart
■ 4 Sharpshooters (4th CLY) – 1 Sherman VC, 1 Stuart, 1 AA Tk

Presumably all the other AA tanks, including 22nd Brigade HQ's 'ALLAHKEEFA' and 1 RTR's 'SKYRAKER', which were both photographed, got ashore as intended.

The 1 RTR 'War Diary' indicates that training on AA tanks began in late February. On 1 April, the regiment had three Crusader AA tanks, though on the 7th this fell to two and remained at this figure until the end of the month. A further list dated 21 May shows they had six, but AA tanks are not included in later statistics and Regimental HQ details appear to be missing.

1 RTR landed in Normandy on 7 June, at which point the 'War Diary' states: 'From 14:00-16:00hrs the tanks of the Regiment were disembarked. This operation was completely successful. The tanks went to SOMMERVIEU 825808, where they leaguered and carried out de-waterproofing. The Unit leaguered at this place for

A Crusader III AA Mark III of 22nd Armoured Brigade's HQ Group disembarks from an LST on the afternoon of 7 June. The tank's name, 'Allahkeefa' also appears in slightly modified form on one of the Fireflies captured at Point 213.

the night.' Again the AA tanks were not mentioned, with the tank strength figures for July covering Cromwells (with CS tanks listed separately), Fireflies and Stuarts only, while those for later months give just a total figure.

ALLIED AIR SUPERIORITY

All the effort that went into the development and deployment of these vehicles was largely wasted. Allied air superiority was such that there was little opportunity for them to be deployed in their primary role. There are no records of the type shooting down any *Luftwaffe* aircraft. Its under-employment led to the disbandment of the AA Troops in July to August 1944.

Reconnaissance Troop

The Reconnaissance Troop was equipped with Stuart V (M3A3) light tanks, generally known as 'Honeys'. The term supposedly originated in 1941 when the first Lend-Lease Stuarts were issued to British armoured units in North Africa. On bringing one back from a test drive, the driver enthusiastically called out 'She's a honey!' and the name stuck.

All versions of the Stuart were well liked for their excellent handling and mechanical reliability, but by mid-1944, the type was vulnerable to virtually all German anti-tank weapons, while its 37mm (1.5in) gun was incapable of penetrating anything other than the lightest German AFVs.

A few Stuarts were fitted with the 'Littlejohn adaptor' in an attempt to improve their armour-piercing capability. This device was invented by the Czech designer Janacek (which translates as 'little John'), who had worked on 'squeeze bore' weapons and ammunition since the late 1930s. The principle was similar to the Gerlich taper bore guns, but

differed in adding an adaptor to the muzzle of an existing gun, rather than using a specially made tapered barrel.

Work continued in Britain on improving the Stuart during the war, leading to the adoption of the 'Littlejohn adaptor' for the 2-pdr gun. Its lightweight shot, known as APSV (armour-piercing super velocity), had a very high muzzle velocity, giving a considerable increase in armour penetration. A slightly modified version was rapidly produced for the US 37mm (1.5in) gun and was fitted to some Staghound armoured cars and Locust air-portable light tanks in addition to a number of Stuarts.

M3A3 Stuart V

CREW

SPECIFICATIONS

Weight: 14.7 tonnes (14.47 tons)
Length: 4.33m (14ft 2in)
Width: 2.47m (8ft 1in)
Height: 2.29m (7ft 6in)
Engine: 190kW (250hp) Continental W-670-9A 7-cylinder radial petrol
Speed: 58km/h (36mph)
Range: 119km (74 miles)
Armament: 1 x 37mm (1.5in) M6 gun, plus 3 x 7.62mm (0.3in) machine guns (1 AA, 1 coaxial, 1 ball-mounted in hull front)

The Stuart V retained the excellent automotive performance of earlier versions and was a popular reconnaissance vehicle. The ineffectiveness of its 37mm (1.5in) gun against anything other than light armour led to a significant number being converted to 'Stuart Recce' vehicles. These had their turrets removed and were fitted with a variety of machine guns on pintle mountings.

Although the Littlejohn adaptor worked well, some units felt that increasing firepower was not the right approach for improving what was supposed to be a 'stealthy' reconnaissance vehicle. The Stuart was a bulky vehicle and its height made it too conspicuous to be used as a 'tracked armoured car'. This led many units to remove the turrets from most of their Stuarts, converting them to what were generally referred to as 'Stuart Recce' vehicles. These vehicles generally retained their 7.62mm (0.3in) ball-mounted hull machine guns and were also armed with a variety of additional pintle-mounted weapons, such as the 12.7mm (0.5in) Browning machine gun.

The reduction in weight and height made these conversions far more effective as reconnaissance vehicles and their versatility was such that they evolved into a range of specialist sub-types, including ammunition carriers, ambulances and Kangaroos (armoured personnel carriers).

Whatever their equipment, all reconnaissance troops had to adapt to the demands of the bocage. They were often as road-bound as other armoured units and devised what became known as the 'snake patrol'. This involved moving along a road until the leading vehicle reached a bend. It would then halt and wait for the second vehicle to come alongside and take up an overwatch position from which it could cover the first vehicle's advance to the next bend. The whole nerve-wracking process was repeated as often as necessary, ideally by patrols operating on two or more parallel routes.

A British M5 Stuart light tank kicks up dust on a road in Normandy, 15 June 1944.

Administration Troop

The Administration Troop was responsible for keeping the regiment fully supplied with everything required to keep it in action.

Squadron Quarter Master Sergeant (SQMS) Doug David of C Squadron, 9 RTR, remembered that: 'The supply echelon comprised many "pack-up" items such as ammunition, petrol, water, rations, mail when available, spare crews, and spares and stores of all kinds. There were people from the ACC [Army Catering Corps], REME LAD [Light Aid Detachment of the Royal Electrical and Mechanical Engineers] and the Signals. In C Squadron the SQMS was normally in charge and in A Squadron the Squadron Sergeant-Major [SSM]. When a battle was being fought a supply package called F1 echelon was put together. This comprised half-tracks, 3-tonners, and the 15-cwt water wagon, and would take ammunition, petrol, compo rations and mail forward to the tanks of F echelon. We would also bring up spare crews if needed and anything

special requested by the Squadron Leader. The SQMS or SSM would re-stock from Royal Army Service Corps Direct Issue Depots, or take what they needed from RASC dumps, literally on a help-yourself basis.'

When a tank regiment was in action, it divided itself into three echelons, F, A and B; under some circumstances, another echelon, F1, was interposed between F and A. Replenishment had to be carried out under many different conditions. When going into action, the tanks moved from a rear area to a forward assembly area (FAA). Depending on the type of move it was sometimes necessary to restock, especially with petrol, food and water, before going into action. Restocking could be done at the FAA or at the forming-up point (FUP).

When in action the echelons remained separate, and F1 or A would move up to the tanks whenever

Ford WOT 3-Tonner

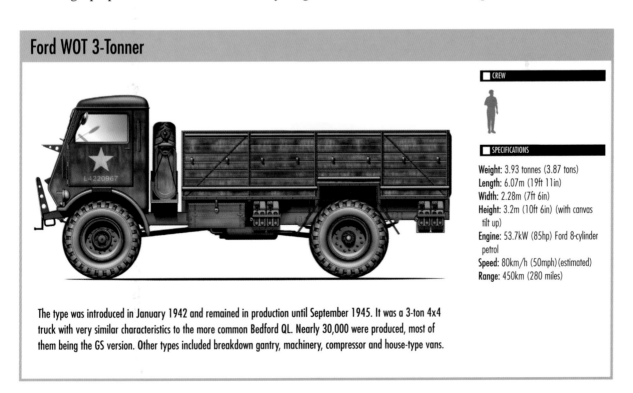

L4220967

CREW

SPECIFICATIONS

Weight: 3.93 tonnes (3.87 tons)
Length: 6.07m (19ft 11in)
Width: 2.28m (7ft 6in)
Height: 3.2m (10ft 6in) (with canvas tilt up)
Engine: 53.7kW (85hp) Ford 8-cylinder petrol
Speed: 80km/h (50mph) (estimated)
Range: 450km (280 miles)

The type was introduced in January 1942 and remained in production until September 1945. It was a 3-ton 4x4 truck with very similar characteristics to the more common Bedford QL. Nearly 30,000 were produced, most of them being the GS version. Other types included breakdown gantry, machinery, compressor and house-type vans.

possible. Depending on the intensity and length of combat, it might be necessary to replenish the tanks during the action. This would often be done by bringing the tanks back from contact with the enemy – possibly one or two troops at a time – to a 'forward rally' area. After replenishment the tanks might return to action or be held in the forward rally area in readiness to reinforce the unit. At the end of the day the tanks generally returned to a rear rally or laager area, where they could be replenished and the crews could get some sleep after carrying out essential routine maintenance on their vehicles. The supporting vehicles of A or F1 echelon could also be included in the laager.

Rear Echelon Replenishment

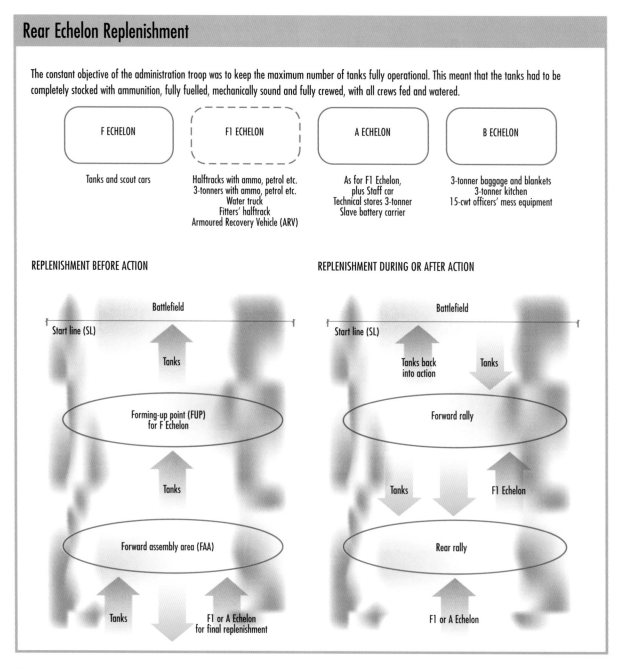

The constant objective of the administration troop was to keep the maximum number of tanks fully operational. This meant that the tanks had to be completely stocked with ammunition, fully fuelled, mechanically sound and fully crewed, with all crews fed and watered.

F ECHELON	F1 ECHELON	A ECHELON	B ECHELON
Tanks and scout cars	Halftracks with ammo, petrol etc. 3-tonners with ammo, petrol etc. Water truck Fitters' halftrack Armoured Recovery Vehicle (ARV)	As for F1 Echelon, plus Staff car Technical stores 3-tonner Slave battery carrier	3-tonner baggage and blankets 3-tonner kitchen 15-cwt officers' mess equipment

REPLENISHMENT BEFORE ACTION

Battlefield

Start line (SL)

Tanks

Forming-up point (FUP) for F Echelon

Tanks

Forward assembly area (FAA)

Tanks | F1 or A Echelon for final replenishment

REPLENISHMENT DURING OR AFTER ACTION

Battlefield

Start line (SL)

Tanks back into action | Tanks

Forward rally

Tanks | F1 Echelon

Rear rally

F1 or A Echelon

'A' Squadron

At full strength, 'A' Squadron of the 4th CLY consisted of 12 Cromwell IVs, three Cromwell VI CS tanks armed with 95mm (3.7in) howitzers, and four Sherman VC Fireflies, with their powerful 17-pdr anti-tank guns. The Fireflies were included as a tacit admission that the Cromwells' Ordnance QF 75mm (2.9in) guns would struggle to deal with the thicker armour of the heavier German tanks, such as the Tiger and Panther.

The Cromwell originated with a General Staff requirement issued in late 1940 for a 6-pdr-armed Cruiser tank as a successor to the Crusader, which was about to enter service. (At the time, it seemed that it would not be possible to fit a larger gun than the 2-pdr in the Crusader's small turret ring.)

The first prototype, the A24 Cavalier (then known as the Cromwell I) built by Nuffield, was plagued by problems. Most of these were attributable to its obsolete Liberty engine, which had been adopted mainly because it was readily available as it was already in production for the Crusader. Leyland and Birmingham Railway Carriage & Wagon Company (BRC&W) had also offered very similar designs, but these were both crippled by the unreliability of their Liberty engines. Once it became clear that there would be a significant delay in developing an entirely new combat-worthy tank, the Crusader was hastily adapted to mount the 6-pdr in a modified turret as the Crusader III.

It had long been apparent that a new tank engine was essential and Rolls-Royce produced a brilliantly successful modification of its Merlin III aero engine designated Meteor. A prototype engine delivering almost 450kW (600hp) gave outstanding performance in a modified Crusader during trials in April 1941. Leyland were scheduled to produce the

'A' Squadron: Personnel

UNIT	OFFICERS	MEN
Squadron HQ Troop	3	12
1 Troop	1	18
2 Troop	1	18
3 Troop	1	18
4 Troop	1	18
Total Strength of 91 all ranks	7	84

Meteor but withdrew from the programme in mid-1941, claiming that it was impractical to provide adequate cooling for the engine in the confines of a tank's hull. As Rolls-Royce were already fully committed to production of the Merlin and could not spare facilities for the Meteor, manufacture of the new engine was passed to the Rover Car Company.

CROMWELL DEVELOPED

New General Staff specifications were issued to cover development of these tanks. The BRC&W design using the Meteor was A27M (or Cromwell III) and Leyland's Liberty-engined version became A27L (Cromwell II). Nuffield's A24 powered by the Liberty was designated Cromwell I. The system was revised in November 1942, with the A24 renamed

ORBAT: 'A' Squadron, 4th County of London Yeomanry

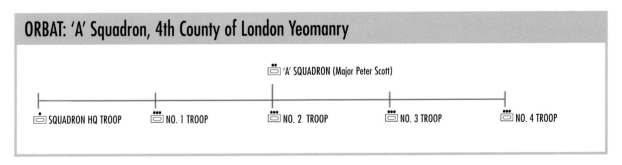

'A' SQUADRON (Major Peter Scott)

SQUADRON HQ TROOP — NO. 1 TROOP — NO. 2 TROOP — NO. 3 TROOP — NO. 4 TROOP

Cavalier, A27L becoming Centaur and A27M was christened Cromwell.

The first Centaurs were completed in November 1942, but Rover had difficulties in tooling up for production of the Meteor, and it was not until January 1943 that sufficient engines were available to allow the A27M Cromwell to enter production. The Centaur design allowed for subsequent refitting with the Meteor engine and many Centaurs were converted to Cromwells before being issued to units. (Only a handful of Centaurs ever saw combat, the vast majority of the 1821 finally produced were used for training.)

In addition to Leyland, a large number of firms were involved in Centaur and Cromwell production, including LMS Railway, Morris Motors, Metro-Cammell, BRC&W and English Electric.

Early Cromwells were of largely riveted construction, although later models incorporated some welding. Almost all versions featured the distinctive slab-sided turret with an inner shell of welded plates and a thicker outer skin secured by huge bolts.

Cavaliers, Centaurs and early Cromwells all had a maximum of 76mm (3in) frontal armour, but later vehicles were up-armoured to a maximum of 101mm (4in). The hull sides were also 'double skinned' with the strengthened Christie suspension units sandwiched between them.

When combined with such a powerful engine, this suspension allowed early Cromwells to reach speeds of up to 64.4km/h (40mph), but this was found to cause excessive wear to the road wheels, and later versions were fitted with governors that restricted them to a maximum of 52km/h (32mph).

Fuel consumption on 67 octane 'pool' petrol was between 0.18km and 0.53km per litre (0.42 and 1.25 miles per gallon), depending on terrain.

'A' Squadron, 4th County of London Yeomanry

Cromwell IV: 12
Cromwell VI CS: 3
M4A4 Sherman Firefly: 4

On the morning of the battle at Point 213, 'A' Squadron fielded 11 Cromwells and four Sherman Fireflies – a number of Cromwells had been lost a few days before and had yet to be replaced.

'A' SQUADRON HQ TROOP

NO 1 TROOP

NO 2 TROOP

NO 3 TROOP

NO 4 TROOP

During the main production run, the original 360mm (14in) wide tracks were replaced with 394mm (15.5in) tracks to decrease ground pressure and improve performance across soft ground and snow.

NEW GUN

The Cromwell's armament caused the greatest concern to most units issued with the type. The vast majority of Cavaliers and Centaurs, together with the early versions of the Cromwell, were armed with the 6-pdr gun. This had a markedly superior armour-piercing (AP) performance to the Sherman's 75mm (2.9in), but its poor HE capability led to the decision to fit a new gun in later production vehicles. This was a 75mm (2.9in) weapon based on the reliable 6-pdr, but firing US 75mm (2.9in) ammunition. Although its AP performance was mediocre, even by the standards of 1943 (and worse than that of the 6-pdr), the US 75mm (2.9in) had the saving grace that it could be fitted to any AFV capable of mounting the 6-pdr. As a result, the type was adopted as the OQF 75mm (2.9in) and armed the majority of Cromwells deployed in Normandy.

Secondary armament comprised two 7.92mm (0.31in) Besa machine guns. The first was mounted coaxially with the 75mm (2.9in) main armament and fired by the gunner, while the second was 'gimbal' mounted in the front of the hull and operated by the co-driver. The gimbal mounting gave 45° of traverse and 25° of elevation – the Besa was aimed by a No. 35 telescopic sight, which was connected through a linkage to the mounting.

The need for more potent armament had been recognized as early as January 1942 when work began on adapting the basic Cromwell design to mount the new 17-pdr. This was designated A30 Challenger and a small production batch of 200 was completed.

The pilot models were overweight and the already inadequate armour had to be reduced to compensate. The type was gradually issued to units from the late summer of 1944, but it was never very popular, as the lengthened Cromwell hull made steering difficult, while the tall, thinly armoured turret presented an uncomfortably large target.

A Cromwell Mk IV from 2nd (Armoured Reconnaissance) Battalion, Welsh Guards, speeds by during an inspection, 31 March 1944.

CROMWELL TYPES

The Cromwell went through eight marks, including an Armoured Observation Post (AOP) version, for artillery observers, which retained the 75mm (2.9in) gun and was equipped with two extra No. 19 radios in the turret and one in the hull at the cost of reduced stowage for machine gun ammunition. The tank was commanded by a Royal Artillery (RA) surveyor, usually a major or captain, with two RA radio operators, plus another from the Armoured Brigade's HQ Squadron. The crew of an AOP could call on the artillery regiment to mark a target with coloured smoke to guide in Typhoons from 2nd Tactical Air Force or they could direct an artillery bombardment themselves.

A command version was also produced that retained its normal armament and closely resembled the AOP tanks. However, one of the Cromwells assigned to 22nd Armoured Brigade was designated as the brigade command tank – this vehicle had its turret stripped out before being welded to the hull. The guns were replaced by wooden dummies and additional radios were fitted, which were operated by Royal Signals personnel. This brigade command tank remained in service until the end of the war. An identical vehicle was also used as the 7th Armoured Division HQ command tank.

Almost 2500 Cromwells were completed and the type remained in British service in dwindling numbers during the immediate post-war period.

It seems likely that the type last saw action in the Korean War with the reconnaissance troop of 8th King's Royal Irish Hussars.

THE SHERMAN FIREFLY

In January 1943, the limitations of the Challenger were stressed in a report by the Chief Inspector, Gunnery at the AFV School, Lulworth. This was instrumental in the decision to restrict Challenger production to just 200 vehicles, but did nothing to solve the increasingly urgent problem of meeting the increasingly urgent need for a 17-pdr-armed tank that would fill the gap until the Comet and Centurion could be brought into service.

In the aftermath of the Challenger's disappointing showing in the Lulworth trials, several unofficial attempts were made to up-gun the Sherman with the 17-pdr. The first of these was made by one of the Gunnery School staff, Major George Brighty of the Royal Tank Regiment (RTR), in early 1943. Despite the fact that the A30 Challenger was undergoing initial trials at Lulworth, Brighty was convinced that the Sherman was a better mount for the 17-pdr.

However, he was stymied by the turret of the Sherman, which was too small to allow for the gun's very long recoil stroke. In desperation, he removed the recoil system and devised a rigid mounting that forced the entire tank to absorb the recoil. While the system worked, it was far from ideal and there was uncertainty that it could have remained operational under frontline conditions.

A Sherman Firefly kicks up dust somewhere in Northern France during the summer of 1944. Note the ammunition storage boxes that have been welded to the glacis plate at the front.

Cromwell IV & Cromwell VI CS

■ CREW

By the time that it went into action in Normandy, the Cromwell had fallen a generation behind the latest German tanks – while it was roughly equivalent to contemporary versions of the Panzer IV, it was far outclassed by the Panther. Despite its relatively poor armour and firepower, the type had some good points, especially its high speed and reliability, which were fully exploited after the breakout from the Normandy beachhead.

■ SPECIFICATIONS

Weight: 27.94 tonnes (27.5 tons)
Length: 6.35m (20ft 10in)
Width: 2.9m (9ft 6in)
Height: 2.49m (8ft 2in)
Engine: 450kW (600hp) Rolls-Royce Meteor V12 petrol
Speed: 52km/h (32mph)
Range: 278km (173 miles)
Armament: 1 x 75mm (2.9in) OQF gun, plus 2 x 7.92mm (0.31in) Besa machine guns (1 coaxial and 1 ball-mounted in hull front)

The Cromwell CS (Close Support) variants were identical to the equivalent marks of 'standard' Cromwells except that they were armed with the 95mm (3.7in) CS Howitzer, which originated in late 1941 as a replacement for the unpopular 76mm (3in) CS Howitzer. At the time, this made sense because until 1943, at least, British tanks were armed with 2-pdr and 6-pdr guns that had a poor performance when firing HE. The new howitzer fired smoke rounds, an 11.34kg (25lb) HE shell to a maximum range of 5486m (6000 yards) and a HEAT round capable of penetrating 100mm (3.94in) of armour. By the time of the Normandy campaign, its value was questionable, as the vast majority of Cromwells in theatre were armed with 75mm (2.9in) guns with adequate HE performance for most tasks. Despite this, Cromwell CS tanks remained in frontline service until well after the end of the war.

■ SPECIFICATIONS

Weight: 27.94 tonnes (27.5 tons)
Length: 6.35m (20ft 10in)
Width: 2.9m (9ft 6in)
Height: 2.49m (8ft 2in)
Engine: 450kW (600hp) Rolls-Royce Meteor V12 petrol
Speed: 52km/h (32mph)
Range: 278km (173 miles)
Armament: 1 x 95mm (3.7in) Ordnance QF 95mm Howitzer, plus 2 x 7.92mm (0.31in) Besa machine guns (1 coaxial and 1 ball-mounted in hull front)

In June 1943, a colleague of Brighty, Lieutenant-Colonel George Witheridge RTR, arrived at Lulworth. A veteran of the North Africa campaign, Witheridge had first-hand experience of the unequal battles between British tanks armed with 2-pdr guns and Rommel's formidable combination of Panzers and anti-tank guns. During the disastrous Battle of Gazala in mid-1942, Witheridge had been blown out of his Grant tank, and although he recovered from his wounds, he was declared unfit to return to combat duty. In January 1943, he was posted to the USA to act as a tank gunnery adviser at Fort Knox, where he formed a highly favourable impression of the Sherman and began to think about the possibilities of up-gunning the design. When he arrived at Lulworth, Witheridge inspected the A30 Challenger and 'joined in the chorus of complaints' about the tank. Working in conjunction with Brighty, he developed a modified turret that allowed the 17-pdr to be fitted in a more conventional mounting.

Not long afterwards, Witheridge and Brighty received a notice from the Department of Tank Design (DTD) ordering them to abandon the project. Witheridge used his connections with such influential people as Major-General Raymond Briggs, the Director of the Royal Armoured Corps, to successfully lobby Claude Gibb, Director General of Weapon and Instrument Production at the Ministry of Supply, to make it an official ministry project.

DESIGN

W.G.K. Kilbourn, a Vickers engineer working for the DTD, transformed the prototype into a combat-worthy tank that would serve the British forces from D-Day onwards. The breech had to be rotated 90° to allow for loading from the left rather than from directly behind the gun. Other difficulties included the 102cm (40in) recoil stroke of the 17-pdr, which was too long for the Sherman's existing turret.

His solution was to redesign the recoil system – the recoil cylinders were shortened and repositioned on both sides of the gun to take advantage of the width of the Sherman's turret instead of being hindered by its limited height. To make room for the gun's recoil, the radio was moved to an armoured box ('bustle') on the rear of the turret, which also acted as a counterweight for

the long barrel. When coupled with a new gun cradle and mantlet, these modifications solved most of the major problems associated with actually firing the 17-pdr.

As the redesign progressed, further difficulties became apparent – the 'standard' Sherman turret had a single hatch for use by the commander, gunner and loader, which made it difficult for the loader to bail out in an emergency, as he had to squeeze behind or under the breech to reach the hatch. The 17-pdr's larger breech and recoil system made escape virtually impossible for the loader in such circumstances and the problem was only solved by fitting a new hatch over his position. This hatch was also useful when it came to 'bombing up' the tank, as 17-pdr ammunition was significantly larger and more awkward to stow than the 75mm (2.9in) rounds of 'standard' Shermans. This factor also led to the decision to remove the hull machine gunner's position to make room for additional ammunition stowage

By late 1943, enthusiasm began to grow for the project – 21st Army Group was informed of the new tank in October 1943 and even before final testing had taken place in February 1944, an order was placed for the conversion of 2100 M4A4 Shermans. This reaction was understandable, as the Challenger programme was suffering from constant delays and it was becoming apparent that the Sherman conversion offered the only realistic option of fielding 17-pdr-armed tanks in time for the Normandy landings. Not surprisingly, it was given the 'highest priority' by Winston Churchill himself.

Although the name 'Firefly' is now generally used for the type, it is not found in wartime official documents. It was sometimes used in unit level (brigade/regiment) war diaries from March 1944, with 'Mayfly' occasionally used as an alternative. During the war, Fireflies were usually known as 1C, 1C Hybrid or VC, depending on the basic mark of the vehicle, with the 'C' suffix indicating a 17-pdr-armed tank.

ARMAMENT

The main armament of the Sherman Firefly was the Ordnance Quick Firing 17-pounder (17-pdr). Designed as the successor to the OQF 6-pounder (6-pdr), the 17-pdr was the most powerful British

Sherman VC Firefly

CREW

At least one Firefly (serial number T212728; above) from the 4th Troop, 'A' Squadron, was captured after the surrender at Point 213, and was photographed a number of times by the Germans following their occupation of the hill. The Firefly was a well-respected tank, and a few were pressed into German service with handpainted markings (below).

Production of the Firefly began in January 1944, and by 31 May a total of 342 Sherman Fireflies had been delivered to the 21st Army Group, sufficient to allow most British armoured units to form tank troops each with three conventional Shermans and one Firefly. The type was issued on the same basis to formations such as 7th Armoured Division, which were primarily equipped with Cromwells, but this complicated maintenance, as each Cromwell troop now needed to be supplied with spares for two different tanks. From D-Day to the end of the Normandy campaign in late August, approximately 550 Fireflies were completed, more than sufficient to replace those lost during the period. As numbers increased in late 1944, British and Canadian units started to receive two Fireflies per troop. By February 1945, almost 2000 Fireflies had been built and the type represented 50 per cent of the tank strength of some British armoured units in Northwest Europe. Production tapered off in the spring of 1945 and the last tank was delivered in May 1945 as later designs (primarily the Comet and Centurion) entered service. While sources are contradictory, at least 2100 Fireflies were completed and the total may have exceeded 2300.

SPECIFICATIONS

Weight: 35.36 tonnes (34.8 tons)
Length: 7.82m (25ft 8in)
Width: 2.67m (8ft 9in)
Height: 2.74m (9ft)
Engine: 316.6kW (425hp) Chrysler Multibank A57 30-cylinder petrol
Speed: 36km/h (22.4mph)
Range: 201km (125 miles)
Armament: 1 x Ordnance QF 17-pdr (76.2mm/3in), plus 1 x coaxial 7.62mm (0.3in) Browning machine gun

tank gun of the war, and one of the most powerful of any nationality, having a better armour-piercing performance than the 8.8cm (3.5in) KwK 36 fitted to the German Tiger I, or the Panther's 7.5cm (2.9in) KwK 42. The 17-pdr could penetrate 140mm (5.5in) of armour at 500m (550 yards) and 131mm (5.15in) at 1000m (1100 yards) using standard armour-piercing, capped, ballistic capped (APCBC) ammunition. When available, armour-piercing, discarding sabot (APDS) ammunition could penetrate 209mm (11.4in) of armour at 500m (550 yards) and 192mm (7.6in) at 1000m (1100 yards), which could theoretically defeat the armour of almost every German AFV at any likely range. However, early-production APDS rounds were inaccurate at long range and their 50mm (2in) penetrators were less destructive after penetrating the target than normal APCBC shot. In any case, 17-pdr APDS ammunition was rarely available until late 1944.

Despite the Firefly's superior anti-tank capabilities, the type was regarded as inferior to the standard Sherman for use against other targets such as enemy infantry and anti-tank guns. The original 17-pdr HE round suffered from poor fragmentation, as it had to be a thick-walled design with an unusually small explosive filling to withstand the high G-forces on firing. The gun's high velocity was also liable to make the shell ricochet off hard ground before exploding some distance beyond the target. Once these problems became apparent a new HE round with a reduced propelling charge and thinner shell wall was designed which proved to be a major improvement over its predecessor, but was still considered to be inferior to the 'standard' Sherman's 75mm (2.9in) HE shell.

Another problem was that in dry weather the powerful muzzle blast from the 17-pdr kicked up a substantial amount of dust and dirt, which could betray the tank's position and made it difficult for the gunner to observe the fall of shot, forcing him to

A Sherman Firefly waits in ambush. Fireflies were arguably at their best in dealing with counter-attacks when they could fire from cover and pick off advancing German AFVs.

A pair of Sherman Fireflies drive through a town somewhere in northern France following the breakout from Normandy.

rely on the commander to order corrections. The cramped turret meant that loading the large 17-pdr ammunition was difficult, so Fireflies had a reduced rate of fire compared to 75mm (2.9in) armed Shermans. These drawbacks were accepted, however, as the type was essentially a stop-gap design intended to be withdrawn from service as the Comet and Centurion became available.

The Firefly's secondary armament was the standard 7.62mm (0.3in) Browning coaxial machine gun. A few vehicles retained a Browning 12.7mm (0.5in) machine gun on the turret roof, although most crews removed it due to the awkward mounting and its position by the commander, which limited his field of vision in combat.

PRODUCTION

Three main variants of the Sherman Firefly entered service, based on the Sherman I (M4), Sherman I Hybrid (M4 Composite) and Sherman V (M4A4) tanks. To complicate matters, a very small number of Canadian licence-built Sherman IIs (M4A1), the Grizzly, were converted to Fireflies in Canada and used for training, but none saw action. The majority of Shermans converted were the Sherman V/M4A4 model, of which the British received about 7200.

The Sherman VC and IC variants are easily distinguished by their lower hulls; the VC had a curved and riveted lower hull, while the IC had a welded and angled lower hull. The Hybrid was distinguished by its cast upper hull, giving it a distinctive curved look in comparison to the more 'boxy' hull of a typical Sherman.

Production of the Firefly began in early 1944, and by 31 May 342 Fireflies had been delivered to Montgomery's 21st Army Group in readiness for the D-Day landings. These equipped British tank troops on the basis of three standard Shermans and one Firefly. Initially, 7th Armoured Division and other Cromwell units also received Fireflies, but this caused problems, because each Cromwell troop had to be supplied with parts for two different tanks. The Fireflies were slowly replaced by Challengers as they became available. Churchill units never received Fireflies, and as a result generally had to rely on attached M10 or M10 'Achilles' units to deal with German AFVs, which were too heavily armoured for their 75mm (2.9in) guns to deal with.

Firefly production was limited by the availability of suitable tanks, as 75mm (2.9in) armed Shermans were being phased out of production and the turrets of later Shermans designed for the US 76mm (3in) gun were incompatible with the 17-pdr. Between D-Day and the end of the Battle of Normandy in late August, 550 Fireflies were completed, more than sufficient to replace losses.

In late 1944, with the issue of the improved HE shell for the 17-pdr, British units started to receive two Fireflies per troop. By February 1945, 2000 Fireflies had been completed and some units were equipped with a 50/50 mix of 75mm (2.9in) and 17-pdr-armed Shermans.

In the spring of 1945, production of the Firefly tapered off as the superior Comet and Centurion entered service, with the last tank being delivered in May 1945. It seems likely that a total of between 2100 and 2200 Fireflies were completed, although the exact numbers will probably never be known, as contemporary sources give contradictory totals.

1st Battalion, the Rifle Brigade

In 1937, the Rifle Brigade together with the King's Royal Rifle Corps (60th Rifles) formed the first motor battalions – the integral infantry for the British Army's new mobile divisions (redesignated armoured divisions in 1939).

By 1944, the motor battalions had acquired US armoured halftracks and were the nearest that the wartime British Army ever came to forming an equivalent to the German *gepanzert* (armoured) Panzergrenadier battalions. Unfortunately, their potential was rarely fully exploited due to a lack of clear tactical doctrine for 'armoured infantry'.

An imaginative brigade or divisional commander (such as 'Pip' Roberts of 11th Armoured Division) could nonetheless achieve good results, but the Rifle Brigade's 1st Battalion (1st RB) was unlucky in that Brigadier 'Looney' Hinde viewed 22nd Armoured Brigade as little more than a mechanized light cavalry formation intended primarily for long-range reconnaissance, raiding and pursuit. This attitude largely relegated 1st RB to 'mopping up' after the armour and guarding the tanks at night – hardly good preparation for fighting through the Normandy bocage.

This was symptomatic of the British Army's failure to absorb the lessons of World War I. By 1918, British officers commanding frontline troops were mainly very young, highly professional and both eager and willing to adopt the highly effective German-style infiltration tactics. The overwhelmingly conscript forces that they led had become almost as efficient as the regular, long-service volunteers of the British Expeditionary Force (BEF) of 1914 and arguably played the key role in the final defeat of the German armies in the '100 Days' – the battles of the autumn of 1918.

This painfully won expertise was largely lost as the wartime conscripts were 'demobbed' and the much-reduced peacetime army returned to what many long-serving officers regarded as 'real soldiering' – the almost constant 'small wars' of Empire.

CUSTOM AND TRADITION

'Real soldiering' marked a return to the pre-World War I attitudes where 'the Regiment' was in a real sense 'home' for all ranks, providing a sense of belonging, with its emphasis on unique and regional differences, a focus for loyalty and a boost to morale in times of crisis – for regimental honour and success meant a lot. However, regimental customs, jargon and traditions could also make it difficult for newcomers to fit into what was essentially an army composed of separate and distinct tribes. This fostering of cliques often also undermined the

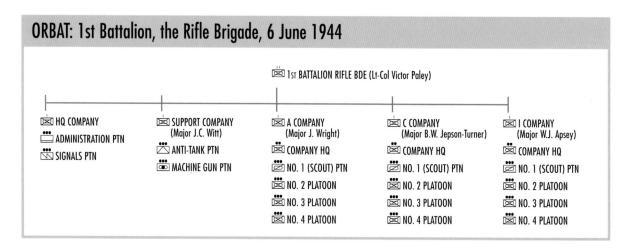

ORBAT: 1st Battalion, the Rifle Brigade, 6 June 1944

1ST BATTALION RIFLE BDE (Lt-Col Victor Paley)

HQ COMPANY
ADMINISTRATION PTN
SIGNALS PTN

SUPPORT COMPANY
(Major J.C. Witt)
ANTI-TANK PTN
MACHINE GUN PTN

A COMPANY
(Major J. Wright)
COMPANY HQ
NO. 1 (SCOUT) PTN
NO. 2 PLATOON
NO. 3 PLATOON
NO. 4 PLATOON

C COMPANY
(Major B.W. Jepson-Turner)
COMPANY HQ
NO. 1 (SCOUT) PTN
NO. 2 PLATOON
NO. 3 PLATOON
NO. 4 PLATOON

I COMPANY
(Major W.J. Apsey)
COMPANY HQ
NO. 1 (SCOUT) PTN
NO. 2 PLATOON
NO. 3 PLATOON
NO. 4 PLATOON

cohesion of larger formations (or even regiments receiving a large influx of replacements), and regimentalism also bred a dislike, suspicion and even, on occasions, hatred of outsiders, whether they be other regiments or services within the British forces. As late as 1944 a British tank officer faced with a difficult mission likely to entail heavy losses asked plaintively: 'Couldn't you send a less well-known regiment?'

ECCENTRIC LEADERSHIP

Even in 1944 there were still a substantial minority of eccentric regimental level officers who, like their Japanese counterparts, believed in adopting a deliberately conspicuous leadership profile despite the obvious hazards from enemy snipers. This included the use of hunting-horns to spur on or rally their men in Normandy and Arnhem, and the major who led his men into battle at Arnhem wearing a bowler-hat and carrying a battered umbrella for, as he later claimed, identification purposes. In Italy, the Commando officer Colonel Jack Churchill wielded both a sword and bowler-hat. It was small wonder that German snipers were easily able to pick off British officers until some at least swallowed their pride and made themselves far less conspicuous.

A combination of regimental pride and eccentricity caused problems for much of the war – there was a strong tendency to dispute inconvenient or unpalatable orders, command being exercised more by conference than obedience in North Africa and later in Normandy. When General Hobart assumed command of the Mobile Division (soon to become 7th Armoured Division) in 1938, he was outraged that its officers preferred playing polo to combat training.

Luckily, the artillery and infantry were less infected by this mental malaise. Certainly, at the junior level in particular, most officers were as good as their Allied counterparts, if usually not quite up to the best German standards, particularly when they began to be recruited from a wider social group through modified selection procedures.

NEW COMMISSIONS

Officer quality in the British Army was also enhanced by the many NCO platoon commanders (sergeant-majors) of 1939 who were later commissioned, some

rising to command battalions or regiments by 1945, as well as some men who received 'commissions in the field' for outstanding bravery or initiative.

However, the commissioning of so many NCOs had drawbacks in the long term because it caused a leadership gap, and the quality of infantry NCOs declined noticeably by 1944, largely because those men with leadership abilities had already become officers. So serious was the shortage of officers that by 1945 some of the newer ones were barely 18 years old. Even this was not enough, especially as the real tactical training of officers was provided only when they joined their units, and this 'in-house training' was often patchy, giving rise to continued complaints about poor officer quality.

Officer casualty rates in 1939–45 were (proportionately) higher than they had been in

1st Battalion, the Rifle Brigade Unit Badge

In September 1939, the battalion formed part of 1st Support Group, 1st Armoured Division. It first saw action in May 1940, when it served as part of 30th Brigade in the defence of Calais, together with 2nd Battalion King's Royal Rifle Corps and 1st Battalion Queen Victoria Rifles. All three battalions were lost after imposing a critical three days' delay on German armoured forces attempting to attack the BEF's fragile perimeter around Dunkirk. After the fall of France, the battalion was re-formed and then sailed to North Africa with 1st Armoured Division. The unit joined 22nd Armoured Brigade as part of 7th Armoured Division for El Alamein and continued to serve with the brigade and division until the end of the war. After the surrender of Hamburg in May 1945, the battalion ended the war in Kiel. The battalion was unique in that it comprised A, C, I and S (Support) Companies – other Rifle Brigade battalions had A, B, C and S (Support) Companies.

1914–18, and roughly double that for other ranks. Yet the need for so many officers was partly self-inflicted – even in 1943 it was unthinkable, at least officially, to have mere NCOs commanding platoons, as was practised so successfully in the German Army.

TACTICAL LIMITATIONS

British training was therefore prescriptive (all tactical problems being categorized into types) and fostered a methodical and set-piece approach to combat, itself a sort of battle of attrition using superior material to compensate for a lack of

1st Battalion, the Rifle Brigade: Vehicles

EQUIPMENT	STRENGTH
Jeeps	2
CMP 15cwt truck	8
Ford WOT 3-ton truck	14
Humber Scout Car	9
Universal Carrier Mk II	47
Loyd Carrier	12
6-pdr AT gun	6
M5A1 halftrack	36

Motor Battalion: Personnel

UNIT	OFFICERS	MEN
Headquarter Company (consisting of):	5	94
Company HQ	1	8
Signals Platoon	1	16
Administration Platoon	3	70
Support Company (consisting of):	7	192
Company HQ	2	25
Three Anti-Tank Platoons, each	1	37
Two Machine Gun Platoons, each	1	28
3 x Motor Companies (each consisting of):	7	168
Company HQ	2	37
Scout Platoon	2	41
3 x Motor Platoons (each composed of):		
Platoon HQ	1	6
3 x Motor Sections (each composed of):	–	8
Total Strength of 854 all ranks	38	816

tactical excellence. British officers complained that it was difficult to get their men to do more than the minimum required, whereas the Germans, who saw all tactical situations as essentially unique, trained men to continually do more than should have been reasonably asked of them.

As the late Richard Holmes put it in his *Battlefields of the Second World War*: '... with the end of the war in sight they were simply not prepared to take unnecessary risks ... the dreadful attrition of junior officers and NCOs in Normandy testified to an increasing need to pull men into battle by personal example. The typical British attack had become a short rush forward, dig in and await the inevitable German counter-attack. These were soldiers who would grind the enemy down, or hold a defensive perimeter to the death, but they had acquired neither the battlefield habits nor the confidence in their leaders necessary for a *blitzkrieg*-style operation ....'

Reports from Normandy cited excessive bunching together by troops and an over-reliance on supporting fire rather than their own weapons (partly because of the British infantry squad's low organic firepower); and the problems of fighting in the Normandy bocage and beyond demonstrated that there were clear limits to the Western Allied policy of expending ammunition rather than lives, particularly if 'ammunition' of whatever sort was scarce or absent.

Even after Montgomery's vigorous efforts to stamp out the false notion of 'independence', it took the infantry (and other arms) a long time to learn to fight in larger, division-sized formations or mixed battle-groups of the sort the Germans wielded so skilfully. The British armour's habit of withdrawing from the battlefield at night to form a defensive leaguer not only put more strain on men and machines and surrendered any gains made to the enemy, but also gave the infantry the impression that they had been abandoned. The Germans remained where they were at dusk to provide, and receive in turn, support from different arms and to recover unmolested any unserviceable or abandoned vehicles.

In Normandy, full coordination in some formations was not achieved until many bitter lessons of the Desert War had been bloodily relearned, and even as late as the Arnhem fiasco,

British inter-arms co-operation was sometimes found wanting. Although British tanks began to be fitted with hull-mounted telephone sets in July 1944 to allow instant communication with their accompanying infantry, the evidence suggests that neither the infantry nor the tank crews made much use of them.

Equally, man-portable infantry radios were generally underused despite being relatively plentiful in 1944, since they were unreliable and a radio 'specialist' meant one less combat soldier in order to carry around a heavy and unwanted piece of equipment at a time when the company strength was often well below the official establishment figure. Instead, orders tended to be issued in time-wasting 'O Group' meetings where concentrations of officers were vulnerable to attack.

MANPOWER SHORTAGES

In most theatres, casualty rates approached or exceeded 1914–18 rates on occasions, and the shortage of infantrymen, who bore the brunt of the losses, could only be partially alleviated by an influx of poorly trained personnel of often inferior quality. These reinforcements were found by disbanding or amalgamating some units and by transferring AFV crews, artillerymen, rear-area personnel, military prison inmates and even surplus RAF or Royal Navy manpower to infantry units, often with only scanty training.

To compensate for this state of affairs, late-war British infantry tactics reverted to simpler World War I-style set-piece advances behind artillery barrages to make up for these training and experience deficiencies. A reduction in the overall proportion of non-combat to combat personnel within units (along German, Japanese or Soviet lines) was not attempted, so that – despite the fact that the official infantry battalion manpower total was reduced – combat strength fell steadily. Prolonged combat reduced infantry companies to

Universal Carriers from the 1st Battalion, the Rifle Brigade park along a country road near Le Bény-Bocage, August 1944.

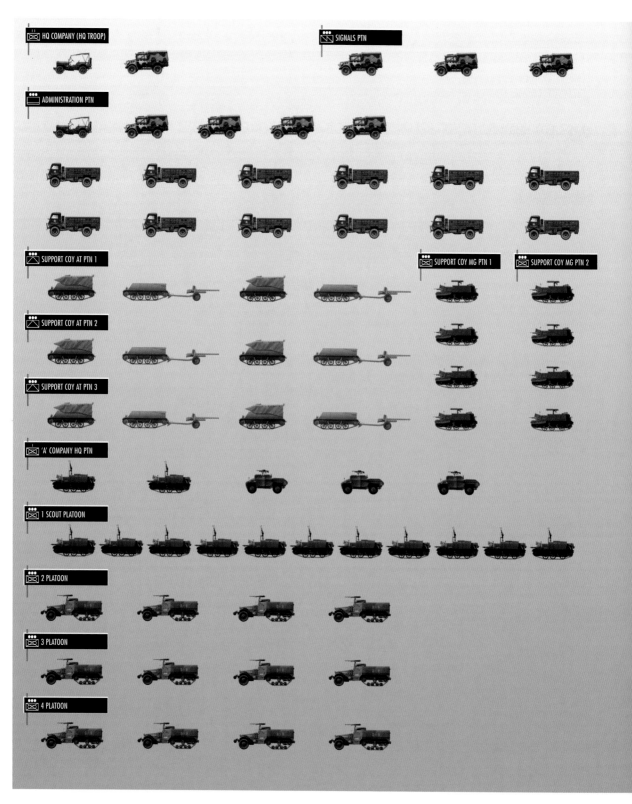

HQ COMPANY (HQ TROOP)

SIGNALS PTN

ADMINISTRATION PTN

SUPPORT COY AT PTN 1

SUPPORT COY MG PTN 1

SUPPORT COY MG PTN 2

SUPPORT COY AT PTN 2

SUPPORT COY AT PTN 3

'A' COMPANY HQ PTN

1 SCOUT PLATOON

2 PLATOON

3 PLATOON

4 PLATOON

1st Battalion, the Rifle Brigade (fighting component)

Jeep: 2
CMP 15cwt truck: 8
Ford WOT 3-ton truck: 12

Humber Scout Car: 9
M5A1 halftrack: 36
Universal Carrier MkII: 47

Loyd Carrier: 6
Loyd Carrier with 6-pdr AT gun: 6

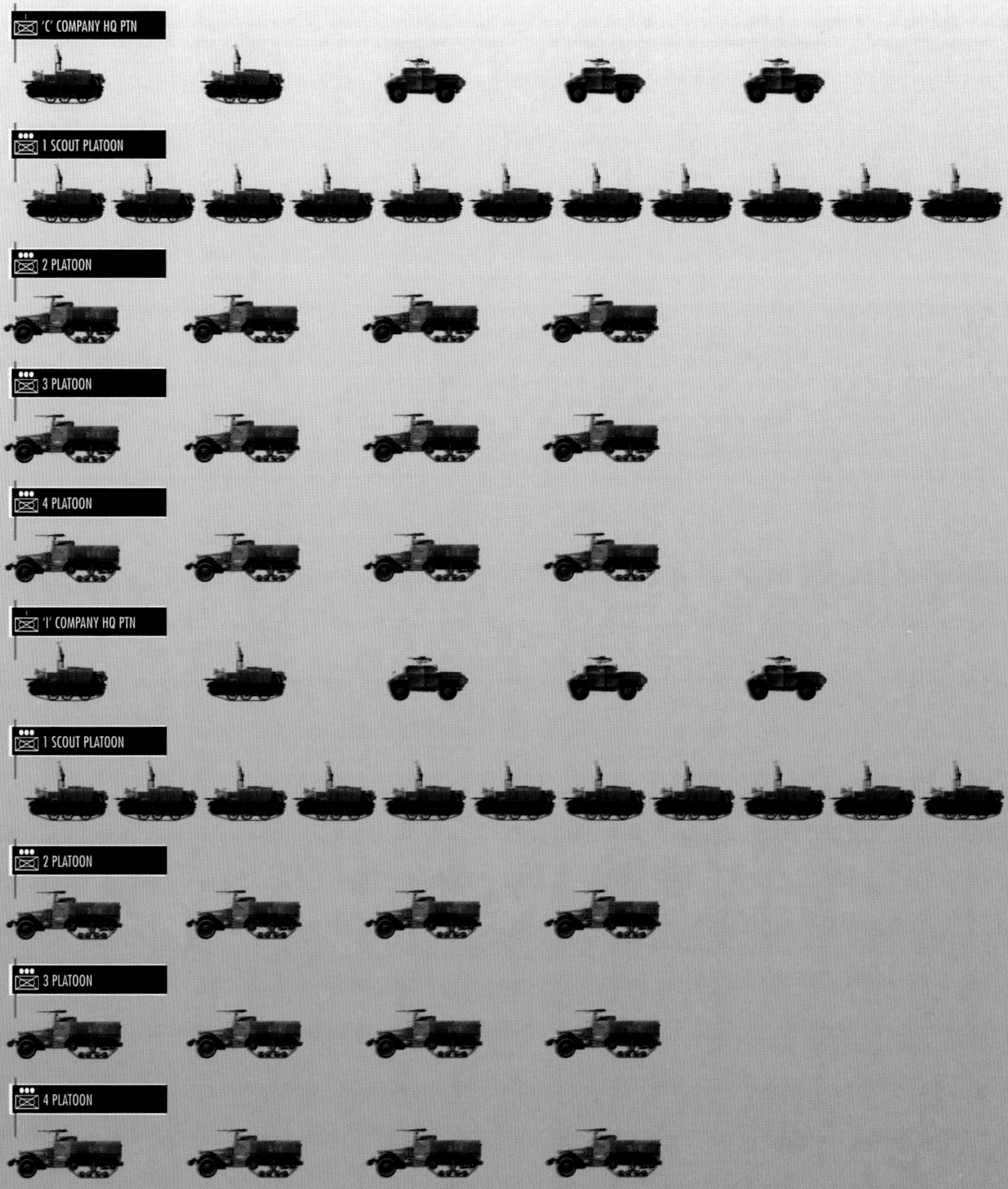

'C' COMPANY HQ PTN

1 SCOUT PLATOON

2 PLATOON

3 PLATOON

4 PLATOON

'I' COMPANY HQ PTN

1 SCOUT PLATOON

2 PLATOON

3 PLATOON

4 PLATOON

40 men or less, and these decimated units were then rebuilt with raw 18- or 19-year-old replacements.

By 1945, most British infantry companies might have just one veteran left, while 45-year-old men, who had previously been deemed too old for active military service, were now being sent to frontline units.

This state of affairs reflects the gradual exhaustion of Britain's finite infantry rather than manpower reserves, and in reality the strength of the British Army actually grew from 2.7 million men in 1944 to 2.9–3 million men in 1945, not counting Commonwealth contributions, which totalled 1.4 million men during the war.

Earlier in the war, the British had reduced the ratio of infantry to armoured and artillery formations so that there were not enough infantry units, and had also raised far more units than could be maintained in the long term. Infantrymen also became scarce because the British and US armies had underestimated the infantry losses that they would suffer in Normandy's bocage, due to an over-reliance on casualty statistics compiled in North Africa, and were therefore unable to rapidly replace their losses.

HQ Company

In a motor battalion such as 1st RB, the HQ Company was especially important due to the tendency to deploy the battalion's rifle companies independently, with one company supporting each of the armoured brigade's three tank regiments.

When on the move or deployed for action, there was no clear-cut distinction between Battalion HQ and the HQ Company. Some of the Battalion HQ personnel would be located at rear HQ and some of the HQ Company's transport was used by Battalion HQ. There would be a Royal Signals vehicle to maintain communications with Brigade HQ.

In action, the Commanding Officer (CO) formed a small Tactical HQ containing only essential command personnel. His operational officers, Adjutant, Signals Officer, Technical Officer and Intelligence Officer (IO), each had their own armoured halftrack (or M3 White scout car) fitted with a Wireless Set No. 19. The CO would normally be at Battalion HQ while the unit was in action but might otherwise be at Brigade HQ or visiting his own companies, holding Order Groups (O Groups) or conducting reconnaissance. The Battalion HQ group could continue to function in his absence.

The Second-in-Command (2IC) was not normally at the Tactical HQ. In action, he assumed responsibility for all administrative matters, thus

HQ Company: Equipment

EQUIPMENT	STRENGTH
HQ Troop	
Jeep	1
Motorcycle	1
CMP 15cwt truck	1
Administration Platoon	
Jeep	1
Motorcycle	2
CMP 15cwt truck	4
Ford WOT 3-ton truck	12
Signals Platoon	
CMP 15cwt truck	3
Motorcycle	5

HQ Company: Personnel

UNIT	OFFICERS	MEN
Company HQ	1	8
Signals Platoon	1	16
Administrative Platoon	3	70
Total Strength of 99 all ranks	5	94

leaving the CO to concentrate on operational tasks. He was responsible for the Rear HQ, which held all the battalion elements that were not actively engaged in an operation. This included the transport, supply and maintenance elements.

The IO was responsible for keeping the unit's 'War Diary' or 'Intelligence Summary'. A motor battalion had a small Intelligence Section of an officer, sergeant and four men, whose responsibility was to know as much as possible about enemy weapons, equipment, formations and units. The IO would work with the CO and the 2IC at Battalion HQ. When the CO visited Brigade HQ to receive orders from the brigadier, he would go with him and be separately briefed by the Brigade IO on the latest information about the enemy. During an attack he would be by the CO's side; and when the battalion was occupying a defensive position, he would accompany him when he went to visit the rifle companies.

The medical establishment allowed for an armoured halftrack ambulance (with four or five stretcher-bearers) to be assigned to each rifle company plus one for the Medical Officer (MO), who would set up a Regimental Aid Post (RAP) to provide initial treatment for the wounded. These four vehicles would travel with the HQ Company on long moves but would normally be dispersed between the rifle and support companies.

In planning each operation, one key function of Battalion HQ was to prepare a list of those to be left out of battle (LOB). These key personnel would form a cadre for rebuilding the battalion if heavy casualties were sustained. Typical LOBs might include two majors (probably the battalion's 2IC and a senior company commander), four captains and five lieutenants. The rifle companies would leave behind a total of perhaps 20 sergeants, corporals and lance-corporals. A range of specialist NCOs and men from the Signals Platoon, Intelligence Section, Sniper Section, as well as all Company Quartermaster Sergeants (CQMS) and stores personnel, would generally also be listed to remain out of battle.

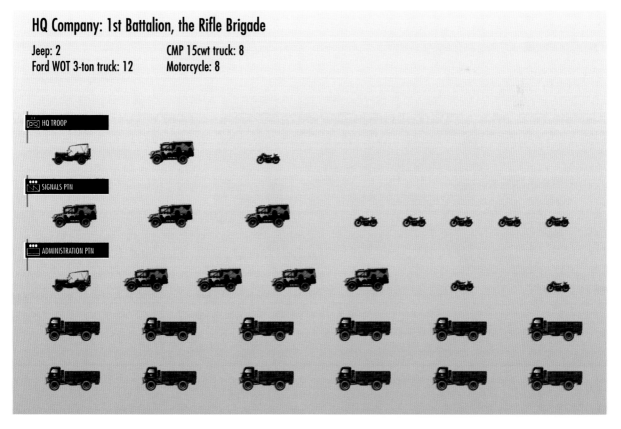

HQ Company: 1st Battalion, the Rifle Brigade

Jeep: 2   CMP 15cwt truck: 8
Ford WOT 3-ton truck: 12   Motorcycle: 8

HQ TROOP

SIGNALS PTN

ADMINISTRATION PTN

Willys MB Jeep

CREW

SPECIFICATIONS

Weight: 1.04 tonnes (1.02 tons)
Length: 3.33m (10ft 11in)
Width: 1.57m (5ft 2in)
Height: 1.83m (6ft) (With canvas
 tilt raised)
Engine: 45kW (60hp) Willys L134
 4-cylinder petrol
Speed: 105km/h (65mph)
Range: 482.8km (300 miles)

The versatile jeep appeared in many guises during (and long after) the war. In British armoured units, it was primarily used as a frontline 'staff car' and liaison vehicle.

Truck, 15cwt, GS, 4x2, Bedford MWD

CREW

SPECIFICATIONS

Weight: 2.13 tonnes (2.09 tons)
Length: 4.38m (14ft 4.5in)
Width: 1.99m (6ft 6.5in)
Height: 2.29m (7ft 6in)
Engine: 53.7kW (72hp) Bedford OHV
 6-cylinder petrol
Speed: 80km/h (50mph) (estimated)
Range: 270km (168 miles) (estimated)

The Bedford MWD was one of the best known of the wartime 15cwts. It entered service just before the war and Vauxhall Motors completed some 66,000 (not all of them GS trucks) by the time production ceased in 1945. In common with other 15cwts of the era, early models had an open cab and no tilt. They were initially issued on the basis of one per infantry platoon, to carry the unit's ammunition, rations and kit. This example is finished in the so-called 'Mickey Mouse ear' camouflage widely used for British 'soft-skinned' support vehicles in 1944.

Support Company

The Support Company provided the battalion's organic anti-tank and sustained fire support with its six 6-pdr anti-tank guns and four Vickers medium machine guns.

The limitations of the small 2-pdr anti-tank guns were apparent even as the type entered service in 1936, and design studies of potential replacements began in 1938. Development of the new weapon was undertaken at Woolwich Arsenal, whose designers calculated that a 57mm (2.2in) gun firing a 6-pdr shot should have greatly improved amour-piercing performance while still being light enough to be easily manoeuvrable.

ORDNANCE QUICK-FIRING 6-PDR 7CWT

The selection of a 57mm (2.2in) weapon was at least partially due to the fact that this had been a standard calibre of the Royal Navy since the late nineteenth century and hence manufacturing equipment was readily available. The design of the gun was complete by 1940 and in April of that year the type was formally accepted as both a tank gun and an anti-tank gun. The Ordnance Board had also been requested to examine the feasibility of heavier anti-tank guns, including 80mm (3.15in), 90mm (3.5in) and 100mm (3.9in) designs. This resulted in the recommendation of an 87.6mm (3.45in) gun, looking rather like the 95mm (3.7in) AA gun firing a 9kg (20lb) shot, which was rejected in March 1940.

The massive loss of equipment (including most of the Army's 2-pdr anti-tank guns) in the Dunkirk evacuation forced a drastic change of plan. The priority was now the rapid re-equipping of home defence forces to face a probable German invasion. At this point in the war, equipment policy had to be one of quantity rather than quality and 6-pdr production would interfere with that of the 2-pdr. (It was estimated that three 2-pdrs could be completed for every two 6-pdrs.) Retention of the 2-pdr also avoided the inevitable delays in retooling factories to produce the 6-pdr and training troops to use the new gun effectively. Only after the

Support Company: Equipment

EQUIPMENT	STRENGTH
HQ Troop	
Motorcycle	3
CMP 15cwt truck	3
Jeep (4x4)	1
Ford WOT 3-ton truck	2
Anti-tank Platoon 1	
Motorcycle	1
CMP 15cwt truck	2
Loyd Carrier	4
6-pdr AT gun	2
Anti-tank Platoon 2	
Motorcycle	1
CMP 15cwt truck	2
Loyd Carrier	4
6-pdr AT gun	2
Anti-Tank Platoon 3	
Motorcycle	1
CMP 15cwt truck	2
Loyd Carrier	4
6-pdr AT gun	2
Machine Gun Platoon 1	
Motorcycle	1
Universal Carrier Mk II	4
Machine Gun Platoon 2	
Motorcycle	1
Universal Carrier Mk II	4

Support Company: Personnel

UNIT	OFFICERS	MEN
Company HQ	2	25
Anti-Tank Platoon 1	1	37
Anti-Tank Platoon 2	1	37
Anti-Tank Platoon 3	1	37
Machine Gun Platoon 1	1	28
Machine Gun Platoon 2	1	28
Total Strength of 198 all ranks	7	191

Support Company: 1st Battalion, the Rifle Brigade

Loyd Carrier: 6
Ford WOT 3-ton truck: 2
Loyd Carrier with 6-pdr AT gun: 6

CMP 15cwt truck: 9
Medium Machine Gun Carriers: 8
Motorcycle: 8

The Support Company's 6-pdrs and Vickers machine guns were frequently deployed by sections (two weapons each) to reinforce whichever rifle companies were most heavily engaged.

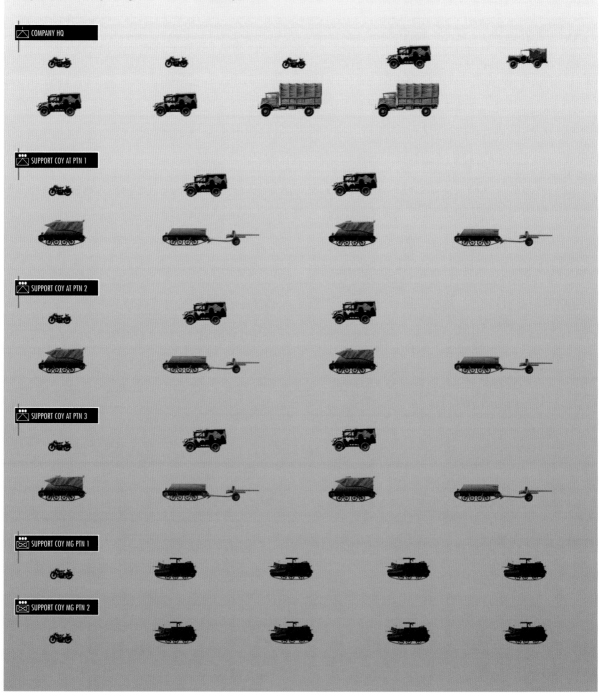

COMPANY HQ

SUPPORT COY AT PTN 1

SUPPORT COY AT PTN 2

SUPPORT COY AT PTN 3

SUPPORT COY MG PTN 1

SUPPORT COY MG PTN 2

invasion scare had passed and the limitations of the 2-pdr were bloodily revealed in North Africa was the decision taken to finally begin production of the 6-pdr.

In 1941, there was initially a drive for '6-pdr tanks at all costs' before priority switched to 6-pdr anti-tank guns. The first tank guns (Mark III) were completed in June, with full production beginning at the end of October, while the first anti-tank guns (Mark II) were completed in July. In contrast to most other weapons, carriage production exceeded gun production quite significantly in 1941 – most guns produced in that year were the tank version, but these were also capable of being mounted on the anti-tank carriage. Shortage of the necessary tooling forced these early versions to be produced with L/43 barrels, but production switched to the Marks IV and V with L/50 barrels as soon as possible.

Anti-tank regiments in North Africa began to re-equip with the 6-pdr in the spring of 1942 and welcomed the new gun as a vast improvement on the outclassed 2-pdr. However, German AFVs were

constantly being updated and the 'gun-armour race' would continue throughout the war. Almost immediately that the 6-pdr first went into action, the performance of its original plain-steel armour-piercing (AP) shot was boosted by a more powerful loading of propellant. From October 1942, this was replaced by armour-piercing capped (APC) shot to improve the performance against face-hardened armour generally used for German AFVs, at the same time as an armour-piercing, capped, ballistic capped shot (APCBC). This was heavier, with a reduced muzzle velocity, but had an improved long-range performance thanks to its streamlined outer 'ballistic cap'. An HE shell was also developed, as was an armour-piercing composite rigid tungsten-cored shot (APCR) but neither saw much use. In June 1944, just in time for the Normandy campaign, the armour-piercing, discarding sabot shot (APDS) was introduced. Although accuracy suffered to a certain extent, the spectacular capabilities of APDS meant that the Tiger I and Panther could be penetrated at ranges up to 1000m (1100 yards).

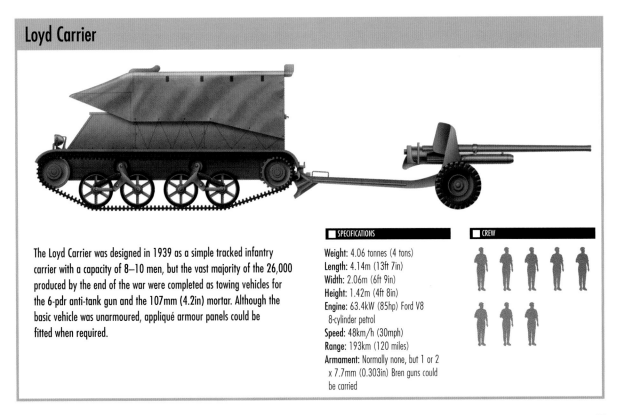

Loyd Carrier

The Loyd Carrier was designed in 1939 as a simple tracked infantry carrier with a capacity of 8–10 men, but the vast majority of the 26,000 produced by the end of the war were completed as towing vehicles for the 6-pdr anti-tank gun and the 107mm (4.2in) mortar. Although the basic vehicle was unarmoured, appliqué armour panels could be fitted when required.

■ SPECIFICATIONS

Weight: 4.06 tonnes (4 tons)
Length: 4.14m (13ft 7in)
Width: 2.06m (6ft 9in)
Height: 1.42m (4ft 8in)
Engine: 63.4kW (85hp) Ford V8
  8-cylinder petrol
Speed: 48km/h (30mph)
Range: 193km (120 miles)
Armament: Normally none, but 1 or 2
  x 7.7mm (0.303in) Bren guns could
  be carried

■ CREW

LOYD CARRIER

In 1939, Captain Vivian Loyd developed a simple cross-country vehicle primarily from existing parts from different manufacturers. The main components were the chassis, engine, gearbox and rear axle of the Ford 2-ton truck combined with tracks and suspension derived from a Vickers light tank. The design used mild steel bodywork with provision for bolting armour plate (referred to as 'BP Plate' in Loyd manuals) to the front and upper sides. The vehicle was open topped, but was issued with a canvas tilt to give the crew some protection in bad weather.

The Army tested the Loyd Carrier in 1939 and placed an initial order for 200 as the 'Carrier, Tracked, Personnel Carrying (TPC)'. This was an armoured personnel carrier (APC) variant fitted with frontal and side armour panels, which could carry up to 10 men. However, the majority of the 26,000 Loyds completed were the five-seat Tracked Towing (TT) version fitted with ammunition stowage racks over the track guards. These were primarily used for towing the 6-pdr or the 107mm (4.2in) mortar and were often fitted with appliqué

7mm (0.27in) armour panels. (In practice, lack of internal space meant that two vehicles were required for each 6-pdr, one for the gun and its crew and the second to carry a reasonable supply of ammunition.)

The Loyd Carrier came in for much criticism for general unreliability – its weak steering was accentuated when towing a heavy load such as the 6-pdr gun and carrying a substantial load of ammunition. Other frequent faults included poor tractive power, weak suspension in rear axle units, and brake fading – all of which were worsened by habitual overloading by frontline users. Despite these problems, the Loyd remained in service throughout the war, but was rapidly phased out of British service in the late 1940s, with many being transferred to the Belgian, Dutch and Danish Armies.

MEDIUM MACHINE GUN CARRIER

The origins of the Medium Machine Gun Carrier can be traced back to the Carden Loyd tankette family, which was developed in the 1920s, and specifically the Mk VI tankette. By 1939, the type

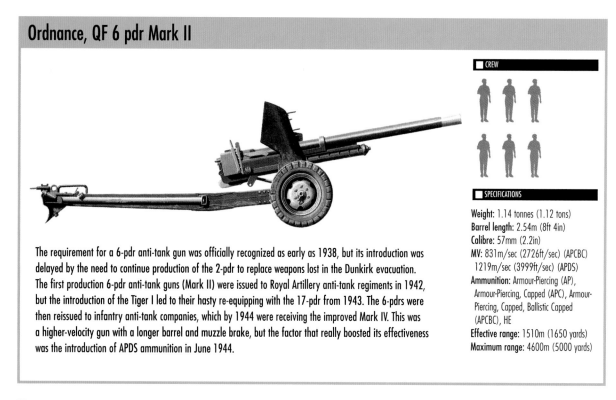

Ordnance, QF 6 pdr Mark II

CREW

SPECIFICATIONS

Weight: 1.14 tonnes (1.12 tons)
Barrel length: 2.54m (8ft 4in)
Calibre: 57mm (2.2in)
MV: 831m/sec (2726ft/sec) (APCBC)
1219m/sec (3999ft/sec) (APDS)
Ammunition: Armour-Piercing (AP), Armour-Piercing, Capped (APC), Armour-Piercing, Capped, Ballistic Capped (APCBC), HE
Effective range: 1510m (1650 yards)
Maximum range: 4600m (5000 yards)

The requirement for a 6-pdr anti-tank gun was officially recognized as early as 1938, but its introduction was delayed by the need to continue production of the 2-pdr to replace weapons lost in the Dunkirk evacuation. The first production 6-pdr anti-tank guns (Mark II) were issued to Royal Artillery anti-tank regiments in 1942, but the introduction of the Tiger I led to their hasty re-equipping with the 17-pdr from 1943. The 6-pdrs were then reissued to infantry anti-tank companies, which by 1944 were receiving the improved Mark IV. This was a higher-velocity gun with a longer barrel and muzzle brake, but the factor that really boosted its effectiveness was the introduction of APDS ammunition in June 1944.

had evolved into a whole family of light AFVs – the Bren Gun Carrier, the Scout Carrier and the Cavalry Carrier.

These were all simple, open-topped vehicles with a thinly armoured crew compartment at the front and a rear-mounted Ford V8 engine. All versions used a unique and highly effective steering system controlled by a steering wheel. Gentle turns were made by moving the front road wheels, which warped the tracks, while track braking was used for sharper turns. While all variants were mechanically similar, each type had its own distinct features and in early 1939 it was decided to simplify production by adopting a single version that was readily adaptable for all the family's roles.

These Universal Carriers entered service in 1940 and rapidly became one of the most popular British wartime vehicles, proving to be almost infinitely adaptable and fulfilling far more roles than had ever been originally envisaged by their designers. One variant that entered service in 1943, the Medium Machine Gun Carrier,

re-created a type that had been pioneered by the Carden Loyds of the 1920s. The new vehicle incorporated minor structural modifications – the engine cover was strengthened to take the weight of a standard 7.7mm (0.303in) Vickers machine gun on a pintle mounting and internal stowage was altered to carry 19 ammunition boxes, each containing a 250-round belt, giving a total of 4750 rounds per vehicle. The gun could be fired from the carrier, or dismounted and ground-fired from the standard tripod, which was stowed in the front compartment.

VICKERS MACINE GUN

The gun itself was the Vickers Mark I, which had been only slightly modified since the very first examples were accepted for service in November 1912. The weight of the water-cooled gun itself varied according to the sights and other accessories used, but was generally about 18kg (40lb) including 4 litres (7.5 pints) of water, while the tripod added a further 22.6kg (50lb).

Medium Machine Gun Carrier

CREW

SPECIFICATIONS

Weight: 4.06 tonnes (4 tons)
Length: 3.76m (12ft 4in)
Width: 2.11m (6ft 11in)
Height: 1.63m (5ft 4in)
Engine: 63.4kW (85hp) Ford V8 8-cylinder petrol
Speed: 52km/h (32mph)
Range: 258km (160 miles)
Armament: 1 x 7.7mm (0.303in) Vickers medium machine gun

This version of the Universal Carrier equipped the Medium Machine Gun platoons, giving the motor battalions a highly mobile source of fire support. The platoons carried range-finders and all the other necessary equipment to allow their guns to exploit the 4115m (4500-yard) range of the Vickers, which was almost twice that of the 76mm (3in) mortar.

The steel boxes for the 250-round ammunition belts weighed 10kg (22lb) each when fully loaded. The cyclic rate of fire was between 450 and 500 rounds per minute, but in practice it was expected that 10,000 rounds would be fired per hour. This would require an hourly barrel change – a two-minute job for a well-trained gun crew.

The guns were usually fitted with dial sights that, combined with high-velocity Mark VIIIz ammunition, allowed sustained indirect fire at ranges of up to approximately 4115m (4500 yards). The Vickers' reliability was near legendary and its capabilities as a sustained fire support weapon so exceptional that it remained in British service until 1968.

Vickers Machine Gun

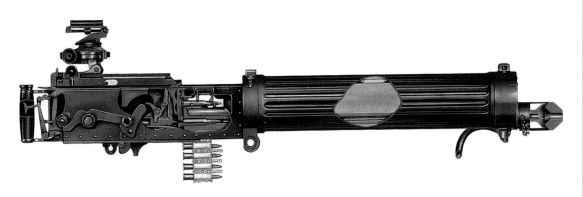

The British Army formally adopted the Vickers gun as its standard machine gun on 26 November 1912, using it alongside the Maxims that had been in service since 1897. It was extensively used in the indirect fire role in 1944–45 and was fitted with a dial sight to engage targets at ranges up to 4115m (4500 yards). Despite its weight and bulk, the Vickers was highly regarded as a support weapon, remaining in service with the British Army until March 1968.

■ CREW

■ SPECIFICATIONS

Calibre: 7.7mm (0.303in)
Length: 1.1556m (3ft 9.5in)
Length of Barrel: 648mm (2ft 4.5in)
Weight: 40.9kg (90.2lb) (gun and tripod)

Feed System: 250-round belt
Rate of Fire: 450–500rpm
Muzzle Velocity: 743.7m/sec
(2440ft/sec)

Effective Range: Direct fire: 2000m
(2187 yards). Indirect fire 4115m
(4500 yards).

'A' Company

'A' Company together with 4th CLY formed the spearhead of 22nd Armoured Brigade's advance and bore the brunt of Wittmann's attack at Villers-Bocage.

Company HQ had responsibility for both command functions and administration/supply duties. These latter, least glamorous, elements of military life were overseen by the

CQMS who commanded a dozen assorted drivers, mechanics, storemen and cooks.

The burden of command was normally shared between two officers, the company commander and his 2IC. When the company was at full strength, the commander would be responsible for 170 men, plus any elements of the Support Company that might be attached for specific operations. It was impossible for him to personally lead so many troops spread over a frontage of possibly several hundred metres. He had to exercise command and control as much through delegation to subordinates as through personal leadership.

The company commander needed to brief his subunit leaders on the mission in hand and ensure that each understood his role. Once his force deployed, he needed to focus on the overall progress of the battle, 'reading' the course of the fighting and reinforcing key sectors as necessary. He would simultaneously be in touch with Battalion HQ, which would be demanding updates and monitoring progress. He would also be acutely aware of developments on his flanks, where the varying fortunes of neighbouring troops might demand his company's intervention. Quite a stressful job all in all.

Helping to ease this demanding workload was his 2IC who in effect allowed the commander to attempt the trick of being in two places at once. One could maintain the company command post while the other went forward to judge the situation for himself. In the event of the loss of the commander, the 2IC naturally took over his role.

Company HQ's staff also included the Company Sergeant-Major (CSM). His role was to assist with issuing orders and intelligence to the forward troops and maintain discipline. In a more intangible but equally important way, he had to set an example within the ranks and ensure that everyone was doing things right, and leave them in no doubt as to when they were doing it wrong.

COMPANY COMMUNICATIONS

A combination of radio operators and runners/motorcycle dispatch riders kept the information flow moving. There would be at least two radios, normally the No. 18, which had a maximum range of 16km (10 miles). One of these would be tuned to the battalion net while the other received reports from the platoon sets. Company radios were more powerful and somewhat more reliable than those issued to platoons, which were generally the No. 38 Mk II with a range of 1.6 km (1 mile).

Whenever it seemed likely that a position would be held for some time, far more reliable landlines and field telephones would be set up to supplement the radio net. (Although landlines were always

'A' Company: Vehicles

EQUIPMENT	STRENGTH
HQ Platoon	
Motorcycle	3
CMP 15cwt truck	2
Universal Carrier Mk II	2
Ford WOT 3-ton truck	3
Humber Scout Car	3
No. 1 Scout Platoon	
Universal Carrier Mk II	11
No. 2 Platoon	
M5 halftrack	4
No. 3 Platoon	
M5 halftrack	4
No. 4 Platoon	
M5 halftrack	4

'A' Company: Personnel

UNIT	OFFICERS	MEN
Company HQ	2	37
Scout Platoon	2	41
Motor Platoon 1		
Platoon HQ	1	6
Motor Section 1	–	8
Motor Section 2	–	8
Motor Section 3	–	8
Motor Platoon 2		
Platoon HQ	1	6
Motor Section 1	–	8
Motor Section 2	–	8
Motor Section 3	–	8
Motor Platoon 3		
Platoon HQ	1	6
Motor Section 1	–	8
Motor Section 2	–	8
Motor Section 3	–	8
Total Strength of 175 all ranks	7	168

vulnerable to enemy artillery fire, telephoned messages were much more secure than radio traffic, which was always liable to be intercepted by German monitoring posts.)

At least three runners/motorcycle dispatch riders were available, sufficient for one per motor platoon, and these could be increased by orderlies, clerks and the like, where they did not already double as signallers.

COMPANY COMMAND POST

The Company Command Post (CP) was normally a fixed position from which the commander could direct his platoons and contact adjacent and higher formations. It was staffed by the commander, CSM, signaller and runners. In the assault, the commander would take its staff with him, together with some men to act as an escort. The 2IC would

establish a reserve post, or in the offensive a fixed position, to which messengers could head in the event they could not find the mobile CP.

THE COMPANY IN THE ATTACK

Although the company would generally work in conjunction with an armoured regiment, it had sufficient integral weaponry to deal with anti-tank ambushes and similar minor defensive positions that might delay the advance. (The two 76mm/3in mortars of each motor platoon were especially valuable – as an Army Training Memorandum of October 1942 noted: 'The 25-pdr gun is able to put down a total of 125lb of projectiles in one minute

This photograph shows infantry from the 6th Battalion, the Green Howards, part of the 50th (Northumbrian) Division, fighting in the Normandy bocage. A damaged M5 halftrack is being used as cover.

at "intense" rate, while one 3in mortar can put down 200lb at rapid rate in the same period … For short periods of time … six 3in mortars can bring down a greater weight of fire than an eight-gun field battery…')

One of the most important factors in the company's effectiveness was its initial deployment – the difficult task of striking the right balance between the assault echelon and the reserve or support element. The company commander had to try to read the likely course of the battle and conserve his assets to enable him to affect its outcome two or more moves further down the line. He could, therefore, only commit a portion of his troops to the initial assault, holding a number in reserve and, mathematically speaking, the decision was deceptively simple – to lead with one platoon or two?

'A' Company: 1st Battalion, the Rifle Brigade

Humber Scout Car: 3
M5A1 halftrack: 12
Universal Carrier MkII: 13
Ford WOT 3-ton truck: 3
Motorcycle: 3
CMP 15cwt truck: 2

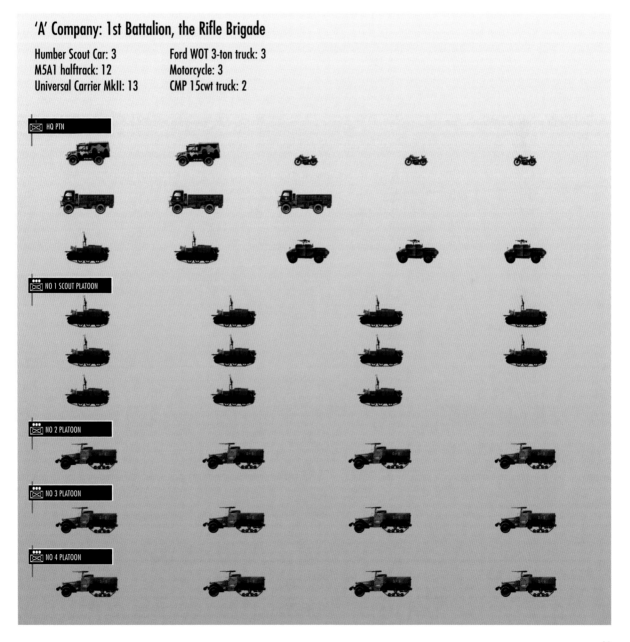

HQ PTN

NO 1 SCOUT PLATOON

NO 2 PLATOON

NO 3 PLATOON

NO 4 PLATOON

V SHAPE

The V shape provided the most popular method of deployment and followed the longstanding principle that a reserve should always constitute at least one third of the force. Two platoons would advance on parallel axes, with the third held back in support. The lead platoons would maintain a boundary between themselves to prevent squads becoming mixed up, but their commanders would still seek to keep in contact with their flank protection. It was felt that this 'two pronged' advance allowed the greatest flexibility. The two platoons could provide mutual fire support, one covering while the second moved. Within each platoon, individual squads would operate in a similar fashion.

The role of the third platoon was pivotal in the development of the assault, and its role varied considerably depending on the tactical situation. At its simplest, it would act as the fire platoon, laying down suppressive fire to allow the two forward platoons to advance on their objective. The fire platoon was encouraged to make use of manoeuvre

to limit the effectiveness of the defenders' return fire, although this had to be somewhat restrained if they were to maintain the necessary volume of covering fire.

As well as being a source of fire support, the third platoon also formed a useful manoeuvre element, capable of outflanking a position suppressed by the fire of the forward platoons.

The third platoon could also be held in reserve, ready to move through one of the forward units to exploit a breakthrough. In this case, the unit it relieved could then become the new reserve while it reorganized. Once the reserve element had been committed, the company commander's priority would be to assemble a new one as quickly as possible.

Other roles of the third platoon included mopping up areas bypassed by the main company advance, or those only discovered after they had passed. Most importantly, when dealing with a typically aggressive German defence, the reserve could be thrown in to reinforce the efforts of the leading units in repelling local counter-attacks.

M5A1 Halftrack

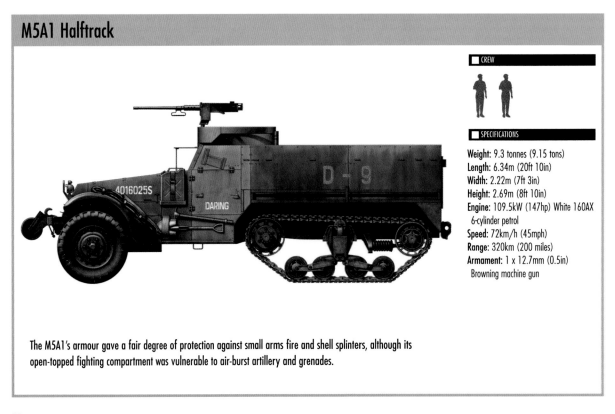

CREW

SPECIFICATIONS

Weight: 9.3 tonnes (9.15 tons)
Length: 6.34m (20ft 10in)
Width: 2.22m (7ft 3in)
Height: 2.69m (8ft 10in)
Engine: 109.5kW (147hp) White 160AX 6-cylinder petrol
Speed: 72km/h (45mph)
Range: 320km (200 miles)
Armament: 1 x 12.7mm (0.5in) Browning machine gun

The M5A1's armour gave a fair degree of protection against small arms fire and shell splinters, although its open-topped fighting compartment was vulnerable to air-burst artillery and grenades.

THE COMPANY IN DEFENCE

A company would normally occupy a frontage of at least two platoons, with the third held in reserve. However, it was not uncommon for the situation to force the company to defend a line in length rather than in depth. This was a particularly unappealing prospect, as it gave the commander few options to respond to an enemy break-in. In a normal defensive position the company would adopt a horseshoe-style deployment, with two platoons forward and the third held in reserve behind and between the forward units. Such a defence in depth gave the company a better chance of repelling attacks.

As always, the commander would position his platoons to take maximum advantage from the terrain, with clear fields of fire. In a well-established position, time could be taken to clear the ground, felling trees, uprooting bushes and levelling anything that could be used as cover by advancing enemy forces. Vulnerable sectors of the front might be protected by obstacles, barbed wire, mines and even tank traps, all covered by the defenders' fire. Artillery and mortars would be deployed to bring down fire on predetermined points where it was likely that the enemy would form up for the assault, and where they would be slowed down by the obstacles.

Outposts would also be set up to provide advance warning of an enemy assault. They could not hope to stall it unaided, but what they could do was to deny the enemy the advantage of surprise. Each outpost would usually be manned by only a small detachment, perhaps including a Bren gun team. Their role was to provide a 'speed bump' that would slow the enemy advance and alert the main line to the attack.

This would also give the defenders time to call in preplanned emergency artillery defensive fire – DF(SOS) in wartime terminology. In theory, the detachment would then withdraw, although this was easier said than done under often intense enemy fire. In extreme situations, a whole platoon could be deployed to hold outpost positions. They were likely to be ordered to hold their ground, and would be heavily dependent on artillery support.

Universal Carrier No. 1 Mark II

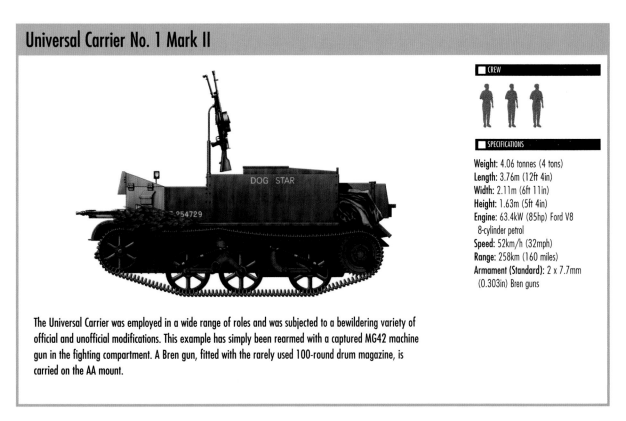

■ CREW

■ SPECIFICATIONS

Weight: 4.06 tonnes (4 tons)
Length: 3.76m (12ft 4in)
Width: 2.11m (6ft 11in)
Height: 1.63m (5ft 4in)
Engine: 63.4kW (85hp) Ford V8
   8-cylinder petrol
Speed: 52km/h (32mph)
Range: 258km (160 miles)
Armament (Standard): 2 x 7.7mm
   (0.303in) Bren guns

The Universal Carrier was employed in a wide range of roles and was subjected to a bewildering variety of official and unofficial modifications. This example has simply been rearmed with a captured MG42 machine gun in the fighting compartment. A Bren gun, fitted with the rarely used 100-round drum magazine, is carried on the AA mount.

Infantry Weapons

By 1944, British and Commonwealth infantry were armed with good, reliable weapons, with the possible exceptions of the Sten and PIAT.

Although the infantry now fielded a far greater variety of weapons than had been available in 1939, the Bren gun and its supporting riflemen still provided the most important element of its firepower at squad and platoon level.

ENFIELD NO. 2 MK I REVOLVER

The standard British service revolver of World War I had been the heavy Webley Mark VI, firing an 11.6mm (0.455in) round. While this was an effective 'manstopper' in the tradition of nineteenth-century handguns optimized for colonial warfare, its fierce recoil meant that it required considerable training to use effectively.

During the 1920s it was decided to adopt a smaller and lighter 9.6mm (0.38in) revolver firing a long, heavy 13g (200 grain) soft lead bullet that would tumble longitudinally on impact, theoretically increasing the wounding and stopping ability against human targets at short ranges. Specifications were issued for a double-action revolver that could be quickly mastered by a soldier after no more than basic training, with a good probability of first-round hits at very close range.

Unsurprisingly, Webley & Scott produced a prototype Webley Mk IV .38 revolver, but rather than adopting the weapon as it stood, the design was passed to the government-run Royal Small Arms Factory (RSAF) at Enfield, which came up with a revolver that was very similar to the Webley Mk IV .38, but with slight internal differences. This Enfield design was quickly accepted as the 'Revolver, No. 2 Mk I', and was adopted in 1931, followed in 1938 by the Mk I* (spurless hammer, double action only), and finally the Mk I** (simplified for wartime production) in 1942. Ironically, wartime demand was such that RSAF Enfield was unable to produce sufficient No. 2 revolvers and Webley's Mk IV had to be accepted as a standard service revolver.

The majority of Enfields produced were either Mk I* or modified to that standard. The second variant was the Mk I**, which was a 1942 variant of the Mk I* simplified in order to boost production, but was discontinued after a short production run as a result of safety concerns over some of the modifications.

The vast majority of Enfield No. 2 Mk I revolvers were modified to Mk I* during World War II, generally as they came in for repair or general maintenance. The official explanation of the change to the Mk I* version was that tank crews had complained that the spur on the hammer was catching on protrusions inside their tanks, but it seems likely that the real reason was that the Mk I* version was cheaper and faster to manufacture. When used in accordance with British training (rapid double-action fire at very close ranges), the No. 2 Mk I* was at least as accurate as any other service handgun of its time, because of the relatively light double-action trigger pull. It was not, however, the best choice for deliberately aimed, long-distance shooting – the double-action pull threw the most competent shooter's aim off enough to noticeably affect accuracy at ranges of more than 14m (15 yards) or so.

Some unit armourers are known to have retrofitted the Enfield No. 2 Mk I* back to the Mk I variant, but this was never an official policy and appears to have been done on an individual basis. The Enfield was not a particularly popular weapon – most users attempted to replace it with other pistols or revolvers such as the Browning Hi-Power, Colt or captured Lugers and Berettas. Despite officially being declared obsolete in 1945, the Enfield (and Webley revolvers) were not completely phased out in favour of the Browning Hi-Power until April 1969.

STEN MARKS II, III & V

Before 1939, submachine guns were widely regarded in Britain as 'gangster weapons' rather than true

22nd Armoured Brigade (advance elements), 13 June 194

The 22nd Armoured Brigade's advance elements at Villers-Bocage was a relatively powerful force, combining tank units from the 4th County of London Yeomanry with motorised infantry from 1st Battalion, the Rifle Brigade. It included 19 Cromwell tanks, four Sherman Fireflies, three OP tanks, seven Stuart light tanks, two scout cars, plus at least 16 assorted halftracks and troop carriers with four anti-tank guns.

KEY

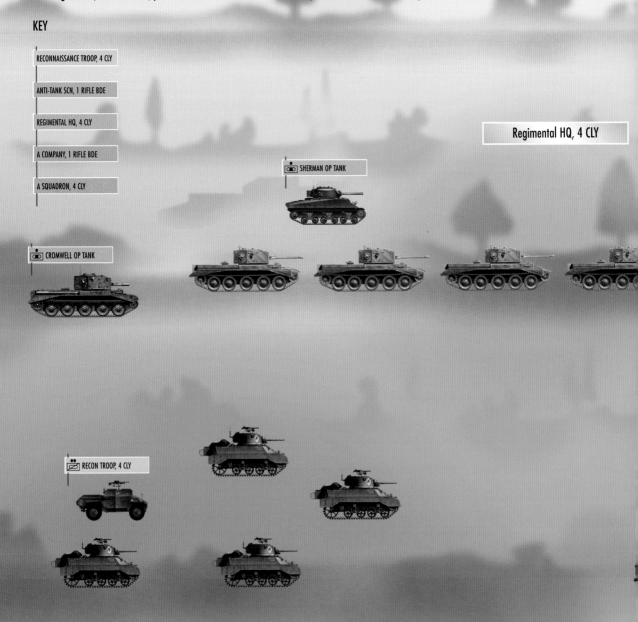

RECONNAISSANCE TROOP, 4 CLY

ANTI-TANK SCN, 1 RIFLE BDE

REGIMENTAL HQ, 4 CLY

A COMPANY, 1 RIFLE BDE

A SQUADRON, 4 CLY

Regimental HQ, 4 CLY

SHERMAN OP TANK

CROMWELL OP TANK

RECON TROOP, 4 CLY

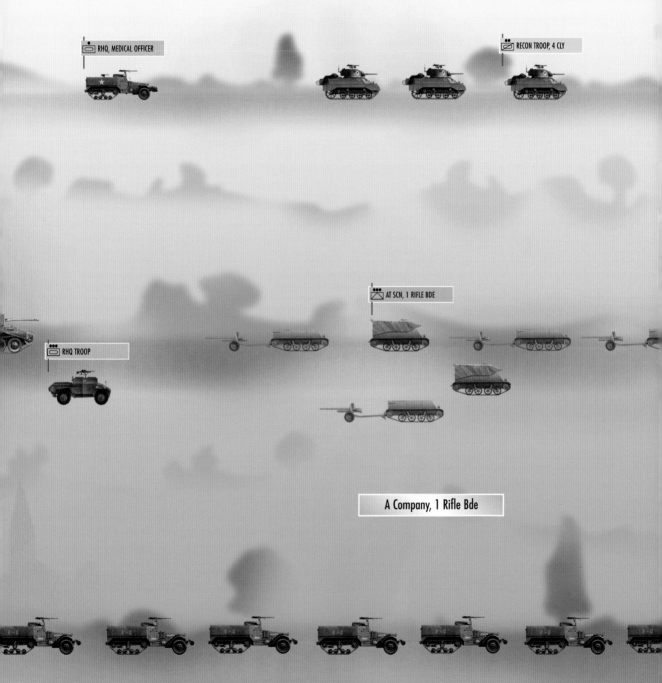

RHQ, MEDICAL OFFICER

RECON TROOP, 4 CLY

AT SCN, 1 RIFLE BDE

RHQ TROOP

A Company, 1 Rifle Bde

NO 4 TROOP

 CROMWELL OP TANK

A COMPANY

NO 1 TROOP

A Squadron, 4 CLY

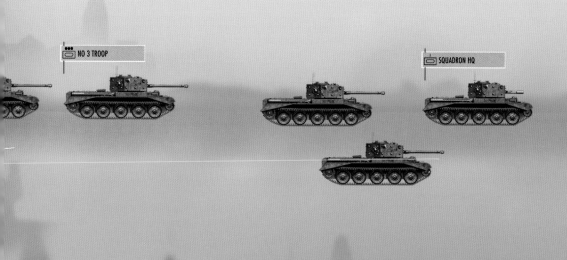

NO 3 TROOP

SQUADRON HQ

NO 2 TROOP

Enfield No. 2 Mk I* Revolver

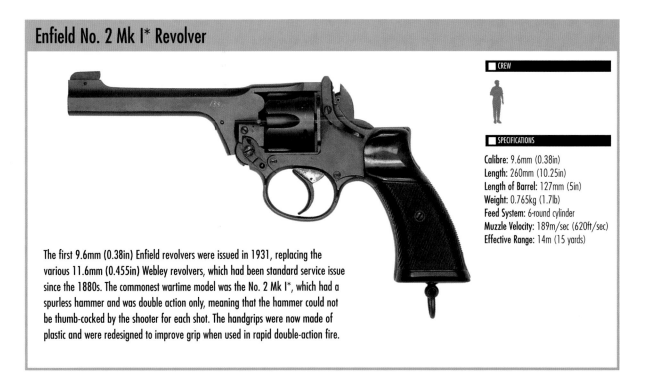

SPECIFICATIONS
Calibre: 9.6mm (0.38in)
Length: 260mm (10.25in)
Length of Barrel: 127mm (5in)
Weight: 0.765kg (1.7lb)
Feed System: 6-round cylinder
Muzzle Velocity: 189m/sec (620ft/sec)
Effective Range: 14m (15 yards)

The first 9.6mm (0.38in) Enfield revolvers were issued in 1931, replacing the various 11.6mm (0.455in) Webley revolvers, which had been standard service issue since the 1880s. The commonest wartime model was the No. 2 Mk I*, which had a spurless hammer and was double action only, meaning that the hammer could not be thumb-cocked by the shooter for each shot. The handgrips were now made of plastic and were redesigned to improve grip when used in rapid double-action fire.

military firearms. Attitudes began to change following the well-publicized German use of the MP38 during the invasion of Poland, and by the time of the Dunkirk evacuation there was a frantic scramble to obtain any sort of submachine gun. A close copy of the pre-war German MP28 was produced as the Lanchester, but this was an expensive weapon that was ill suited for mass production. Considerable quantities of the US Thompson submachine gun were also bought, but these were even more expensive and there was a desperate need for a cheaper alternative.

The chosen weapon, the Sten, was jointly designed by Major R. V. Shepherd, OBE, Inspector of Armaments in the Ministry of Supply's Design Department at the Royal Arsenal, Woolwich (later Assistant Chief Superintendent at the Armaments Design Department), and Mr Harold Turpin, Senior Draughtsman of the Design Department of the RSAF, Enfield. Although the two weapons could hardly have been a greater contrast, the Sten shared some design features, such as its side-mounted magazine configuration, with the Lanchester, and their magazines were interchangeable. In most respects, however, the two guns were poles apart, with the Lanchester being virtually hand-built using the finest materials, whereas the Sten was a simple, almost crude, weapon.

The Sten used welded stamped metal components with a minimum of machining and finishing. Many components were made in small workshops and then sent to the Enfield site for final checking and assembly. The Mk I had a folding foregrip, but most later versions were further simplified: the most basic model, the Mark III, could be completed in five man-hours and contained only 47 different parts. Its stark appearance (it was little more than a pipe with a metal loop for a stock) and its horizontal magazine were distinctive.

The Sten, especially the Mk II, tended to attract affection and loathing in equal measure. Its peculiar appearance when compared to other firearms of the era, combined with doubtful reliability, made it unpopular with some frontline troops, who gave it nicknames such as 'Plumber's Nightmare', 'Plumber's Abortion', or 'Stench Gun'. Made by a variety of manufacturers, often with subcontracted parts, some early Sten guns were liable to malfunction in combat. The double-column, single-feed magazine copied from the German MP28 was never entirely satisfactory, and poor quality control often exacerbated misfeed problems inherent in the design. It was widely held that the Sten was made 'by Marks and Spencer out of Woolworth'. Bitter experience led units to thoroughly test-fire their weapons in training to weed out bad examples; a last-minute issue of new Stens prior to going into action was rarely welcomed.

The Mk II and Mk III Stens were very temperamental, and could accidentally discharge if dropped or even laid on the ground while the gun was cocked. This was largely due to the original inadequate safety mechanism, which was replaced with the Mk 4 cocking handle, which allowed the bolt to be locked in its forward position. Other common faults were guns firing full-automatic when set on 'single', or single shots when placed on 'automatic'. This was particularly true of early Stens using bronze bolts, where the sear projection underneath the bolt could wear down more easily than ones made of case-hardened steel.

The Sten was a blowback-operated submachine gun firing from an open bolt with a fixed firing pin on the face of the bolt. This meant that the bolt remained to the rear when the weapon was cocked, and on pulling the trigger the bolt flew forward under spring pressure, stripping the round from the magazine, chambering it and firing the weapon all in the same movement. There was no breech-locking mechanism, the rearward movement of the bolt caused by the recoil was arrested only by the mainspring and the bolt's inertia. The basic operating principles were similar to those of most other wartime submachine guns – like them, the Sten's open-bolt firing and use of pistol ammunition severely restricted accuracy, with an effective range of around 100m (109 yards).

In an attempt to produce a more reliable weapon, the Mk V was introduced in 1944 – this was essentially a better-quality, more elaborate version of the Mk II. Changes included a wooden pistol grip, a vertical wooden foregrip (deleted on later examples), a wooden stock and a bayonet mount. There was a No. 4 Lee Enfield foresight and the weapon benefited from higher standards of quality control than those applied to both the Mks II and III.

Sten Mk II

The Sten was designed in the period immediately after Dunkirk as a cheap and simple alternative to the excellent, but very expensive, Thompson submachine gun, which was not available in the quantities required. The name was derived from the names of the weapon's chief designers, Major Reginald V. Shepherd and Harold Turpin, and EN for Enfield, the site of the Royal Small Arms Factory, where it was first produced in quantity. Over four million Stens in various versions were made in the 1940s.

■ CREW

■ SPECIFICATIONS

Calibre: 9mm (0.35in)	Weight: 3.2kg (7.1lb)	Rate of Fire: 500rpm
Length: 760mm (2ft 6in)	Feed System: 32-round detachable box	Muzzle Velocity: 365m/sec (1198ft/sec)
Length of Barrel: 196mm (7.7in)	magazine	Effective Range: 100m (109 yards)

Despite its faults, the Sten was a cheap and effective weapon – besides its service use, tens of thousands were supplied to various Resistance movements in occupied Europe, many of which produced their own copies.

RIFLE, NO. 4 MARK I

The British Army's standard rifle throughout much of the interwar period was the Short Magazine Lee-Enfield (SMLE) Mk III★. This was a simplified version of the SMLE Mk III, which had been introduced on 26 January 1907. Although the SMLE Mk III★ (redesignated Rifle, No. 1 Mk III★ in 1926) saw extensive service throughout World War II, especially in the North African, Italian, Pacific and Burmese theatres, it was clear by the 1930s that a newer version was needed.

By the late 1930s, the need for new rifles was becoming urgent, and the Rifle, No. 4 Mk I was developed from a number of experimental models.

A British soldier points his Sten gun from behind a hedgerow somewhere in Normandy.

This type was easier to mass produce than the SMLE, but retained its superb handling. Its rear locking lugs allowed a bolt movement of the same length as the cartridge case and the design of the locking surfaces gave a particularly easy movement to the bolt handle. These features, combined with the cock-on-closing striker, which split the effort of extraction and cocking, made its bolt action exceptionally fast and easy to operate. (While very few of the conscripts of 1944 could match the 1914 British Army standards of 15 aimed rounds per minute, they could still outshoot their opponents armed with the slower-firing Mauser Kar 98k.) Other major benefits of the design were the removable bolt head, which could be threaded off and changed to compensate for varying headspace, and the 10-round magazine, twice the capacity of many other military rifles of the time. Another well-designed feature was the generous chamber dimensions, which allowed loading dirty ammunition and aided in easier extraction of spent cases when the rifle was fouled or heated up from rapid firing.

During the war years, the No. 4 rifle was further simplified for mass production with the creation of the No. 4 Mk I* in 1942, with the bolt-release catch replaced by a simpler notch on the bolt track of the rifle's receiver. It was produced only in North America, by Long Branch Arsenal in Canada and Savage-Stevens Firearms in the USA. (The No. 4 Mk I was primarily produced in British factories.)

The No. 4 became the standard British sniper rifle of the latter half of the war. Every rifle was checked for accuracy at the factory and the best were sent to the London gunsmiths Holland & Holland, who converted them by the addition of a wooden cheek-piece and telescopic sight mounts designed to accept a No. 32 3.5x telescopic sight. (This sight was produced in three marks – the Mk 1 in 1942, the Mk 2 in 1943 and finally the Mk 3 in

1944.) Although the standard No. 4 rifles were officially superseded in British service by the L1A1 Self-Loading Rifle (SLR) in 1957, the sniper versions were converted to fire NATO 7.62mm (0.3in) ammunition, becoming the L42A1 and remaining in service until the 1990s.

BREN GUN

By the early 1930s, the Lewis gun, which had been the British Army's standard light machine gun since 1915, was showing its age and a series of competitive trials were held to select a replacement. A wide variety of weapons were submitted, including the Czech ZB vz. 26, the Danish Madsen, the Browning Automatic Rifle (BAR), the Neuhausen KE7 and the Vickers-Berthier. (The Vickers-Berthier was later adopted by the Indian Army and also saw extensive service throughout World War II.)

Following these trials, the Czech ZB vz. 27, a slightly modified version of the ZB vz. 26, was adopted for production under licence in Britain. The British insistence on retaining the rimmed 7.7mm (0.303in) round for the new gun did

Lee Enfield No. 4 Mk I

By the late 1930s, there was a growing need for new rifles to replace the SMLE, which had been in service since 1904, and the No. 4 Mk I was first issued in 1939 but not officially adopted until 1941. Its action was similar to that of experimental pre-war types, but it was lighter, stronger and, most importantly, easier to mass produce. Unlike the SMLE, the barrel protruded from the end of the forestock and the new rifle was considerably heavier than its predecessor, largely due to its heavier barrel. A new bayonet was designed for the rifle: a spike bayonet, which was essentially a steel rod with a sharp point, and was promptly nicknamed the 'pig-sticker'. It was generally disliked, as it was useless for opening tins, cutting wood and all the other mundane tasks for which bayonets were really needed. Perhaps this drawback was tacitly recognized, as a bladed bayonet was developed towards the end of the war.

■ CREW	■ SPECIFICATIONS		
	Calibre: 7.7mm (0.303in)	Weight: 3.99kg (8.8lb)	Muzzle Velocity: 744m/sec (2441ft/sec)
	Length: 1.13m (3ft 8.5in)	Feed System: 10-round detachable box	Effective Range: 548m (600 yards)
	Length of Barrel: 640mm (2ft 1.2in)	magazine	

cause problems, however, as the Czech weapons were designed for 7.92mm (0.31in) Mauser rimless ammunition. A series of prototypes were then produced under the designations ZB vz. 30, ZB vz. 32, and finally the ZB vz. 33, which became the Bren.

The most obvious result of these modifications was the characteristic 30-round curved box magazine, which was generally loaded with only 27 or 28 rounds to minimize the risk of jamming and prevent undue wear of the magazine spring.

The Bren was a gas-operated weapon, firing at a rate of between 480 and 540 rounds per minute (rpm), depending on the model. Propellant gases vented from a port towards the muzzle end of the barrel through a regulator with four quick-adjustment apertures of different sizes, intended to tailor the gas volume to different ambient temperatures, with the smallest flow at high temperature and the largest at low temperature. (This was also a useful device when it came to keeping a badly fouled gun in action, as turning up

Bren Light Machine Gun

The Bren was derived from a series of Czechoslovakian-designed light machine guns, the ZB vz. 26 and its descendants, which had been tested in an extensive series of official British trials in the 1930s. Its name was derived from Brno, the Czechoslovak city where the ZB vz. 26 was originally designed, and Enfield, site of the Royal Small Arms Factory. The Bren featured a distinctive 30-round curved box magazine to accommodate the standard British rimmed 7.7mm (0.303in) ammunition, a conical flash hider and quick-change barrel. The first Brens were issued in 1938 and British production was soon running at 300 guns per month, rising to 400 per month between 1939 and 1945. The type was reliable and exceptionally accurate – it remained in British Army service until 1958, after which thousands were converted to fire 7.62mm (0.3in) NATO ammunition and reissued as L4 light machine guns, which remained in service until the 1990s.

■ CREW

■ SPECIFICATIONS

Calibre: 7.7mm (0.303in)
Length: 1.156m (3ft 6.9in)
Length of Barrel: 635mm (2ft 1in)

Weight: 8.68kg (19lb)
Feed System: 30-round detachable box magazine. (A rarely used 100-round drum magazine was also available.)

Rate of Fire: 520rpm
Muzzle Velocity: 743.7m/sec (2440ft/sec)
Effective Range: 550m (600 yards)

British infantry armed with a Bren gun and Lee Enfield No. 4 Mk I rifles take up a firing position somewhere in the Normandy bocage.

the setting helped clear debris from the barrel. It was even said that all problems with the Bren could simply be cleared by hitting the gun, turning the regulator, or doing both.) The vented gas drove a piston which in turn operated the breech block. Each gun was issued with a spare 'quick-change' barrel to prevent overheating during sustained fire, although later guns featured a chrome-lined bore, which reduced the need for a spare. Barrel changes were remarkably easy due to a well-designed release catch and a barrel-carrying handle that allowed the removal of hot barrels without the risk of burnt hands.

Although it could never match the sheer volume of fire produced by the MG34 and MG42, the Bren's effectiveness and popularity were such that by 1944 it was not uncommon for two to be fielded by each infantry section – one for every four infantrymen. The Bren was officially operated by a two-man crew, sometimes commanded by a lance-corporal as an infantry section's 'gun group', the remainder of the section forming the 'rifle group'.

The gunner or 'Number 1' carried and fired the Bren, while the loader or 'Number 2' carried extra magazines and a spare barrel and tool kit, and reloaded the gun and replaced the barrel when it overheated. (The large ammunition pouches of the 1937 Pattern Web Equipment were specifically designed to carry up to two Bren magazines each, and in addition to their rifle or submachine gun ammunition, all the infantrymen in a section carried at least two Bren magazines.)

Generally, the Bren was fired from the prone position using the folding bipod, which gave it an effective range of about 550m (600 yards). It was issued with a sling, which allowed it to be fired from the hip while advancing, although this naturally resulted in a greatly reduced effective range. Its accuracy was phenomenal – in fact it was sometimes felt to be too accurate and it was not uncommon for badly worn barrels to be retained to give a better dispersal of fire.

NO. 36M GRENADE (MILLS BOMB)

In 1915, William Mills, an engineer from Sunderland, patented, developed and manufactured the original 'Mills bomb' at the Mills Munition Factory in Birmingham. This was formally adopted for service as the No. 5 Mills in 1915. This original grenade underwent considerable development – the No. 23 was a variant of the No. 5 with a rodded base plug that allowed it to be fired from a rifle. This evolved into the No. 36, a version with a detachable baseplate to allow use with a rifle discharger cup. The final variation of the Mills bomb, the No. 36M, was specially designed and waterproofed with shellac. It was originally intended for use in the extreme conditions of Mesopotamia in 1917, but outlived all other Mills bombs. The No. 5 and No. 23 grenades were declared obsolete in 1918 and the No. 36 (but not the 36M) followed in 1932.

The Mills was a classic design: a segmented cast iron 'pineapple' with a central striker held by a hand lever and secured with a pin. Mills designed the segmented casing to provide a secure grip for the thrower rather than to aid fragmentation. (He was later proved right when tests showed that only internal segmentation had any effect on fragmentation.) The type was a highly effective defensive grenade – a competent thrower could manage 15m (16.4 yards) with reasonable accuracy, but as the grenade could hurl lethal fragments well beyond this range, users had to take cover immediately after throwing.

The Mills could be fitted with a flat base and fired from a rifle with a 'cup discharger' attachment, to a maximum range of about 150m (164 yards). The grenades in service at the beginning of the war were fitted with seven-second fuses to permit both hand and rifle launch, but during combat in the Battle of France in 1940, this delay proved to be too long – sufficient to give the defenders time to escape the explosion or even to throw the grenade back – and was reduced to four seconds. (The Mills seems to have been rarely used as a rifle grenade after 1940.)

The No. 36M Mk I was an extremely reliable grenade and remained the standard British grenade until 1972, when it was completely replaced by the lighter L2 series.

GRENADE, HAND, ANTI-TANK, NO. 75 (HAWKINS GRENADE)
In the autumn of 1940, Captain Hawkins submitted a design for a light anti-tank mine that could be thrown in the path of oncoming tanks. His proposal included the following description: 'The container is a standard commercial rectangular tin, 4.75in x 3.75in x 2.25in, filled with 2lb of gelignite and bound with wire to keep the lid on. Down the length of the largest side is soldered a tinplate pocket to take the firing mechanism. The latter is a cartridge, 4.25 x

No. 36M Mk I Grenade (Mills Bomb)

The Mills bomb of 1944 was almost identical to those of 1918. It was a reliable and effective defensive grenade, which was sometimes also used as tripwired booby trap. Total production of all variants may well have exceeded 70,000,000.

■ CREW

■ SPECIFICATIONS

Length: 95mm (3.75in)
Diameter: 58mm (2.3in)
Weight: 765g (1.69lb)
Explosive: Baratol
Fragmentation/Blast Radius: 91.44m (100 yards)
Fuse: 7 seconds (later reduced to 4 seconds)
Throwing Range: 18m (19.7 yards)

0.625in diameter, containing a cut-down No. 27 detonator, glass phials of sulphuric acid, sugar and potassium chlorate. Flash holes are drilled between the pocket and the main compartment of the tin.'

Preliminary trials were carried out on 23 October 1940; these showed that the detonators were not set off by the impact of landing on hard road surfaces and that the grenade always came to rest on its largest face – the position in which it would most likely go off under the weight of a tank's tracks. A live grenade containing 1kg (2lb) of gelignite was tested against the tracks of an A13 Cruiser tank and completely destroyed two track plates. In a second trial, a grenade was placed askew in the path of an A9 Cruiser tank's tracks, and when struck it moved sideways and then detonated – one track plate was completely destroyed and another cracked right across. These trials also confirmed that a tank's weight would reliably detonate the grenade on anything other than very soft ground and that the grenades were a reasonable size and weight to throw accurately.

After a final series of trials in the summer of 1941, orders were placed for a total of 2.5 million grenades and the type remained in service until the mid-1950s. It proved to be a highly versatile weapon that could be used in clusters to immobilize even the heaviest German AFVs. (It could also be used as a demolition charge when fitted with a detonator and length of safety fuse. In this role, it was especially useful for cutting railway lines as it was just the right size to fit into the side of a railway track.)

GRENADE NO. 82 'GAMMON BOMB'

Designed by Captain R.S. Gammon MC of the 1st Parachute Regiment, the Gammon bomb was developed as a replacement for the temperamental and highly dangerous 'sticky bomb' grenade. It consisted of a stockingette bag made of dark coloured material, a metal cap, and an 'Allways fuse'. The grenade was unique in that unlike conventional grenades, it could be filled with variable amounts of explosive. For anti-personnel use, a small amount of plastic explosive (about half a stick), together with any available improvised fragmentation material such as nails, would be placed in the bag. However, against AFVs or other 'hard' targets, the bag could be completely filled

with explosives, making an unusually powerful grenade that could only be thrown safely from behind cover.

Using the Gammon bomb was very simple. After filling the stockingette bag with explosive, the screw-off cap was removed and discarded. This revealed a stout linen tape wound around the circumference of the fuse. The tape had a curved lead weight on the end, which was held in place with one finger until the grenade was thrown. The weighted linen tape automatically unwrapped in flight, pulling out a retaining pin from the fuse mechanism. Removal of the retaining pin freed a heavy ball-bearing and striker inside the fuse, which were then held back from the percussion cap only by a creep spring. On impact with the target, the weight of the ball-bearing overcame the weak resistance of the creep spring and slammed the striker against the percussion cap, which in turn ignited the detonator.

Gammon grenades were primarily issued to airborne units who were issued with plastic explosive as standard equipment. However, its popularity was such that it was also widely used by infantry units, and the type remained in service until the early 1950s.

PROJECTOR, INFANTRY, ANTI-TANK (PIAT)

The first hollow charge (HEAT) anti-tank weapon to enter British service was the No. 68 rifle grenade. At the time of its introduction in mid-1940, it was a tremendous improvement on the Boys anti-tank rifle, but its poorly designed warhead limited armour penetration to no more than 52mm (2in). The grenade's flat nose and low velocity made it too inaccurate to be of much use at ranges beyond 46m (50 yards) and it was relegated to Home Guard use after 1942.

Its successor, the PIAT, was inspired by the work of Lieutenant-Colonel Stewart Blacker of the Royal Artillery, who pioneered the development of the spigot mortar. His first such design dating back to the mid-1930s was for a lightweight platoon mortar. This replaced the conventional barrel with a steel rod known as a 'spigot' fixed to a baseplate, while the bomb itself had a propellant charge inside its tail. The mortar was fired by dropping the bomb onto the spigot, which detonated the propellant and launched the bomb. By effectively putting the barrel on the inside of the weapon, warhead size was no longer restricted to the barrel's diameter. Blacker's design was submitted to the War Office as the 'Arbalest', but it was turned down in favour of a more conventional Spanish design that formed the basis for the development of the 50mm (2in) mortar.

Blacker was undeterred and began experimental work on a hand-held anti-tank weapon based on the spigot design, but found that spigot-launched rounds could not be fired at sufficient velocity to penetrate armour. During the invasion scare of 1940, he devised the Blacker Bombard, a crew-served, anti-tank spigot mortar, which fired a 9kg (20lb) anti-tank bomb to a maximum range of approximately 91m (100 yards). (The bomb was purely a blast weapon, but the heavy explosive payload stood a fair chance of disabling light AFVs.)

The Bombard was widely issued to the Home Guard and some regular units in 1941, but Blacker realized that there was a dire need for a man-portable anti-tank weapon. When he became aware of the newly developed No. 68 grenade, he appreciated that a HEAT bomb fired from a spigot launcher might meet this requirement.

In early 1941, he developed the Baby Bombard, a simple shoulder-fired launcher consisting of little more than a metal casing containing a large spring and a spigot. The bomb was placed in a trough at the front of the casing, and when the trigger was pulled, the spigot rammed into the tail of the bomb and fired it to a maximum range of approximately 140m (150 yards). Initial trials were discouraging – a War Office report of June 1941 stated that the casing was flimsy, the spigot did not always fire when the trigger was pulled, and none of the bombs provided exploded on contact with the target.

At the time that he developed the Baby Bombard, Blacker was working for MD1, a government department responsible for devising weapons for use by guerrilla and Resistance groups

Projector, Infantry, Anti-Tank (PIAT)

CREW

SPECIFICATIONS

Length: 0.99m (3ft 3in)
Weight: 15kg (33lb)
Bomb Weight: 1.4kg (3lb) (HEAT)
Muzzle Velocity: 76m/sec (250ft/sec)
Effective Anti-Tank Range: 91m
  (100 yards)
Armour Penetration: 100mm (3.9in)

The PIAT was derived from Lieutenant-Colonel Blacker's spigot mortar, the Blacker Bombard, which had been hastily developed as an anti-tank weapon in 1940 during the post-Dunkirk invasion scare. The PIAT was essentially a sheet-steel tube containing the trigger mechanism, firing spring and spigot, with a launching trough at the front for the fin-stabilized HEAT bomb. On firing, the steel spigot was driven forward to strike a propelling cartridge in the bomb's hollow tail, blowing it off the spigot and recocking the weapon. Whilst it worked, it was heavy and awkward, with a ferocious recoil. Despite these problems, it did have certain advantages over contemporary bazookas and *Panzerfaust*, notably the lack of dangerous back-blast, which made it far easier to use within buildings and other confined spaces. A total of 115,000 PIATs were produced – the type entered British service in 1943 and it remained the standard infantry anti-tank weapon until 1950.

in Occupied Europe. Shortly after the trials of the Baby Bombard, Blacker was posted to other duties, and left the prototype with a colleague, Major Millis Jefferis, who rebuilt it and combined it with a HEAT mortar bomb to create what he called the 'Jefferis Shoulder Gun'.

The initial trials at the Small Arms School, Bisley, got off to a bad start when a warrant officer firing the Shoulder Gun was wounded by a fragment of the exploding bomb in a freak accident. Jefferis himself then took over and fired off several more rounds, all of which pierced the armoured target. Impressed with the weapon, the Ordnance Board of the Small Arms School modified the ammunition, renamed the Shoulder Gun as the Projector, Infantry, Anti-Tank (PIAT), and approved its issue as a standard infantry anti-tank weapon.

Preparing the PIAT for firing was at best awkward and sometimes almost impossible – it had to be cocked, which entailed standing the weapon on the ground, pointing upwards, and placing both feet on the butt. The PIAT's body was then twisted to unlock it and pulled upwards to compress the

A British infantryman shoulders a PIAT anti-tank weapon somewhere in Northwest Europe, 1944.

firing spring and cock the weapon before lowering the body and relocking it. The process required considerable strength and resulted in a significant number of injuries, especially to shorter users who found it particularly difficult to lift the body high enough against the pressure of the very strong spring. (Cocking the PIAT while under fire in the confines of a slit trench was even more demanding – the 'textbook method' was for the gunner to lie on his back and use his feet.)

Pulling the trigger released the spring, which drove the spigot forward to detonate the propellant in the bomb's tail. As the bomb was fired, the recoil blew the spigot backwards, compressing the spring and cocking the weapon for the next shot. Although training naturally concentrated on the PIAT's primary anti-tank role, it could be used as a crude mortar against other targets at ranges up to 275m (300 yards) by twisting the butt to lie sideways on the ground and extending the monopod.

The PIAT was first used in combat during the invasion of Sicily in mid-1943, where its limitations rapidly became apparent. It had a ferocious recoil and would fail to recock unless gripped firmly when fired. There were also complaints about its inaccuracy and faulty ammunition, which led to a

series of trials to gauge the true extent of the problems. The results confirmed that even a skilled gunner only stood a 60 per cent chance of hitting an AFV at 91m (100 yards), whilst unreliable fuses meant that there was a 25 per cent chance of the bomb failing to detonate on hitting the target. (When everything did work properly, it could penetrate up to 105mm/4in of armour, sufficient to deal with most German AFVs with flank or rear shots.)

Although it was never a popular weapon, the PIAT was effective. Operational analysis of the early stages of the Normandy campaign indicated that seven per cent of all German AFVs destroyed by British forces were knocked out by PIATs, compared to six per cent attributable to rockets fired by aircraft. A contemporary Canadian Army survey questioned over 150 officers with recent combat experience about the effectiveness of 31 different infantry weapons. Perhaps surprisingly, the PIAT achieved top place as the most 'outstandingly effective' weapon, followed by the Bren gun in second place.

ORDNANCE SMOOTH BORE MUZZLE LOADING (SBML) 2-INCH MORTAR

During the 1930s many European armies introduced light mortars to supplement their infantry's rifle grenades. A number of these designs were evaluated in Britain and a Spanish 50mm (2in) mortar was selected as the basis for further development. By late 1937, 10 prototypes of the new 50mm (2in) mortar had been completed together with HE and smoke bombs (1600 rounds of each type).

Initial field trials were highly successful and the type went into production in February 1938, only four months after the first trials. By 1939, there were 500 in service under the designation Mk II.

The Mk II was little more than a simple barrel mounted on a baseplate – the bombs were muzzle loaded and fired at a rate of up to eight rounds per minute by a small trigger lever near the breech. (Trigger operation was particularly useful as it allowed the mortar to be fired almost horizontally against buildings and similar targets.) The standard impact-fused HE bomb weighed 1.02kg (2.25lb) and had a maximum range of 457m (500 yards). The smoke round weighed the same, but the illuminating round was significantly lighter at 0.45kg (1lb). A wide range of other ammunition

was also developed including a specialized bomb that threw a lightweight explosive-filled net over minefields which was then detonated to clear a path. The Mk II was originally fitted with a large collimating sight with elevating and cross-level bubbles, but it was soon found that this was unnecessary and it was replaced by a simple white line painted up the length of the barrel. The firer only had to line this up in the direction of the target and fire a number of aiming shots.

During the war the 50mm (2in) mortar evolved into no fewer than eight separate marks, plus a number of other sub-types, including the Mk VII★ with a shortened barrel for use by airborne units, the Mk VII for Universal Carriers and the Mk III used as a smoke discharger in tanks.

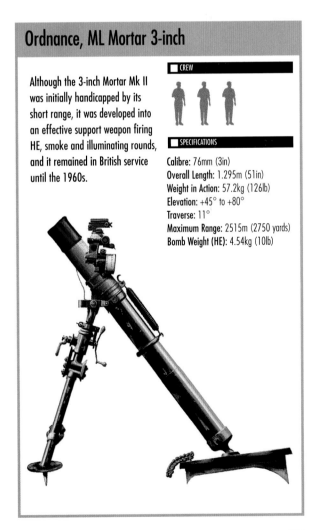

Ordnance, ML Mortar 3-inch

Although the 3-inch Mortar Mk II was initially handicapped by its short range, it was developed into an effective support weapon firing HE, smoke and illuminating rounds, and it remained in British service until the 1960s.

CREW

SPECIFICATIONS

Calibre: 76mm (3in)
Overall Length: 1.295m (51in)
Weight in Action: 57.2kg (126lb)
Elevation: +45° to +80°
Traverse: 11°
Maximum Range: 2515m (2750 yards)
Bomb Weight (HE): 4.54kg (10lb)

ORDNANCE, ML MORTAR 3-INCH

The first British 76mm (3in) mortar was the original Stokes Mortar, which was first used in 1916. Improved versions of this weapon remained in service for much of the interwar period, but in the early 1930s it was decided that it was in need of complete modernization. Both the mortar and its ammunition were thoroughly updated, incorporating many features of the French Brandt mortars. The new design was formally adopted as the Ordnance, ML Mortar, 3-inch Mk II in the late 1930s.

1st Dorsets with 76mm (3in) mortars in Normandy. A 'textbook' mortar pit took the crew at least four hours of hard digging, but this was frequently reduced to half an hour's work by blasting a basic pit using six No. 75 grenades.

Although the Mk II was a sturdy and reliable weapon, it lacked the range of many of its foreign counterparts. The early versions had a range of only some 1463m (1600 yards), which compared badly with the 2400m (2625 yards) of its German equivalent, the 8-cm GrW 34. An extensive series of experiments and trials with new propellants increased the range to 2515m (2750 yards), which overcame many of the original drawbacks. In addition to the improved ammunition, later marks had a strengthened baseplate to absorb the greater recoil and improved sighting arrangements. A special lightweight version (Mortar, 3-inch Mk V) was developed for use in the Far East, but only 5000 were produced, some of which equipped airborne units.

5th Royal Horse Artillery

In mid-1943, the Royal Artillery (including the RHA) reached its peak strength of 700,000 (about 26 per cent of total British Army strength and roughly the same size as the Royal Navy), in 630 regiments, 65 training regiments and six officer cadet training units. Although the need to replace infantry casualties led to the disbandment of some units (mainly AA regiments) in 1944, artillery remained a vital part of 21st Army Group's offensive capability.

Normandy marked the combat debut of the Sexton self-propelled 25-pdr, which proved to be so successful that the type remained in British service until well into the 1950s. Although the 25-pdr was inferior to contemporary US and German 105mm (4.1in) howitzers in terms of shell weight, its range and rate of fire more than made up for this theoretical disadvantage. Good as the towed guns were, the need for a self-propelled version of the 25-pdr had been recognized since 1941, and this was initially met by a crude conversion of the Valentine. This was accepted for service as the Bishop and began to be issued to artillery units in North Africa in 1942. However, rushed development left the type with such severe shortcomings that it was rapidly phased out of service as the US M7 Priest self-propelled 105mm (4.1in) howitzers became available.

THE PRIEST, THE RAM AND THE SEXTON

Priests were highly effective and well-liked vehicles, but the 105mm (4.1in) howitzer was not a standard British weapon and required special supply arrangements for its ammunition and spares. The obvious solution seemed to be a 25-pdr-armed version of the Priest and a US prototype was completed in 1942, but suffered severe damage when the gun mount broke during test-firing. This setback, coupled with doubts that American

5th Royal Horse Artillery Unit Badge

The unit formed in March 1901 in South Africa as the 11th Brigade Royal Horse Artillery, comprising G and O Batteries. In 1903, it was transferred to India, with G Battery stationed at Bangalore and O Battery at Lucknow. It was renamed 5th Brigade Royal Horse Artillery in October 1906. It returned to the UK in 1911 and by 1919 it comprised E, G and O Batteries, all stationed in Aldershot. The regiment then served in India in 1920–22 but was disbanded in October 1926. It was re-formed in November 1939 as 5th Field Regiment Royal Horse Artillery, initially with G and K Batteries, which were joined by CC Battery in late 1940. The regiment then saw service in the Middle East, Italy and Northwest Europe, initially with 8th Armoured Brigade and then 7th Armoured Division (from November 1942 until the end of the war).*

ORBAT: 5th Royal Horse Artillery, Regimental Headquarters

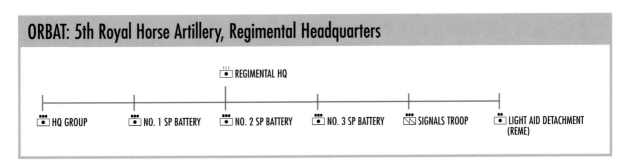

REGIMENTAL HQ

HQ GROUP | NO. 1 SP BATTERY | NO. 2 SP BATTERY | NO. 3 SP BATTERY | SIGNALS TROOP | LIGHT AID DETACHMENT (REME)

production facilities would be assigned to a vehicle that would not be adopted for US service, was sufficient to kill off the proposal in favour of an alternative Canadian design.

The Canadian Department of Munitions and Supply and the Canadian Army Engineering Design Branch were asked to build another prototype, using the 25-pdr on a Ram tank chassis, with the same basic layout as that of the Priest. There were a number of problems with mounting the gun, and its controls had to be modified to give a faster rate of traverse for emergency anti-tank use (25° left and 15° right). The recoil system was adjusted and locked to give a constant recoil stroke of 508mm (20in) in order to provide 40° of elevation, so that the gun's maximum range was almost as great as that of the towed version. The prototype was completed in late 1942 and was shipped to Larkhill for trials in January 1943. These were highly successful and, after minor changes, full series production began at the Tank Arsenal, Montreal Locomotive Works, in 1943. The gun and its mounting were manufactured at Marine Industries' Sorel Works, near Montreal.

The first 124 vehicles (Sexton I) were based on the hull of the Ram tank and were issued to Canadian artillery units. The main production run of over 2000 vehicles (Sexton II) used the hull of the Canadian-produced Grizzly tank – a modified M4A1 Sherman. Both versions carried a crew of six (commander, driver, gunner, gun layer, loader and radio operator) in an open-topped fighting compartment. There was stowage for a total of 112 rounds of 25-pdr ammunition (normally 94 HE/smoke shells and 18 armour-piercing shot.) Standard secondary armament comprised two Bren guns, which could be fitted on to a removable pedestal mount, but some vehicles also carried a pintle-mounted 12.7mm (0.5in) Browning machine gun on the left front corner of the fighting compartment.

COMMAND MODELS

A number of command-post versions were completed from late 1943 under the designation Sexton Gun Position Officer (GPO). This type was identical to the Sexton Mk II except that the gun was removed and the aperture in the hull front was plated over. This created the necessary space for map tables, plotting tables, seats for the Gun Position Officer and his staff, plus an extra radio.

Many Sexton units received four Ram Observation Post (OP) tanks apiece. These were conversions of the Canadian Ram II medium tank in which the main armament and turret basket were deleted and a dummy mantlet and gun fitted. The turret could traverse 45° either side of the centre line, so that the observer had a reasonably wide field of view through the vision port located under the dummy barrel.

Internally, the space was used to accommodate six crew plus radios and map boards. However,

5th Royal Horse Artillery: Weapons

TYPE	NUMBER
25-pdr SP Sexton	24
OTHER	
Bren 7.7mm (0·303in) LMG	27
PIAT	14
Signal pistol	9

5th Royal Horse Artillery: Vehicles/Trailers

EQUIPMENT	STRENGTH
Motorcycle	32 + 4 + 2
Car, 5-cwt, 4x4	14 + 4 + 3
Car, 4-seater, 4x4	1
Truck, 15-cwt, 4x2, GS	6
Truck, 15-cwt, 4x2, office	1
Truck, 15-cwt, 4x4, personnel	1 + 2 + 3
Truck, 15-cwt, 4x2, water	4
Truck, 15-cwt, 4x2, wireless house	1
Truck, 15-cwt, 4x2, machinery, type KL	1
Halftrack, fitted with winch	12
Halftrack, fitted for wireless	34
Lorry, 3-ton, 4x4, GS	28 + 1
Lorry, 3-ton, 4x4, signal office	1
Tractor, 6x4, breakdown	1
OP Tank	13
Carriers, tracked, starting and charging	3
Sexton SP gun carriages	24
Trailer, 1-ton, 2-wheeled, GS	15 + 3
Trailer, 15-cwt, 2-wheeled	1

Self-Propelled Field Battery

Sherman OP Tank: 4
25-pdr SP Sexton: 8
15cwt truck, 4x2: 2

15cwt truck, half-tracked: 13
5cwt car: 3
3-ton lorry, 4x4: 8

Universal Carrier: 1
Motorcycle: 9

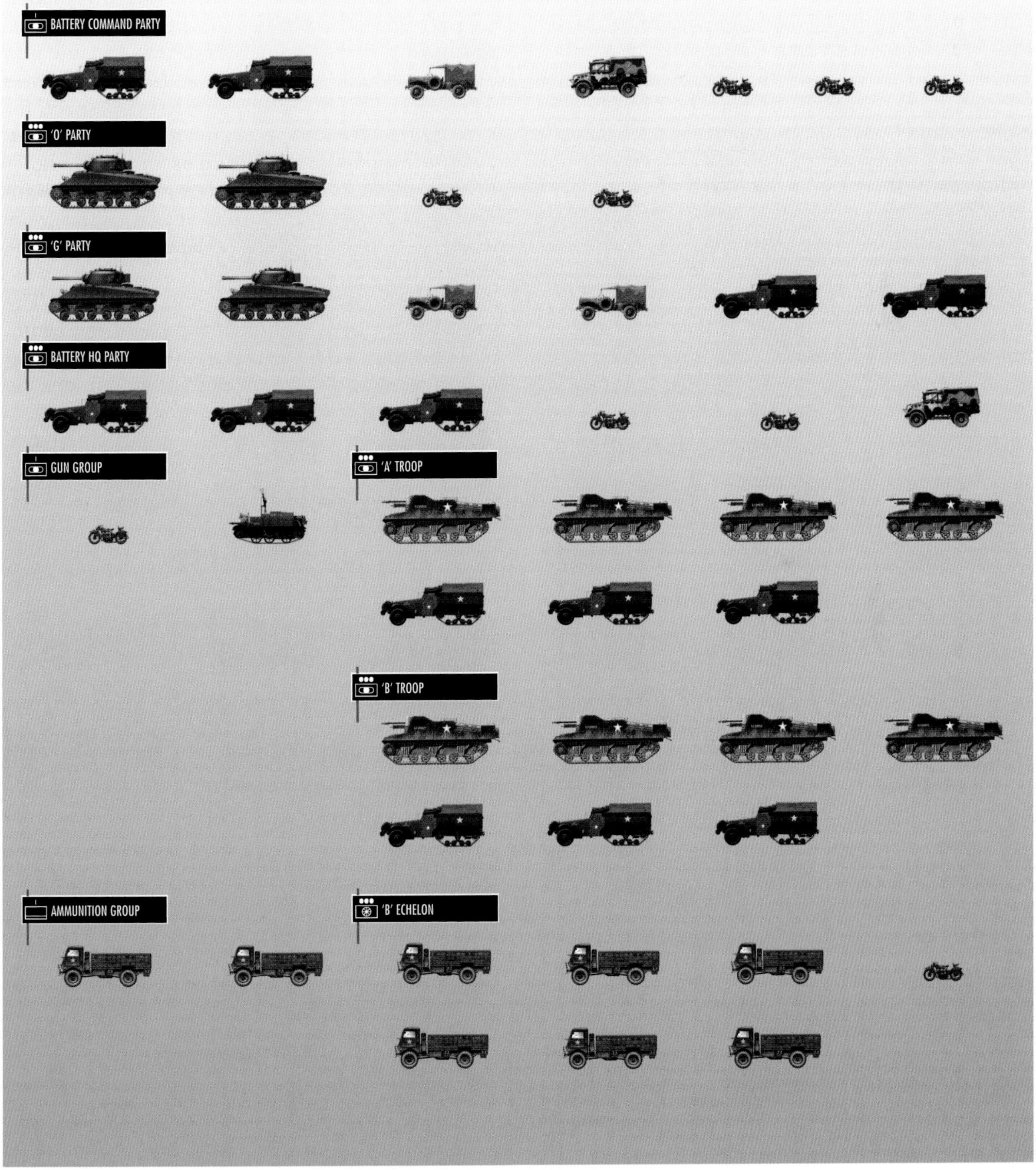

BATTERY COMMAND PARTY

'O' PARTY

'G' PARTY

BATTERY HQ PARTY

GUN GROUP

'A' TROOP

'B' TROOP

AMMUNITION GROUP

'B' ECHELON

5th RHA were issued with Sherman OPs instead – these were converted in a very similar manner to the Ram OPs, losing their main armament but retaining their turret and hull machine guns.

ARTILLERY TACTICS

Despite its smaller shell, the 25-pdr was at least as effective as US artillery due to the ability of the British and Canadian gunners to concentrate their fire more efficiently. In Normandy, the organization of artillery was generally the same as it had been in North Africa, with 24 guns per regiment and 72 guns (three regiments) per division.

Forward Observation Officers (FOOs) were normally officers from each battery in OP tanks who deployed with the frontline troops, although there were artillery officers at various levels within each division who could call down the fire of a single artillery regiment or the entire corps' artillery if needed. (From December 1942, the FOOs were relatively senior officers who had the authority to make the necessary rapid decisions and to issue orders for fire support, rather than having to pass time-consuming requests up through the chain of command.) All the guns within a division were

BELOW: A regiment's establishment included attached officers and soldiers from other corps. These were: the Medical Officer (MO) of the Royal Army Medical Corps (RAMC) – several soldiers in each battery were trained as stretcher-bearers; an armourer and electricians from the Royal Electrical and Mechanical Engineers (REME); cooks from the Army Catering Corps (ACC).

Besides the attached troops there were two elements with their own establishments which formed part of every artillery regiment:
■ The Light Aid Detachment (LAD) from the REME which was responsible for the more major repairs and maintenance of the regiment's vehicles and other equipment, apart from the guns. The guns and fire control instruments were the responsibility of RA artificers and fitters who were not part of the LAD. In SP regiments such as 5th RHA, the LAD was much larger and provided a section to support each battery.
■ The other major element was the HQ Signals Troop manned by Royal Signals personnel. The Regimental Signals Officer was a Royal Signals officer.

The unit's establishment tables listed the numbers of officers and soldiers by ranks and 'skills' in each type of regiment and its batteries. Soldiers were divided into 'Tradesmen' (who received higher pay) and 'Non-Tradesmen'.

RHA Field Regiment: Typical Personnel, May 1944

RANK	LT-COL	MAJ	CAPT	SUB	Warrant Officer	Senior NCO	Junior NCO	Gunner/ PTE	TOTAL
Officers RA	1	4	12+1	20+4					37
Tradesmen RA						5	10	152+3	167
Non-Tradesmen/ Unspecified RA					11	32+1	95+6	277+40	415
RAMC Attached			1						1
ACC Attached							3	18	21
REME Attached						1	3		4
TOTALS	1	4	13	20	11	38	111	447	645

RHA Field Regiment, Signals Troop: Typical Personnel, May 1944

RANK	LT-COL	MAJ	CAPT	SUB	Warrant Officer	Senior NCO	Junior NCO	Gunner/ PTE	TOTAL
Officers				1					1
Tradesmen						1	12	21	34
Non-Tradesmen							1	2	3
TOTAL				1		1	13	23	38

surveyed into a map grid where their location and the location of any enemy targets were plotted, and that information shared across the division. The key to the rapid concentration of fire on a target was the rapidity with which the guns could be surveyed onto a map grid, a task that was carried out by dedicated survey troops.

Although British artillery tactics up to regimental level were devised in the pre-war period and did not change much during the war, in 1941 Brigadier Parham, 38th Division's Commander Royal Artillery (CRA), invented and tested new procedures for co-ordinating fire from larger formations. These culminated with a demonstration of a 144-gun concentration (approximately six regiments) against an opportunity target within five minutes of the target being called.

AGRA

In mid-1942, XIII Corps conducted further trials and new doctrine was formulated under which each

corps had an Army Group Royal Artillery (AGRA) directly attached to it. Each AGRA was a brigade-sized formation comprised entirely of artillery, and was designed to provide swift and devastating fire support to all Allied units within its range. An AGRA in Northwest Europe typically consisted of one field regiment, four medium regiments and a heavy regiment. (By the end of the war, these were supplemented by a super heavy regiment and Land Mattress salvo rocket launchers.)

A call for regimental support (24 guns against an 'Uncle' target) could be answered in just 60 seconds, and divisional support (72 guns against a 'Mike' target) in three minutes, and even heavier fire concentrations included 'Yoke' for AGRA level, 'Victor' for corps level fire by 150–250 guns, and 'William' for army level bombardments. It was estimated that, once it had been located, a German artillery battery in Normandy could expect to be obliterated by a bombardment averaging 20.3 tonnes (20 tons) of shells.

Sherman OP

CREW

SPECIFICATIONS

Weight: 35.36 tonnes (34.8 tons)
Length: 7.82m (25ft 8in)
Width: 2.67m (8ft 9in)
Height: 2.74m (9ft)
Engine: 316.6kW (425hp) Chrysler Multibank A57 30-cylinder petrol
Speed: 36km/h (22.4mph)
Range: 201km (125 miles)
Armament: 2 x 7.62mm (0.3in) Browning machine guns

In British service, Shermans were adapted to fulfil a vast number of specialized roles, including acting as artillery observation vehicles. This conversion was designated Sherman OP (Observation Post). The main modifications involved the replacement of the 75mm (2.9in) main armament with a dummy gun and the installation of map boards and additional radio equipment. (The coaxial and bow machine guns were usually retained and some vehicles seem to have kept the 12.7mm/0.5in Browning AA MG as well.)

25-pdr SP, Tracked, Sexton

CREW

SPECIFICATIONS

Weight: 25.86 tonnes (25 tons)
Length: 6.12m (20ft 1in)
Width: 2.71m (8ft 11in)
Height: 2.43m (8ft)
Engine: 298kW (400hp) Continental
R-975 9-cylinder radial petrol
Speed: 40km/h (25mph)
Range: 201km (125 miles)
Armament: 1 x Ordnance QF 25-pdr
(87.6mm/3.45in) gun/howitzer, plus 2
x 7.7mm (0.303in) Bren machine guns

Although the US Priest was popular with British artillery units, its 105mm (4.1in) howitzer was not a standard British weapon, which complicated the supply of ammunition and spares. A 'Commonwealth equivalent' armed with the 25-pdr was urgently needed, and the Canadian Department of Munitions and Supply designed the highly successful Sexton, which entered British and Canadian service in September 1943. A total of 2150 vehicles were completed before production ended in 1945, with the type remaining in service until 1956.

Artillery Support

The 7th Armoured Division's two artillery regiments, 3rd RHA and 5th RHA, collectively fired 550,000 rounds of 25-pdr ammunition during the Normandy campaign, equivalent to an average of 30 rounds per gun per day.

This average was dwarfed by the ammunition expenditure during critical engagements such as the Battle of the Brigade Box, when the regiments fired off anything up to 400 rounds per gun in a single day. So rapid and heavy was the British shelling that many German prisoners in Northwest Europe were convinced that the 25-pdr (firing at up to eight rounds per minute) had power-loading or was belt fed.

In addition to engaging targets of opportunity, British and Canadian artillery units were heavily committed to the carefully planned bombardments in support of 21st Army Group's major offensives. For these operations, their fire was supplemented by Allied naval gunfire support – during the Normandy campaign, the bombarding ships fired a total of 68,251 rounds of ammunition, including a substantial number of very large calibre shells – up to 406mm (16in) – from battleships and monitors.

ARTILLERY EFFECTIVENESS

In July 1944, 2nd Panzer Division reported that their sector of the front was under constant British bombardment by an average of 4000 artillery rounds and 5000 mortar bombs per day. When British forces attacked, the intensity of fire dramatically increased, with up to 3500 rounds being fired in a matter of two hours.

In preparation for a minor attack by 49th (West Riding) Division on Cristot on 16 June, German positions were subjected to harassing fire throughout the night of the 15th to 16th. On the morning of the 16th, the defences were:

- Bombarded by naval gunfire between H-35 and H-20
- Rocketed and strafed by Typhoons from H-15 to H-Hour
- Bombarded by a company of 107mm (4.2in) mortars from H-15 to H-Hour

The attack itself was supported by the fire of seven RA field regiments (25-pdr guns) and four medium regiments (140mm/5.5in guns). The attacking infantry found 17 dead Germans in the village, together with two wrecked armoured cars and the remains of a single unidentifiable 'soft-skin' vehicle. British casualties were: three killed and 24

Ammunition Expenditure, 12–30 June 1944		
WEAPONS	TOTAL FIRED	PER WEAPON PER DAY
183mm/7.2in Howitzer (HE)	6166	15.1
140mm/5.5in Gun (HE)	101,453	35.2
114mm/4.5in Gun (HE)	20,746	N/k
25-pdr (All Types)	516,400	46.3
Ordnance QF 75mm/2.9in	35,558	0.7
17-pdr	6426	0.3
6-pdr	9735	0.5
107mm/4.2in Mortar	131,283	7.5
76mm/3in Mortar	192,881	16.9

wounded (almost all due to German mortar fire). Subsequent analysis concluded that a total of 25,500 rounds had been fired at the village.

A British artillery crew fire a 114mm (4.5in) Medium Gun Mk 2 as the Allies advance on Tilly-sur-Seulles, July 1944. The gun required a crew of eight to manhandle and operate it effectively.

Chapter 4
Villers-Bocage:
The Test of Battle

Villers-Bocage was an unexpected battle in both strategic and tactical terms. Allied strategic planning had expected that German forces would fight a logical campaign, retreating from one defence line to the next as Allied forces exploited their superiority in numbers and firepower. Based on this assumption, maps were prepared showing a series of 'phase lines' indicating the anticipated progress of the Allied advance during the first 90 days of the campaign. While these were essential for planning the logistic support of the Allied armies, their very existence caused immense controversy when elite German units such as I SS Panzer Corps reduced the Allied advance to a crawl in a series of actions, including that at Villers-Bocage.

At the tactical level, Villers-Bocage was a complete surprise for both sides — neither was expecting to fight there at that time. As far as 22nd Armoured Brigade was concerned, it had reached its objective after encountering only minimal opposition and it seemed likely that the enemy would take some time to gather sufficient forces to make a serious counter-attack. Michael Wittmann was as thoroughly surprised as his opponents and was only in position to make his initial attack because he had been forced to move twice during the previous night to avoid Allied artillery fire. The crucial factor was his seizure of the initiative and masterly exploitation of the advantage of surprise.

OPPOSITE: A Cromwell VI CS tank kicks up dust somewhere in Normandy. This one has been identified as belonging to the 7th Armoured Division.

Normandy Campaign: Plans and Practice

In the words of *Generalfeldmarschall* Helmuth von Moltke, 'No plan survives contact with the enemy.' In the Normandy campaign, the plan and the practice turned out to be very different affairs.

In the immediate aftermath of the initial British landings it was planned that XXX Corps would secure Villers-Bocage, astride the Caen–Avranches road and rail routes, and make contact with V US Corps at Caumont. Meanwhile, I Corps would pivot on Caen, maintaining contact with XXX Corps to its right. The latter would then continue its southerly advance to secure key terrain features, including the vital Mont Pinçon.

I Corps would perform a similar task on the left (eastern) flank, gaining ground to allow the construction of airfields southeast of Caen – a particularly high priority. In subsequent operations, Second Army would secure high ground running through St Pierre d'Entremont, Mont de Cérisi, Condé-sur-Noireau and Falaise, over 48km (30 miles) inland from the beaches. During these operations, I Corps would pivot on Argences and take Falaise.

It was emphasized that the 'ultimate object' of the Second Army was to protect the flank of the US forces committed to the capture of Cherbourg, Angers, Nantes, and the Brittany ports: 'There is no intention of carrying out a major advance until the Brittany ports have been captured.'

AMERICAN FRONT

On the American front, while one of General Bradley's corps captured Cherbourg – which it was calculated should fall about D+15 – two others were to begin a southerly drive towards St-Lô. First US Army would then advance to a line running through Avranches and Domfront, at the junction of the Cotentin and Brittany peninsulas. It was expected that this line would be reached about D+20, at which time Third US Army would become operational and First US Army Group (afterwards the Twelfth, under Bradley) would assume command of all American ground forces in France. After clearing the Brittany peninsula, the US forces would face east and 'pivot on the British position like a windlass in the direction of Paris'. This great turning movement would bring the Allied line forward to the Seine on a 225km (140-mile) front.

Montgomery later remarked that such forecasts were 'academic' in an operation of this magnitude. Nevertheless, the Allied planners had some hope, if no real expectation, that their troops would reach the Seine and the Loire by D+90. This provisional schedule had primarily been devised to form a framework for planning the enormous logistic effort required to transport men and materiel – by the end of 11 June (D+5), 326,547 troops, 54,186 vehicles and 106,099 tonnes (104,428 tons) of supplies had been landed, and by 30 June (D+24) the figures had risen to over 850,000 men, 148,000 vehicles and 579,120 tonnes (570,000 tons) of supplies.

Montgomery's 'excessive caution' has been heavily criticized both by his contemporaries and by later historians. This ignores the critical shortage of manpower that forced him to disband 59th Division in August 1944 to keep the remaining infantry formations up to something approaching full strength. As he put it: 'The good general must not only win his battles; he must win them with a minimum of casualties and loss of life.'

THE CAMPAIGN IN PRACTICE

The Allied planning assumptions had failed to allow for the determination of two very different characters – Hitler and Rommel. Hitler intuitively felt that the Allied landings would indeed be made in Normandy, but uncharacteristically failed to insist on priority being given to the preparation of defences in that sector.

However, immediately after the invasion, he reverted to his usual spate of 'no retreat' orders, backed with sufficient reinforcements to keep the Allies penned up in a confined beachhead for far longer than they had anticipated. Although much of Rommel's work in preparing the 'Atlantic Wall' was wasted in the construction of fortifications in sectors where no major landings could realistically be expected, his emphasis on defeating the invasion 'on the beaches' did ensure that sufficient forces were in position to prevent a rapid Allied breakout.

This was most marked in the fighting for Caen – Montgomery had hoped to take the city on D-Day, but it was not entirely cleared until 18 July, largely because of the exceptional, skilful defence by I SS Panzer Corps.

Despite this skill, Hitler's insistence on holding ground at all costs prevented a rapid Allied breakout, but committed elite Panzer formations to inevitable defeat in a prolonged battle of attrition.

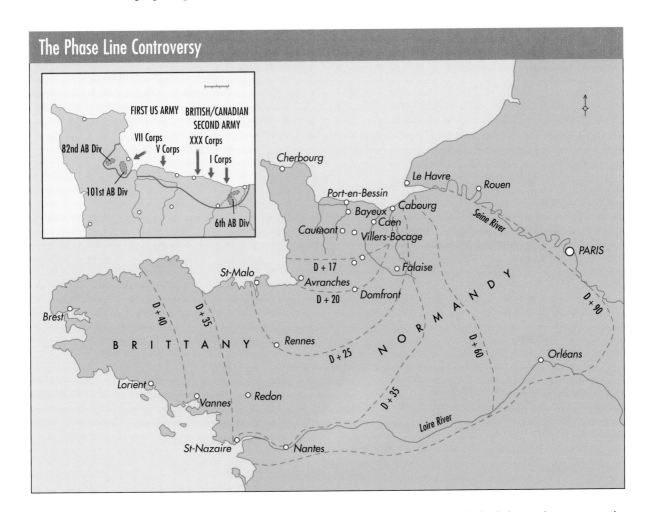

The Phase Line Controversy

When 21st Army Group's advance stalled in the face of the determined German defence of Caen, Montgomery's enemies within the Allied command structure were quick to compare his slow advance unfavourably with the progress predicted in this pre-invasion briefing map. Lieutenant-General Omar Bradley, commanding the First US Army, was furious when he saw these 'phase lines', refused to be committed to them and demanded that they be removed from the American sector of the front.

7th Armoured Division Arrives in Normandy

The division's intended role reflected the optimistic assessments typical of pre-invasion planning. 22nd Armoured Brigade were to land on the beaches already secured by 50th (Northumbrian) Division and to concentrate around Ryes, 4km (2.5 miles) from the beaches, starting on the evening of D-Day.

Meanwhile, 50th Division was assumed to have captured Bayeux and secured the road to Tilly-sur-Seulles. 22nd Armoured Brigade, with as much of the Division as was available, was then to pass through to Mont Pinçon, via Villers-Bocage and Aunay-sur-Odon. Having secured a firm base on the Mont Pinçon feature, the armour was then to turn east to take Thury-Harcourt and the crossings over the Orne.

22nd Armoured Brigade landed successfully during the morning of D+1, 7 June, having been delayed 12 hours by the weather, which steadily worsened until the landing programme was running 48 hours late. Nevertheless, few vehicles were lost. 22nd Armoured Brigade (less 1st Rifle Brigade and much of its transport) successfully concentrated by the evening of 7 June, but was then committed to a series of what should have been purely infantry operations until 12 June. 50th Division had captured Bayeux and advanced south on the Tilly and Caen roads for about 5km (3 miles), with their flanks resting on the Rivers Aure and Seulles.

However, there were still enemy strongpoints north of Bayeux at Sully and Port-en-Bessin, which had to be cleared by 56th Brigade, supported by 5th Royal Tank Regiment (5 RTR). This provided a harrowing introduction to armoured operations in the bocage. The close terrain meant that tanks and anti-tank guns commonly opened fire at ranges of 45m (50 yards) or less. Enemy infantry could approach unprotected tanks unseen, and on one occasion succeeded in boarding a tank; and snipers were extremely active. However, the regiment, after much hard fighting, succeeded in destroying four 88mm (3.5in) guns, one 75mm (2.9in) gun and one self-propelled 37mm (1.5in). Meanwhile, 1st Royal Tank Regiment (1 RTR) and 4th County of London Yeomanry (4th CLY) were supporting 69th Infantry Brigade in the St-Léger area and 151st Brigade in the area of the Jerusalem crossroads.

By 10 June, it was assessed that the build-up had reached a stage where an armoured offensive could be launched against Tilly-sur-Seulles and Villers-Bocage. 8th Armoured Brigade had made good progress and was now in the outskirts of St Pierre less than 1.6km (1 mile) from Tilly. The plan was to pass 22nd Armoured Brigade through 50th Division, and to follow up with 56th Brigade, which was to advance on the right to Verrières, through Blary, Ellon and Folliott, and 4th CLY, on the left, down the main road to Tilly and Juvigny. 1 RTR had been badly delayed in landing and was ordered to stay behind, guarding the bridges over the Seulles. Artillery support was to be provided by 3rd and 5th Royal Horse Artillery, 86th Field Regiment and 64th Medium Regiment, and the infantry had under its command a self-propelled anti-tank battery of the Norfolk Yeomanry.

ARMOURED ADVANCE

The advance began at 05:45 hours on 10 June and the leading tanks of 5 RTR made slow progress down the sunken roads towards Ellon, although one troop, somewhat to its own astonishment, and to the enemy's complete surprise, succeeded in entering a German leaguer, where they destroyed a Panzer IV. Once again, however, the tanks were up against infiltrating enemy infantry, snipers and a strongly held roadblock near Ellon.

An attempt to work round farther to the left towards Bernières-Bocage met with no greater success, two Cromwells being lost to a Panther in the village. The next morning an attempt was again made towards Bernières-Bocage. The reconnaissance troop moved on beyond the village and opposition seemed to be fading; but German reinforcements supported by a self-propelled gun advanced through the woods and destroyed one of the leading Stuarts of the reconnaissance troop.

A platoon of the Rifle Brigade that attempted to clear part of the woods without armoured support was rushed by German infantry and suffered severe casualties. More infantry was brought up, including a company of the 2nd Battalion, the Essex Regiment, which cleared the village and the surrounding woodland, while the advance continued through Ellon and Folliott until it emerged into open cornfields east of the road from Bernières-Bocage to Folliott.

Here, the going seemed to be more promising, but Panthers were concealed in the thick woods east of Bernières-Bocage; a Sherman Firefly was hit, and a Panther stalked the tanks of the right-hand troop along a sunken road, destroying two tanks with two rounds. Once again, the Essex Regiment attacked and secured its objective, but was heavily counter-attacked during the night by a company of infantry, supported by two flamethrowing tanks (probably Flammpanzer IIIs). The 2nd Essex managed to hold its ground despite heavy casualties, destroying

one tank with a PIAT and damaging the other. Thereafter, 5 RTR, with 8th Hussars and 2nd Essex, remained in position to cover the right flank.

4TH CLY ADVANCE

On the left, 4th CLY were fighting the same sort of battle. Opposition was first encountered in the woods and houses around the crossroads at Jerusalem. Three platoons of 1st Rifle Brigade's 'A' Company then moved in to clear the area. They spotted a Panzer IV on the road just to the north of the crossroads and warned the tanks, who were able to destroy it before it could open fire. The riflemen also came under fire from a further two tanks deployed amongst the houses, which then retreated. German snipers were active throughout

A British Sherman Crab flail tank rises, nose up, over a hedgerow in the early weeks of the Normandy campaign.

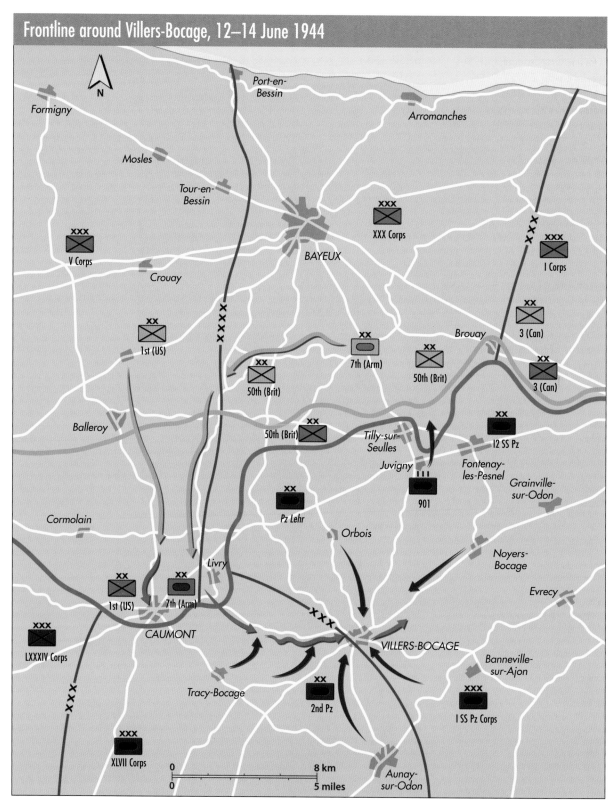

Frontline around Villers-Bocage, 12–14 June 1944

N

Formigny

Port-en-Bessin

Arromanches

Mosles

Tour-en-Bessin

XXX Corps

BAYEUX

I Corps

V Corps

Crouay

3 (Can)

1st (US)

Brouay

7th (Arm)

50th (Brit)

50th (Brit)

3 (Can)

50th (Brit)

Tilly-sur-Seulles

12 SS Pz

Juvigny

Fontenay-les-Pesnel

Grainville-sur-Odon

Pz Lehr

901

Balleroy

Cormolain

Orbois

Noyers-Bocage

Evrecy

Livry

1st (US)

7th (Arm)

VILLERS-BOCAGE

LXXXIV Corps

CAUMONT

Banneville-sur-Ajon

Tracy-Bocage

I SS Pz Corps

2nd Pz

XLVII Corps

0   8 km
0   5 miles

Aunay-sur-Odon

OPPOSITE: The Allied failure to take Caen on D-Day was to exercise a baleful influence on the entire Normandy campaign. Operation 'Perch', which culminated in the reverse at Villers-Bocage, was the first in a succession of Allied offensives intended to rectify that failure. Although the German hold on the southern suburbs of Caen was not finally broken until 18 July, the constant pressure applied by Montgomery's 21st Army Group 'fixed' the bulk of the Panzer divisions in that sector of the front, paving the way for the US breakout further west.

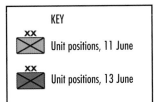

KEY

XX
Unit positions, 11 June

XX
Unit positions, 13 June

the day until the village was cleared that evening by 1st South Wales Borderers.

Meanwhile, having secured the right flank towards 5 RTR, the remainder of 4th CLY attempted a flanking movement towards Ste-Bazaire, to the northeast of Jerusalem. They lost two Cromwells to friendly fire from 8th Armoured Brigade before they were recognized – a reminder of the difficulty in distinguishing the Cromwell from a Panzer IV when glimpsed briefly through the thick foliage of the bocage. The Rifle Brigade, supported by 5th Royal Horse Artillery (5th RHA), occupied Ste-Bazaire and later, closely supported by the tanks, worked down to the woods north of Buceels.

It was clear by now that more infantry would be required to press the attack down the main road through Buceels, and 2nd Glosters, supported by 'A' Squadron, entered the village and secured the bridges to the south, knocking out one Panzer IV and taking some prisoners. By this time the light was fading, and with no very clear idea of the

enemy's strength in Tilly, it was decided to leaguer for the night, and push on over the bridges with the reconnaissance troop the next morning.

The night passed without incident, and at first light the advance continued, meeting two Panthers and an anti-tank gun on the road north of Tilly. The Cromwells were able work their way around the German position and destroyed one Panther and the anti-tank gun with flanking fire. The second Panther attacked the infantry but was destroyed by a PIAT. After this promising start, any further advance proved to be impossible. 4th CLY attempted a flanking movement to the west, only to lose a complete troop to well-sited anti-tank guns, and the infantry's attack from the north was pinned down by accurate mortar and artillery fire.

A troop of Cromwells did, however, get across the main road to the east of the town and shot up some enemy infantry and an anti-tank gun. Meanwhile, the Germans' skilful infiltration tactics allowed them to work back round the bridges at Buceels, delaying the advance until the lost ground could be recaptured. The next morning, a further attempt was made to outflank Tilly from the west via Verrières. Enemy infantry held the village, supported by a tank and an anti-tank gun, which destroyed one Cromwell and fought the advance to a standstill.

A final attempt was made to renew the advance on Tilly and Hottot on the morning of 12 June with two battalions of 131st Brigade, who had now arrived, supported by 1 RTR, but this met with no more success than the attacks of the previous day.

German Dispositions and the Caumont Gap

In contrast to the lack of Allied progress around Caen in the first few days of the invasion, the position at the junction between the British Second and US First Armies was far more promising.

Since D-Day, the steady whittling away of the German LXXXIV Corps had left the battered 352nd Infantry Division covering the Trévières–Agy sector virtually single-handed. By 9 June, constant pressure by the US 1st and 2nd Infantry Divisions led to a collapse of the 352nd's

left flank, and that night it was withdrawn to cover the key road centred on St-Lô.

This withdrawal left a gaping hole in the German lines more than 12km (7.5-miles) wide from Bérigny due east to Longraye, which was held by elements of *Panzer Lehr*. The corridor opened the way through Caumont to the high wooded terrain in the vicinity of the Bois du Homme and Le Bény-Bocage. Seizure of that high ground would have placed the US V Corps in a deep salient that the Germans feared could be reinforced and exploited either to outflank Caen or as the springboard for an offensive towards Avranches.

Generaloberst Dollmann commanding the Seventh Army foresaw this development on the morning of 9 June, but LXXXIV Corps no longer had any troops to plug the gap. Dollmann therefore proposed that II Parachute Corps should be assembled south of Balleroy to counter-attack northwards in conjunction with I SS Panzer Corps. Although the order for this offensive was passed by General Meindl of II Parachute Corps, Dollmann was doubtful if it was feasible, since there was no realistic estimate of when the various elements of the corps might arrive. (Given the badly damaged state of the transport system and continuous Allied air attacks, it was probable that they would straggle into the battle area, making a concerted counter-attack virtually impossible.)

REDEPLOYMENT

Of the units originally attached to Meindl's corps, the 77th Infantry Division had already been diverted to the Cotentin. The increasing urgency of blocking a threatened penetration at Montebourg made it imperative that the 77th Infantry Division should continue with that mission. Meindl was thus left with only two fresh formations, 17th SS Panzergrenadier Division *Götz von Berlichingen* and 3rd Parachute Division.

By the evening of 9 June the bulk of 3rd Parachute Division had only reached Brécey, east of Avranches. The 17th's 37th SS Panzergrenadier Regiment was in the same general area, while the

German infantry man a heavily camouflaged Pak 36 (Panzerabwehrkanone 36) 3.7cm (1.5in) anti-tank gun somewhere in Normandy. By 1944, the Pak 36 was outdated and struggled to penetrate Allied armour except at point-blank range.

An SS Tiger I moving up to the front, June 1944. From the beginning of the Normandy campaign all German vehicles made extensive use of foliage as camouflage in an attempt to avoid the attentions of Allied fighter-bombers.

38th SS Panzergrenadier Regiment was east of Laval. The 17th's tracked vehicles were being moved up by rail and on 9 June were strung out between La Flèche and Saumur. The move suffered further delay when air attacks forced the last two trains to be unloaded south of the Loire. Only advance elements of the 17th, including the reconnaissance battalion, had reached Balleroy by the 9th, but these were able to begin preparations for the division's deployment in that sector.

In the meantime, however, plans were changed. Rommel believed that German weakness in the Carentan area was more dangerous than the gap on the right of LXXXIV Corps. II Parachute Corps was diverted to hold the sector between Carentan and St-Lô, which was given priority over supporting 352nd Division despite its desperate condition. 3rd Parachute Division was still earmarked for deployment in the St-Lô area with the tentative mission of holding the northern edge of the Forêt de Cerisy.

353rd Infantry Division, the last mobile unit in Brittany, was also ordered to St-Lô to come under command of Meindl's corps. However, the chief concern was the situation along the Vire. Most of 17th SS Panzergrenadier Division was deployed southwest of Carentan, while *Kampfgruppe Heintz* (a mobile battle-group of the 275th Infantry Division) was to move on arrival into the St-Jean-de-Daye area.

STOP-GAP MEASURES

The only immediate step to plug the Caumont Gap on 10 June was the decision to leave the 17th's reconnaissance battalion in the vicinity of Balleroy. Although the move does not seem to have been intended as a deception, it had that effect. The US

1st Infantry Division immediately took prisoners and located forward positions of elements of the 17th south of Balleroy east to St-Paul-du-Verney. Unidentified medium tanks were also reported on the afternoon of 10 June in the vicinity of La Londe. The light mixed units actually in contact were recognized to be incapable of launching any major counter-attack, but from prisoner interrogations, US V Corps deduced that the 17th might be in position to attack, probably from the direction of the Forêt de Cerisy by 11 June.

US intelligence warned of a long-term risk that 11th Panzer and 1st SS Panzer Divisions, which were reported to be moving up from the south and northeast respectively, might be used to spearhead an offensive against V Corps, although it was highly uncertain when either would arrive.

STRENGTH AND DECEPTION

At this time, Allied intelligence staff were preoccupied with the knowledge that the Germans now had at least a theoretical 'window of opportunity' to achieve sufficient local armoured superiority to launch serious counter-attacks. The signs seemed ominous and US First Army's report on the fighting of 9 June noted that: 'Enemy forces pursued their delaying tactics pending the arrival of armored counterattack forces.'

Throughout 10 June, the Caumont Gap was held by nothing more than the thin screening forces of 17th SS Panzergrenadier Division's reconnaissance battalion. Their extreme vulnerability to any serious

Allied attack was obvious and 2nd Panzer Division, from General Hans Freiherr von Funck's XLVII Panzer Corps, was earmarked to reinforce the sector. 2nd Panzer Division had in fact begun its move from Amiens to the battle area during the night of 9–10 June. Its leading elements had reached Paris, but daylight movements were subjected to near constant air attacks, which inflicted a steadily rising toll of losses.

By the evening of 10 June, the wheeled elements were nearing Alençon, but the tanks had only just begun to move from Amiens by rail. Mindful of the problems caused by the ineffective piecemeal commitment of *Panzer Lehr*, 12th SS and 21st Panzer Divisions, Funck wanted to delay commitment of 2nd Panzer Division until 13 June, by which time it should have fully assembled. In the meantime, its reconnaissance battalion was rushed to Caumont with orders to hold the high ground there.

In addition, I SS Panzer Corps commander Sepp Dietrich ordered his only reserve, the 101st SS Heavy Panzer Battalion, to take up position behind *Panzer Lehr* and 12th SS Panzer Division to cover his open left flank. Anticipating the importance the British would place on seizing the high ground near Villers-Bocage, the six serviceable Tigers of the 101st's 2nd Company, under the command of Michael Wittmann, were directed to a position just south of Point 213 on the Villers-Bocage ridge and arrived on 12 June after a five-day drive from Beauvais.

22nd Armoured Brigade's Advance to Villers-Bocage

Allied pre-invasion planning had expected that Caen would be taken on D-Day and that a series of Allied offensives would then rapidly enlarge the beachhead. This assumption gave rise to the earliest version of Operation 'Perch', which was then intended to be a major Allied breakthrough to the southwest of Caen.

This was to be an operation carried out by XXX Corps; 50th (Northumbrian) Division was due to land on Gold Beach on 6 June, capture Bayeux and the road to Tilly-sur-Seulles. For the next stage of the operation 7th Armoured Division, reinforced by 8th Armoured Brigade, would

spearhead a further advance from Tilly-sur-Seulles to Villers-Bocage and on to Mont Pinçon.

However, the stubborn German defence of Caen and Tilly-sur-Seulles rendered such plans irrelevant. In response to the new situation, Montgomery devised a pincer movement to take

Caen, code-named Operation 'Wild Oats'. The eastern arm of the pincer would consist of I Corps' 51st (Highland) Division and 4th Armoured Brigade. The armour and Highlanders would cross into the Orne bridgehead, the ground gained east of the Orne by 6th Airborne Division during Operation 'Tonga', and attack southwards to Cagny, almost 10km (6 miles) to the southeast of Caen. XXX Corps would form the pincer's western arm. In an alteration to Operation 'Perch', instead of making for Mont Pinçon the 7th Armoured Division would now swing east, crossing the Odon River to take Evrecy and the high ground near the town (Hill 112).

To complete the encirclement, it was suggested that 1st Airborne Division should be dropped southwest of Caen around Evrecy, but the Allied air commander, Air Marshal Sir Trafford Leigh-

Mallory, vehemently opposed the idea. He refused to fly the division into Normandy, arguing that the drop would scatter the division too widely to fulfil its objectives, and that the drop zone was in any case too dangerous for his pilots. (He allegedly added that there was an unacceptable risk of losses due to 'friendly fire' from Allied shipping in the Channel.)

Montgomery was furious, describing Leigh-Mallory as 'a gutless bugger, who refuses to take a chance and plays for safety on all occasions'. However, Montgomery had to accept the veto and the offensive went ahead without its airborne element – at this point it seems to have been incorporated into a revised version of Operation 'Perch', and 'Wild Oats' was dropped as a separate operation.

The planned offensive quickly became impractical – XXX Corps became bogged down in repeated attacks on the town of Tilly-sur-Seulles, which was fiercely defended by *Panzer Lehr* and elements of 12th SS Panzer Division. It proved impossible for 51st Highland Division to attack until 12 June and this broke down almost

A heavily camouflaged Sherman in a Normandy lane. The dust seen here was a constant problem during dry spells, frequently alerting German artillery observers in time to bring down devastating bombardments on Allied columns. In an attempt to minimize the risk, thousands of warning signs reading 'DUST BRINGS SHELLS!' were put up along Normandy roadsides.

immediately in the face of determined opposition by 21st Panzer Division – by the following day, the offensive east of Caen was called off.

By 12 June, Operation 'Perch' was revived in an amended form. The Caumont Gap was an obvious weak spot in the German lines and a far more attractive target than the well-defended area around Tilly-sur-Seulles. Conscious that this might well be a fleeting opportunity that required rapid exploitation, Dempsey had conferred with Lieutenant-General Gerard Bucknall commanding XXX Corps and Major-General George Erskine commanding the 7th Armoured Division. Erskine was ordered to be prepared to disengage his armour from the fighting around Tilly-sur-Seulles so that it could exploit the opening in the German lines, seize the town of Villers-Bocage and advance against *Panzer Lehr*'s left flank.

The initial objective was Point 213 – the highest point of a ridge immediately to the east of the town, which, if taken, would force *Panzer Lehr*'s withdrawal and outflank the defences of Caen. In support of the 7th Armoured's flanking manoeuvre, 50th (Northumbrian) Division would maintain pressure against the *Panzer Lehr* Division around Tilly-sur-Seulles. Elements of the US V Corps would advance to cover the British right flank – 1st US Infantry Division was tasked with taking Caumont, while the 2nd US Infantry Division would attack towards St-Lô.

FLAWED COMMAND

One of the problems that bedevilled the operation was that so many senior officers held different views regarding its objectives. Montgomery and Dempsey saw it as the means of breaking the stalemate around Caen. They saw the seizure of Villers-Bocage and Point 213 as the preliminaries to an advance on Evrecy that had the potential to unhinge the entire German line west of Caen.

In contrast, Bucknall seems to have regarded the offensive solely as a means of breaking the stalemate on XXX Corps' sector of the front. He believed it was a subsidiary operation to the main battle for Caen and was intended (at least partly) to act as a diversion from the main offensive. As a result, XXX Corps was ordered to restrict its ammunition expenditure and to avoid a 'Corps battle' that might compromise the Army commander's plan.

Erskine later wrote that: 'After some unsuccessful stabs at Tilly, I suggested the use of the Division's mobility round the right flank of 50 Div. I was sure there was a soft spot here and had in fact reconnoitred routes and had a cut and dried plan for a swoop on Villers-Bocage.' His view was heavily influenced by his experience in North Africa, where mobility, speed and surprise were critical factors in battlefield success, but there was no real appreciation of anything beyond the tactical level and crucially no thought of how to adapt 'desert style' armoured tactics to the very different terrain of Normandy.

The 'man on the spot', Brigadier Hinde, commanding 22nd Armoured Brigade, was therefore given the impression that his objectives were limited to the rapid capture of Villers-Bocage and Point 213. This pressure led to a rushed deployment and lack of proper reconnaissance, which were major factors contributing to the success of Wittmann's initial attack.

ADVANCING AT LAST

Despite the urgency of the 'new' Operation 'Perch', it seems that Bucknall and his staff at XXX Corps HQ were less than dynamic in getting it under way. Dempsey himself had to visit the HQ to prod them into action and Erskine was fuming at the delay – he later noted that 24 hours had been wasted in what he believed was 'spurious planning'. In the absence of any confirmation that the operation was 'on', 7th Armoured Division spent the morning of 12 June continuing attempts to advance on Tilly-sur-Seulles. It was midday before Erskine was able to pass on orders for 22nd Armoured Brigade to move immediately on Villers-Bocage.

The Cromwells of 8th King's Royal Irish Hussars – 7th Armoured Division's armoured reconnaissance regiment – began to reconnoitre the route the brigade would take; the main body of 22nd Armoured Brigade left the village of Trungy at about 16:00 hours. Four hours later, the main body was approaching Livry after a 19km (12-mile) unopposed advance, the last 9.5km (6 miles) of which were through what was nominally German-held territory. Minor resistance was encountered north of Livry when the 8th Hussars' leading tank was destroyed by an anti-tank gun supported by a small infantry detachment. A platoon of the Rifle Brigade's 1st Battalion was brought forward and within two hours the position was cleared.

Hoping to keep the Germans uncertain about his objective, Hinde ordered a halt for the night just north of Livry. While the main force conducted routine maintenance, the 8th and 11th (Prince Albert's Own) Hussars (the divisional armoured car regiment) patrolled both flanks. The 11th Hussars encountered no resistance on the right flank and linked up with the 1st US Infantry Division near Caumont, meeting 'a US patrol in armoured cars and jeeps, looking very dusty and excited'.

On the left flank the 8th Hussars located elements of *Panzer Lehr* roughly 3km (just under 2 miles) away, losing another two Cromwells in the process, but making sufficient progress for their commander, Lieutenant-Colonel Goulbourn, to

note in his diary that: 'We are all beginning to think we have obtained a complete breakthrough.'

PLAN OF ACTION

During the night Hinde finalized his plans, making provision for his force to hold both Villers-Bocage and Point 213 in strength. 4th County of London Yeomanry (4th CLY), with 'A' Company, 1st Battalion, the Rifle Brigade (1st RB), was to pass through Villers-Bocage and occupy Point 213, whilst 1/7th Queen's Royal Regiment (West Surrey) (1/7th QRR) would follow up and occupy the town itself. At the same time, 5th Royal Tank Regiment (5 RTR), with a further company of the Rifle Brigade, was to take up positions on a second area

A column of British Cromwell Mk IV tanks advance somewhere in the Caen area, July 1944.

22nd Armoured Brigade: Route to Villers-Bocage, 12–13 June 1944

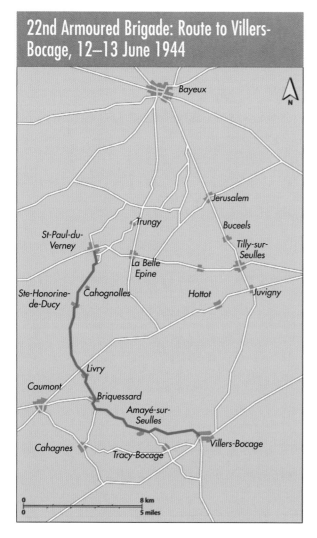

Large scale cross-country movement was virtually impossible in the bocage, which forced all major operations to follow the road network. The advance of 22nd Armoured Brigade was confined to a single road, as the route to the west ran through the US sector, while the roads to the east led straight into *Panzer Lehr* Division's frontline. The limitations of the road system favoured the defence, frequently allowing vastly outnumbered German *Kampfgruppen* to halt the Allied advance.

of high ground to the southwest of the town at Maisoncelles-Pelvey. The M10 Achilles self-propelled 17-pdr anti-tank guns of the Norfolk Yeomanry's 260th Anti-Tank Battery would cover the gap between 4th CLY and 5 RTR. Meanwhile, 5th RHA, equipped with Sexton self-propelled 25-pdrs, would advance behind the rest of the brigade. 5th RHA and the brigade's Tactical HQ

were established to the west of the town at Amayé-sur-Seulles. Hinde's two Hussar regiments were to provide flank protection, screen the British advance and seek out enemy positions on either side of the line of advance. It was intended that the remainder of the division – 131st Infantry Brigade with the 1st Royal Tank Regiment (1 RTR) and the 1/5th and 1/6th QRR – should take up positions around Livry to hold a 'firm base', protecting the brigade group's line of communications.

ROUTE IS CLEAR

During the early hours of 13 June, 1st RB sent out reconnaissance patrols along the first 0.9km (0.5 miles) of the intended British route. Livry was reported to be clear of Germans and the advance resumed at 05:30, with 4th CLY in the lead. Moving cautiously, the column was met at the farms and hamlets along its route by jubilant French civilians, leading to a mood of general relaxation among the troops. Contradictory rumours were rife, including one – later found to be incorrect – that German tanks were stranded in Tracy-Bocage, and another that more tanks, without fuel or infantry support, were similarly immobilized at the Château de Villers-Bocage. (Two of *Panzer Lehr*'s medical companies had established a field hospital at the château, but this position had been abandoned by first light on 13 June. However, given subsequent events, it is likely that a handful of German combat troops remained in and around the town.)

As Hinde's force neared Villers-Bocage a German eight-wheeled armoured car (possibly one of *Panzer Lehr*'s Pumas) was spotted shadowing the column from a distance. Its commander had clearly observed the advance, but the closest Cromwell was so festooned with external stowage that it was unable to traverse its turret to engage, and by the time a second tank had moved into position the armoured car had prudently withdrawn at speed. At 08:30, having safely covered the 8km (5 miles) from its overnight position, 22nd Armoured Brigade group entered the town to be greeted by celebrating residents as two German soldiers left at high speed in a Kübelwagen.

The two Hussar regiments made contact with German forces on either side of the line of advance, with the 8th Hussars engaging eight-wheeled armoured cars. They also reported seeing German tanks heading towards Villers-Bocage but Lieutenant Charles Pearce of 4th CLY believed that these were probably misidentified self-propelled guns.

ON TO POINT 213

In contrast to the previous cautious advance, 'A' Squadron, 4th CLY, drove straight on to Point 213. A German staff car encountered on the road was engaged and destroyed, and the tanks began to take up hull down positions to form a defensive perimeter. Along the road between the town and the ridge, 1st RB's halftracks were ordered to pull over and park to allow reinforcements for Point 213 to pass. The riflemen dismounted and posted sentries, although they could see less than 230m (250 yards) to either side of the road. Crucially, too, there was no proper local reconnaissance – 'A' Company's No. 1 (Scout) Platoon had not arrived in Normandy in time for Operation 'Perch'.

Its Universal Carriers were small enough to use the narrowest country lanes and might well have found Wittmann's Tigers before they could make their attack.

Major Wright, commanding 1st RB's 'A' Company, called all his officers and senior NCOs (SNCOs) to an 'O' Group (briefing and orders session) on Point 213. As they moved towards the ridge in a single halftrack, it was belatedly realized that one enemy shell could wipe out the company's entire command capability, so the halftrack's occupants were rapidly dispersed among several other vehicles. In Villers-Bocage, Lt-Colonel the Viscount Arthur Cranley, the commanding officer of 4th CLY, expressed concern about the lack of adequate local reconnaissance, feeling that his men were 'out on a limb'. He was assured by Brigadier Hinde that all was well, and ordered to Point 213 to ensure that his men had taken up good defensive positions. Hinde then left Villers-Bocage for his HQ.

101st SS Heavy Panzer Battalion

In mid-1944, the Tiger I remained a formidable heavy tank, although it was being phased out of production in favour of the far more powerful Tiger II. The three heavy Panzer battalions committed to Normandy proved to be dangerous opponents, although even at full strength, they fielded only 135 Tigers between them.

The 101st SS Heavy Panzer Battalion had been formed at Sennelager in July 1943, incorporating *Leibstandarte*'s Tiger company and two newly raised companies, but it did not see action as a battalion until the Normandy campaign. The unit was intended to provide I SS Panzer Corps with integral Tiger support, but by the time of the Normandy campaign, its original function of spearheading corps-level offensives had been overtaken by the need to act in a 'fire-brigade' role to seal off Allied penetrations of increasingly fragile German defences.

A succession of crises on the Eastern Front forced elements of the battalion to be deployed in Russia until the spring of 1944, when it finally moved to the Beauvais area to begin anti-invasion training. Much of this training concentrated on

countering major Allied airborne operations, as it was assumed that these would be an important part of any invasion. Although the 101st was not called upon to operate in this particular role, the exercises were useful in forcing its tank crews to adapt their tactics from those optimized for the long-range engagements typical of the rolling Russian steppe to the far more cautious approach needed in the very different terrain of Normandy. (Even so, the Beauvais area was relatively open in comparison to the bocage, where every move had to be carefully planned due to the threat posed by Allied AFVs, anti-tank guns and infantry anti-tank teams concealed amongst the innumerable thick hedgerows and sunken lanes.)

Allied air power proved to be the other major constraint on the 101st's operational freedom throughout the Normandy campaign. The tanks were ordered to keep 50m (54.7 yards) apart whenever they were on the move behind the frontline, to minimize the risk from air attacks.

In practice, the heavily armoured Tigers were virtually invulnerable to most air-launched weapons apart from the notoriously inaccurate rockets or a chance direct hit from a bomb. A few vehicles did fall victim to these weapons, notably *SS-Untersturmführer* Alfred Günther's Tiger 311, which was totally destroyed by a bomb in an air raid

during the night of 14–15 June. While the Tigers themselves were well protected, their crews were always vulnerable if caught outside their tanks, and the battalion suffered a steady trickle of casualties as a result.

The greatest impact of Allied air superiority on the battalion's operational effectiveness was indirect – the cumulative effect of a range of factors such as the time lost in carefully camouflaging all tanks, coupled with the delays in refuelling and resupply caused by the loss of thinly armoured or soft-skin support vehicles to incessant strafing attacks. Equally seriously, Allied bombing of the French transport system imposed further delays on units heading for the Normandy front.

The 101st was alerted on 6 June and started to move the following day. Normally, such a move would have been made by rail, but Allied bombing had severely disrupted the French railway system and it was believed that movement by road would be quicker and less vulnerable to air attack. The inevitable breakdowns resulting from such a long road march were accepted, given the urgency of reinforcing the hard-pressed German forces in Normandy. Although the battalion moved primarily at night to minimize the threat from Allied aircraft, it still came under repeated air attack and its lead elements only arrived on the evening of 12 June, leaving many vehicles broken down en route.

Despite these problems, the 101st was to demonstrate the Tiger's effectiveness, especially in the hands of Panzer *Experten* such as Michael Wittmann, who had almost two years' combat experience of the type and a total of 109 'AFV kills'.

Michael Wittmann sits on top of a Tiger tank in this posed photo in Normandy in 1944. Wittmann's tankman's uniform is adorned with many honours, including the Knight's Cross, Iron Cross First Class, *Verwundetenabzeichen* (Wound Badge) and the *Panzerkampfabzeichen* (Tank Battle Badge).

Surprise Attack

The 101st SS Heavy Panzer Battalion arrived in Normandy on 12 June, after a five-day, 260km (160-mile) drive from Beauvais.

Mustering 45 Tiger I tanks at full strength, the battalion had been subjected to air attacks en route and was reduced to around 17 serviceable tanks. *SS-Hauptsturmführer* Rolf Möbius' 1st Company was 9km (5.6 miles) northeast of Villers-Bocage. The 2nd Company, under the command of *SS-Obersturmführer* Michael Wittmann, was just south of Point 213 on the Villers-Bocage ridge, while the 3rd, with only a single operational Tiger, was near Falaise and would not reach the front for another two days. Wittmann's 2nd Company had a nominal strength of 12 tanks, but due to a combination of losses and mechanical failures, only Tigers 211, 221, 222, 223, 233 and 234 were present on 13 June.

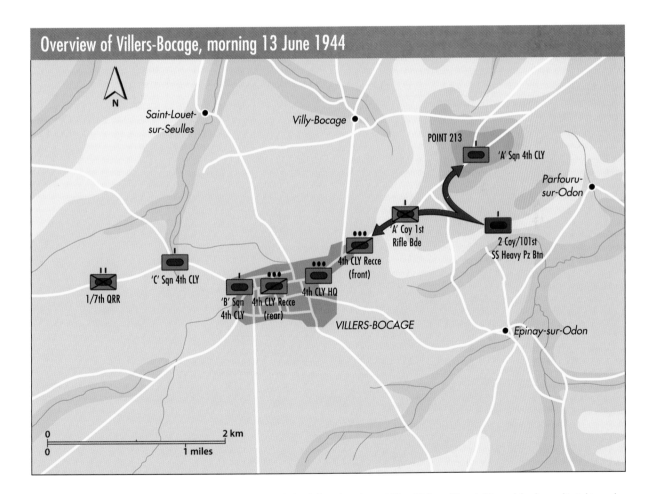

Overview of Villers-Bocage, morning 13 June 1944

Unit positions in and around Villers-Bocage as Wittmann made his single-handed attack at about 09:00 on 13 June. Although this attack has been subjected to much criticism, it brilliantly exploited the advantage of surprise, preventing the British force from effectively deploying its vast numerical superiority. The shock effect of Wittmann's charge temporarily paralyzed the local British command structure, gaining the Germans invaluable time to reinforce the sector.

The area around Villers-Bocage came under heavy naval bombardment during the night of 12–13th June and, fearing that he had been spotted, Wittmann relocated his company twice, finally taking up heavily camouflaged positions along the 'Ancienne Route de Caen'. This was the old road to Caen, which had deteriorated into little more than a narrow country lane, running roughly parallel to and 200m (218.7 yards) south of the main Caen road, the Route Nationale 175 (RN 175). At this time Wittmann had no knowledge of the British advance and anticipated spending the next day or so carrying out badly needed maintenance and repairs to his vehicles.

WITTMANN'S ATTACK

The details of Wittmann's attack have been the subject of considerable research and debate, but there is still a degree of uncertainty regarding the precise sequence of events, the number of vehicles and guns that he destroyed and exactly where his Tiger was finally immobilized. The following account is an attempt to give a logical interpretation of frequently conflicting sources.

At about 08:45, Wittmann was working in his command post when the alarm was raised by one of his men, who warned him that unidentified tanks were driving past outside. Wittmann was in no doubt that they were Allied AFVs and initially estimated that he was opposed by a British armoured regiment.

He made for the nearest tank, Tiger 234, only to find that it was one of those still suffering engine trouble and immediately ran across to take command of Tiger 222, ordering the rest of the tanks to hold their ground. Although most of the remaining Tigers were suffering mechanical problems, it seems that they all managed to manoeuvre into positions from which they could engage the 'target-rich environment' on Point 213.

The timing of Wittmann's single-handed attack could hardly have been better, as virtually the entire British force was 'off-guard':

■ Colonel Cranley was at Point 213, supervising 'A' Squadron's deployment.
■ Major Wright was also at Point 213, awaiting the arrival of his officers and SNCOs for his O Group.
■ 1st RB's 'A' Company's vehicles were parked

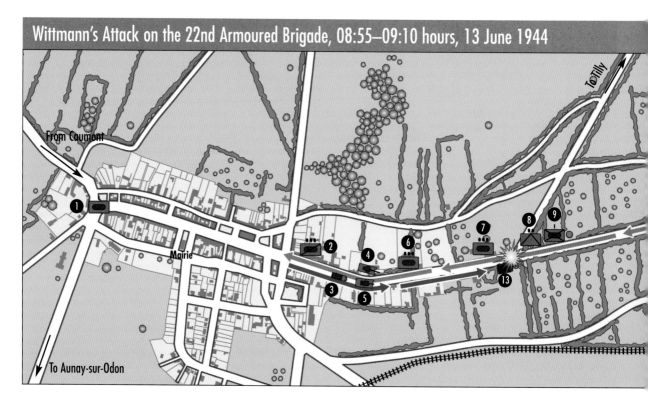

Wittmann's Attack on the 22nd Armoured Brigade, 08:55–09:10 hours, 13 June 1944

along the roadside between Villers-Bocage and Point 213 to keep the road clear for a further squadron of 4th CLY and 1/7th Queens Royal Regiment (1/7th QRR), which was scheduled to support 'A' Squadron's position. Although sentries had been posted, they had a very limited field of vision and none of the riflemen were seriously expecting trouble. (In the absence of their officers and SNCOs, some of them had allegedly taken the opportunity to dismount and start brewing hasty cups of tea.)

■ The remainder of 4th CLY, including its Regimental HQ (RHQ), was strung out in Villers-Bocage and several crews had dismounted to take a break.

PARALYZED COMMAND

Thus the commanders of both 4th CLY and 1st RB were isolated from the bulk of their units, 1st RB's 'A' Company was virtually leaderless, and much of 4th CLY was more intent on taking a break (and speculating on the availability of freshly baked bread from the town's *patisseries*) than preparing for action. Years later, Captain Charles Pearce, RHQ's

1 'B' Squadron, 4th CLY (advance elements)
2 Recce Troop, 4th CLY (4 x M3A3 Stuarts, 1 x Humber Scout Car)
3 M5A1 halftrack (Captain MacLean, Medical Officer 4th CLY)
4 Cromwell OP tank (Captain Victory, 5th RHA)
5 Sherman OP tank (Major Wells, 5th RHA)
6 RHQ, 4th CLY (4 x Cromwell IVs, 1 x Humber Scout Car)
7 Recce Troop, 4th CLY (3 x M3A3 Stuarts)
8 Anti-tank Section, 1st Btn, Rifle Bde (4 Loyd carriers + 2 x 6pdr AT guns)
9 'A' Company, 1st Btn, Rifle Bde (9 x M9A1 halftracks)
10 Cromwell OP tank (Captain Dunlop, 5th RHA)
11 'A' Squadron, 4th CLY (4 x Sherman Fireflies, 10 x Cromwell IVs and Cromwell VI CS tanks)
12 2nd Company, 101st Heavy SS Panzer Battalion (6 x Tiger I Ausf Es)
13 Wittmann's Tiger I immobilized and abandoned

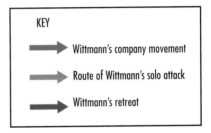

KEY
→ Wittmann's company movement
→ Route of Wittmann's solo attack
→ Wittmann's retreat

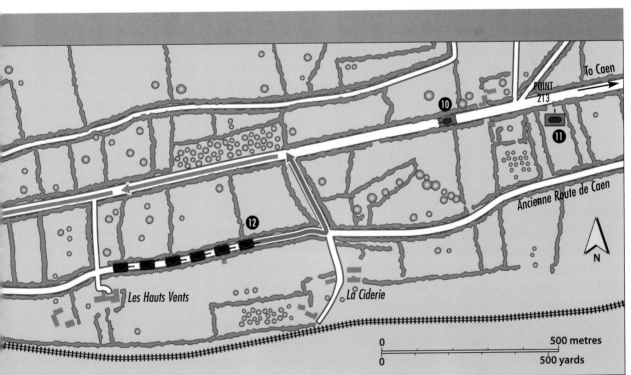

liaison officer, recalled his unease at their casual attitude, while: 'I was in my scout car looking all round for enemy infantry, as I felt sure we would be attacked.' He went on to summarize his thoughts on what should have been done: 'Once having reached the objective … immediate deployment and consolidation must be put into effect at once as the role changes over from one of attack to defence. It is essential that infantry dig in and tanks must take up defensive positions. All ranks should stand to, as this is the most critical time. It is not a question of if a counter-attack comes, but when. Support in depth is important if sufficient troops are available.'

Wittmann's Tiger was spotted at approximately 09:00 by Sergeant O'Connor of 1st RB, who was travelling towards Point 213 in a halftrack and broke radio silence, yelling: 'For Christ's sake get a move on! There's a Tiger running alongside us 50 yards away.' This seems to have been the only warning that the British force received. As Wittmann emerged from the lane onto RN 175, he

engaged and destroyed the rearmost Cromwell of 'A' Squadron, 4th CLY, at Point 213 before it was aware of his presence. He was spotted by a Sherman Firefly, but managed to fire first, wrecking the Firefly, which burst into flames and slewed across the road, seriously impeding any attempt to either reinforce the ridge or to withdraw from it. At this point the British force at Point 213 came under fire from the remaining Tigers, losing three more tanks.

WITTMANN TURNS ON THE TOWN

Wittmann now turned towards Villers-Bocage. Along the RN 175 riflemen desperately hunted for the PIAT anti-tank weapons stowed away in their vehicles and tried to deploy a 6-pdr anti-tank gun, but were forced to take cover as the Tiger advanced on their positions. Many of 'A' Company's M9 halftracks were burnt out when their fuel tanks were ruptured by machine gun and heavy explosive (HE) fire. However, the unit's casualties were surprisingly light, largely due to the fact that most riflemen were already sheltering in roadside ditches and hedgerows.

The M9 halftrack's maximum armour thickness was only 10mm (0.393in) – armour-piercing (AP) rounds from the Tiger's bow and coaxial 7.92mm (0.31in) MG34 machine guns could penetrate at least 12mm (0.47in) of armour at ranges of up to 150m (164 yards). Most of the M9s destroyed by Wittmann were probably hit at ranges well below 50m (54.7 yards). In cases where the main armament was used, the blast effect of an impact-fused 88mm (3.5in) HE shell would be ample to wreck such thinly armoured vehicles.

On reaching the eastern outskirts of Villers-Bocage, Wittmann fought a brief and very one-sided action against three Stuart light tanks of 4th CLY's reconnaissance troop near the junction with the road to Tilly. The Stuarts' thin armour of no more than 51mm (2in) offered no protection against 88mm (3.5in) AP rounds, while even at point-blank range, the Tiger was effectively invulnerable to their puny 37mm (1.5in) guns. (By the time of the Normandy campaign, the Stuart was at best obsolescent and was described as an 'atrocity on tracks' with a gun incapable of harming 'anything

A close-up of Major Wells' knocked-out Sherman OP tank. A round from Wittmann's '88' penetrated the turret, blowing off both the mantlet and the wooden dummy 75mm (2.9in) gun which lie on the ground just in front of the tank.

The gun that knocked out Wittmann's Tiger? There is circumstantial evidence to suggest that this 6-pdr of 1st RB, commanded by Sergeant Bray, was responsible for immobilizing Wittmann's Tiger close to the junction of the Tilly-sur-Seulles road.

tougher than a water-truck'.) One Stuart, commanded by Lieutenant Ingram, attempted to block the road into the town, but was hit and exploded violently. The other two were also quickly destroyed and Wittmann moved into the town along the Rue Georges Clemenceau towards the Cromwells of 4th CLY's RHQ, which attempted to escape by reversing into cover; but in contrast to its high road speed, the Cromwell was 'painfully slow' in reverse, managing no more than 3.2km/h (2mph) at best.

Some crew members had very lucky escapes when their tanks were destroyed – Lieutenant Cloudsley-Thompson recalled that: '... a high-velocity shell whizzed between my wireless operator's head and mine. It passed so close that, although I was wearing headphones, it made me slightly deaf in my right ear for 24 hours afterwards. It was terrifying! The sound was so vicious. Our tank had scarcely left the road before Michael Wittmann's Tiger loomed through the smoke, less than 35 yards away. There was insufficient time to

undo the 75mm travel lock, so I fired the 2in bomb thrower to provide cover, but the short range smoke shell passed way overhead. At the same time, the Tiger traversed its huge 88mm very slightly and fired. I felt a tingling between my legs as the shot passed between them, and wondered if I had been wounded again. A sheet of flame licked over the turret and my mouth was full of grit and burnt paint. "Bale out," I yelled, and leaped clear.'

4th CLY's Adjutant, Captain Pat Dyas, also reversed off the road into a garden and found that his Cromwell was further screened by a small barn. Major Carr, commanding 'A' Squadron 4th CLY, was slightly ahead of the RHQ and pulled up on the right-hand side of the road, firing two shots that bounced off the Tiger's frontal armour. It returned fire, knocking out Carr's tank, which began to burn, adding to the smoke already drifting down the road.

INFANTRY SUPPORT

Scattered groups of German infantry, which had either just infiltrated the town or remained in hiding since the British arrived that morning, now opened fire from the upper floors of nearby buildings. Captain Dyas was wounded in the eye by metal

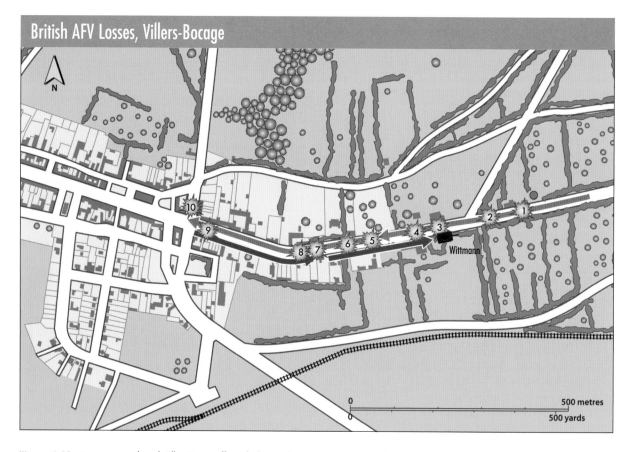

British AFV Losses, Villers-Bocage

Wittmann's 15-minute rampage through Villers-Bocage effectively destroyed the HQ element of 4th CLY, elements of 'A' Troop, 4th CLY, the forward component of the Reconnaissance Troop, as well as an anti-tank platoon and a significant part of 'A' Company, 1st RB.

1. 9 x M5A1 halftracks ('A' Company, 1st Rifle Bde)
2. 4 x Loyd carriers, 2 x 6-pdr AT guns (AT Section, 1st Rifle Bde)
3. 3 x M3A3 Stuarts (Recce Troop, 4th CLY, Lt Ingram)
4. 1 x M5 halftrack (4th CLY, Medical Officer)
5. Cromwell IV (Major Carr, 'A' Squadron, 4th CLY, Commanding Officer)
6. Cromwell IV (Lt Cloudsley-Thompson, 4th CLY, RHQ Troop Leader)
7. Cromwell IV (RSM Holloway, 4th CLY, RHQ)
8. Cromwell IV (Captain Dyas, 4th CLY, RHQ, Adjutant)
9. Sherman OP (Major Wells, 5th RHA)
10. Cromwell OP (Captain Victory, 5th RHA)

splinters thrown up as their shots ricocheted from the turret roof and hatches. It was fortunate for the British that there were too few German infantry in position to effectively support Wittmann's attack – even a handful of *Panzerfaust* or *Panzerschreck* teams could have inflicted severe losses. However, at this stage, it seems that there were no more than a small number of snipers and machine gunners in the town who did no more than keep up harassing fire at any targets of opportunity.

After destroying Cloudsley-Thompson's Cromwell, Wittmann failed to spot Dyas in the thickening smoke and continued towards the centre of Villers-Bocage. Captain Charles Pearce escaped in his Humber Scout Car and warned the rest of the RHQ in the town centre. While they quickly pulled off the road Pearce continued further west to alert 'B' Squadron.

Meanwhile, Wittmann had also accounted for RSM Holloway's Cromwell, before heading further into the town on the Rue Pasteur, where he knocked out two artillery Observation Post (OP) tanks – a Cromwell and a Sherman – both of 5th RHA. His next victims were the Intelligence Officer's Humber Scout Car and the Medical Officer's halftrack.

After these easy victims, Wittmann came up against a far more dangerous opponent in the form of Sergeant Lockwood's Sherman Firefly. By this time, visibility was worsening due to smoke from burning vehicles, together with the dust and debris thrown up by muzzle blast from the high-velocity 17-pdr and 88mm (3.5in) guns, which made accurate shooting very difficult. A combination of the Firefly's muzzle blast and shots from Wittmann's Tiger caused the partial collapse of a nearby building, creating yet more dust and dislodging a German sniper who had taken up position in the roof space. It seems likely that one of Lockwood's shots scored a non-penetrating hit on the front of the Tiger, near the driver's visor, which was sufficient to persuade Wittmann to withdraw. (He was very lucky to survive this hit, as the 17-pdr, even firing conventional armour-piercing, capped, ballistic capped (APCBC) ammunition could easily penetrate the Tiger's 100mm (3.94in) frontal hull armour at ranges up to 1000m (1100 yards). The likeliest explanation is that the hit was at such an extreme angle that the shot ricocheted off.)

Having turned to make better speed out of the town, Wittmann met Dyas' Cromwell head-on. Dyas had been following the Tiger in the hope of getting a shot against its thinner rear armour, which was the Cromwell's only real chance of success with its inadequate 75mm (2.9in) gun. Despite the near impossibility of causing any significant damage to its frontal armour, he managed to fire twice before his Cromwell was destroyed.

WITTMANN IMMOBILIZED

The Tiger then continued eastwards to the outskirts of Villers-Bocage before being immobilized near the junction of the RN 175 and the road to Tilly-sur-Seulles by a 6-pdr anti-tank gun commanded by Sergeant Bray of 1st RB. Once again, luck was on Wittmann's side – it seems probable that this was a close-range shot that hit the Tiger's running gear. Even conventional 6-pdr APCBC shot was likely to penetrate the 80mm (3.14in) armour of the hull or turret sides at anything up to a 500m (550-yard) range, with a fair chance of detonating the stowed ammunition. If any of the new armour-piercing, discarding sabot (APDS) rounds had been available, a hit on the turret or hull would almost certainly have resulted in a devastating 'kill'.

However, Wittmann was still very much in action and sprayed the area with fire from his main armament and machine guns to force his opponents to keep their heads down while he and his crew

Two more views of Sergeant Bray's 6-pdr, surrounded by the wreckage of burnt-out Loyd Carriers.

bailed out. (Although this interpretation of events does contradict Wittmann's own account that his tank was disabled by an anti-tank gun in the town centre, it seems to be the likeliest scenario, as he and all his crew escaped unscathed. Evading a relatively small force of infantry (who would still have been disorganized from his attack) near RN 175 to escape through the bocage was certainly risky, but rather more feasible than trying to dodge the increasingly numerous British forces in the town.)

Wittmann and his crew took all the weapons that they could manage (probably pistols, one or two MP40 submachine guns and grenades) but made no attempt to destroy the tank, believing that it could be recovered. They managed to make their way to *Panzer Lehr*'s HQ at the Château d'Orbois, 6km (3.7 miles) north of Villers-Bocage, to make their report.

In under 15 minutes, Wittmann had destroyed a probable total of seven gun tanks (including a Firefly and a Cromwell OP), three Stuarts, one Sherman OP, nine halftracks, four Loyd Carriers and two 6-pdr anti-tank guns.

Cut Off at Point 213

After the loss of three Cromwells to the Tigers of Wittmann's company, Cranley still had nine operational tanks (including two Fireflies and a Cromwell OP tank) although some were without their full crews.

The defenders were scarcely a balanced fighting force – 4th CLY's Colonel Cranley and Major Scott were trapped there together with Major Wright, Captain Milner, Lieutenants Campbell, Coop and Parker, and a few sergeants of 1st RB who now commanded no more than 10 riflemen. In addition to the tanks, a total of

The view looking down the former RN 175 towards Villers-Bocage from Point 213 today, the road along which 'A' Squadron would have travelled on the morning of 13 June 1944.

two Scout Cars, three halftracks and four motorcycles were within the perimeter, and these were moved onto the roadside.

It was decided to hold the position until reinforcements could fight their way through and, in the meantime, the riflemen were divided into two groups. One, comprising six men commanded by Corporal Nicholson, deployed along the southern side of RN 175, while Lieutenant Campbell took four men to occupy the junction with the road heading east from Point 213, which

Taken by a German photographer after the capture of the positions, this photograph shows Captain Roy Dunlop's abandoned Cromwell OP tank of 5th RHA, captured intact near Point 213.

was dubbed 'Campbell's Corner'. Captain Milner kept watch from a farmhouse on a lane running north, which was also covered by a Cromwell, while Sergeant Gale watched a nearby farm track. Most of 'A' Squadron's tanks were deployed in an orchard just south of Point 213 and Lieutenant Butler conducted a one-man patrol along the hedgerows of the adjoining field. At the same time, Lieutenant Coop took up position just forward of Campbell's Corner to give early warning of any attack from the east.

Elements of the 101st's 4th Company (probably the armoured reconnaissance and scout platoons) arrived at about 10:00 hours and started to round up surviving riflemen who had taken cover in ditches and hedgerows along RN 175 after failing to reach Point 213 or to escape into Villers-Bocage. (A total of 30 managed to avoid capture and made their way back to Allied lines during the next 24 hours or so.)

TOWN OCCUPIED

As this was going on, 1/7th QRR began to enter Villers-Bocage. (On its way to the town, 1/7th QRR's 'D' Company captured an advance party of three men from 2nd Panzer Division, which was moving up from the south. The possibility of 2nd Panzer Division's advance cutting off 22nd Armoured Brigade was a factor that influenced British decision-making throughout the remainder of the battle.) The initial intention was that 4th CLY's 'B' Squadron should attempt to break through to Point 213 in conjunction with one of QRR's companies, but this idea was soon abandoned.

Throughout the morning, the defenders of Point 213 were under fire from both Tigers and infantry. The remaining four more or less serviceable Tigers

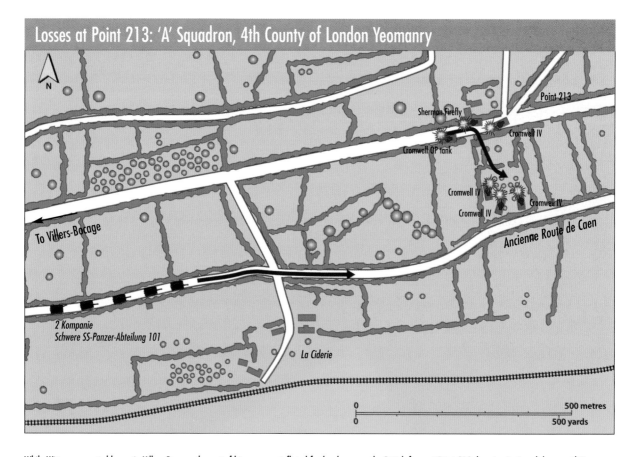

Losses at Point 213: 'A' Squadron, 4th County of London Yeomanry

Point 213

Sherman Firefly

Cromwell IV

Cromwell OP tank

Cromwell IV

Cromwell IV

Cromwell IV

To Villers-Bocage

Ancienne Route de Caen

*2 Kompanie
Schwere SS-Panzer-Abteilung 101*

La Ciderie

| 0 | 500 metres |
| 0 | 500 yards |

While Wittmann created havoc in Villers-Bocage, the rest of his company inflicted further losses on the British force at Point 213, keeping it pinned down until German reinforcements arrived. Wittmann's company's kills at Point 213 included one Cromwell OP tank (Captain Dunlop), one Sherman Firefly and four Cromwell IVs.

of Wittmann's 2nd Company were joined by *SS-Hauptsturmführer* Karl Möbius' 1st Company at about mid-morning. It was rarely possible to accurately identify the source of this fire and the defenders' most effective form of retaliation consisted of short, sharp artillery bombardments by the Sexton SP 25-pdrs of 5th RHA directed by Captain Dunlop's OP Cromwell.

At about 10:30, Colonel Cranley reported over the radio that the position on Point 213 was becoming untenable, and that withdrawal was now impossible. Nevertheless, a breakout was planned and two hours later one of 'A' Squadron's Cromwells attempted to work its way northwards along the lane from Point 213 in the hope of finding an alternative route back to Villers-Bocage. It had only just moved off when it was knocked out by a Tiger that had been concealed further along the lane.

SURRENDER

The Germans then began shelling the trees near RN 175, creating air-bursts which sprayed shell splinters over a wide area. After about five minutes of this bombardment, the defenders decided to surrender at about 13:30. They attempted to burn their remaining tanks, but German troops were on the scene quickly enough to capture several vehicles virtually intact. (As photographs taken by the Germans after the battle testify, at least one Sherman Firefly and a Cromwell CS were evaluated and test-driven by the Germans.)

At least 30 members of 4th CLY were taken prisoner, together with some riflemen and gunners from 1st RB. A few men managed to escape capture in the confusion, including Captain Christopher Milner of 1st RB, who spent the rest of the day on the run and crossed back into British lines after dark.

Two Cromwells of 'A' Squadron's No. 3 Troop lie abandoned in an orchard just south of Point 213. The open stowage bins indicate thorough German searches for rations, documents and 'souvenirs'.

22nd Armoured Brigade Occupy the Town

Wittmann's attack had caused massive disruption to 22nd Armoured Brigade's advance and had badly shaken Brigadier Hinde, who seems to have exercised little real control for the rest of the day.

The 1/7th QRR's deployment in Villers-Bocage was far from straightforward. Their anti-tank and carrier platoons had been sent on ahead to ward off any further German armoured attacks on the town, while the rest of the battalion encountered such dire problems in trying to manoeuvre its cumbersome trucks (Troop Carrying Vehicles – TCVs) past 4th CLY's 'C' and 'B' Squadrons that it was decided that it would be quicker to 'debus' and march the rest of the way. Speed was certainly needed as German forces were

converging on Villers-Bocage. Although the town was officially claimed to have been cleared by 10:00, German snipers were still at large and were soon reinforced by small detachments of Panzergrenadiers from *Panzer Lehr* (and possibly 2nd Panzer Division). German armour was also on its way – on his arrival at *Panzer Lehr*'s HQ, Wittmann had briefed the division's Intelligence Officer, *Oberstleutnant* Kauffmann, on the situation. He was then provided with a Schwimmwagen and drove off to join the German forces surrounding Point 213. By the time

143

he arrived, *SS-Hauptsturmführer* Rolf Möbius' 1st Company was on the scene, but although the two discussed the situation, Wittmann was not allowed to play any further part in the battle.

Meanwhile, Kauffmann ordered *Hauptmann* Helmut Ritgen to assemble what forces he could and block the northern exits from the town. Ritgen assembled a force of 15 Panzer IVs, mainly from the 6th Company of *Panzer Lehr*'s 2nd Panzer Battalion and set off. On arriving at Villy-Bocage, he was briefed by *Generalleutnant* Fritz Bayerlein, who joined the column, but as the tanks moved towards Villers-Bocage they ran into a screen of British anti-tank guns, losing one tank that burst into flames. Lacking infantry support, Bayerlein concluded that it would be suicidal to press home an attack on the town and ordered the force to fall back to Villy-Bocage.

HARASSING FIRE

The Panzers were also active in the town itself – as the main body of 1/7th QRR deployed, it came under harassing fire from German infantry that had infiltrated the eastern end of the town. A Panzer IV advanced far enough down the Rue Pasteur to shell 'C' and 'D' Companies as they were forming up in the Place Jeanne d'Arc. The tank hastily withdrew as the infantry spread out, working their way through the buildings on each side of the street, covered by the battalion's 6-pdr anti-tank guns. This succeeded in temporarily driving back the German forces and damaged two Panzer IVs.

Private Albert Kingston of 1/7th QRR recalled that: 'We were in the town centre, a little square and not much else. There were a few shops open, cafes, I think and we were just standing about waiting for orders when we heard the sound of gunfire coming

The old railway station at Villers-Bocage, which was defended by 'A' Company 1/7th QRR, during the afternoon of 13 June.

from the road out of town. There seemed from the noise to be a big battle going on and presently we saw black clouds of smoke in the air. One of our soldiers said they were tanks blowing up. All of a sudden our anti-tank platoons were ordered into action – to take post. The ammo trucks were driven into side streets and all the rifle sections were told to take up positions in windows of houses on the 'enemy' side of the village. There were several loud bangs which were our 6-pdr anti-tank guns going off and then one very loud explosion … a Bren carrier full of ammo went up. The firing seemed to spread … Jerry infantry were working their way into the town. Then there was some tank gun fire, some machine-gun fire and then dead silence. We waited … The street was a mess. Bricks and rubble all over the place. A couple of hundred yards up the road was the biggest tank I have ever seen. It looked undamaged. One of our 6-pdrs was lying on its side just opposite our house.'

Such actions were repeated throughout the late morning, leading to 'C' and 'D' Companies becoming scattered over a wide area of the town. They were ordered to fall back as all four companies were redployed – 'A' Company was sent to secure the area around the railway station, while 'C' Company was ordered to occupy the northeastern edge of the town, and 'D' Company sent to occupy the southeastern outskirts. This redeployment was hampered by difficulties in re-forming units that had become fragmented as they hunted equally scattered German detachments. 'B' Company was placed in reserve and the battalion's 6-pdr anti-tank guns were deployed to cover key points.

1/7th QRR had to be thinly spread across Villers-Bocage to counter the threat posed by German infantry which infiltrated the town throughout most of the day. Command and control of the battalion was exceptionally difficult in these circumstances and it was fortunate that the German attacks were so poorly coordinated.

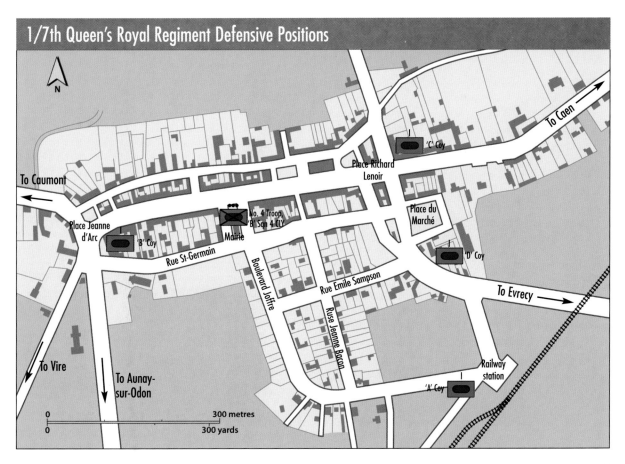

145

Ambush at the Mairie

Frustrated at the impossibility of a straightforward attack along RN 175 to rescue the beleaguered garrison of Point 213, Major Aird, commanding 4th CLY's 'B' Squadron, decided to try to find an alternative route.

To find an alternative route to RN 175, Major Aird selected Lieutenant Bill Cotton's No. 4 Troop for the task, which comprised Cotton's Cromwell CS, armed with a 95mm (3.7in) howitzer, the two 75mm (2.9in) armed Cromwells of Sergeant Grant and Corporal Horne, and a single Firefly commanded by Sergeant Bramall. The troop set off from the Place Jeanne d'Arc and headed south down the road to Aunay, briefly engaging a German armoured car, before cutting across country towards the railway line. Cotton halted the tanks in a field before going forward on foot to carry out a thorough reconnaissance.

Infuriatingly, steep embankments ruled out any attempt to use the line to outflank the Germans and reach Point 213. Cotton therefore decided to head back to the town, moving almost due north to the square around the *Mairie* (town hall), where he deployed his troop in ambush positions covering the Rue Pasteur. Shortly afterwards, he was reinforced by one of the QRR's 6-pdr anti-tank guns. To the west of the town further fighting took place as the Germans attacked 1/5th QRR near Livry, losing one tank in the process.

Villers-Bocage today, facing west along the Rue Georges Clemenceau towards the town centre.

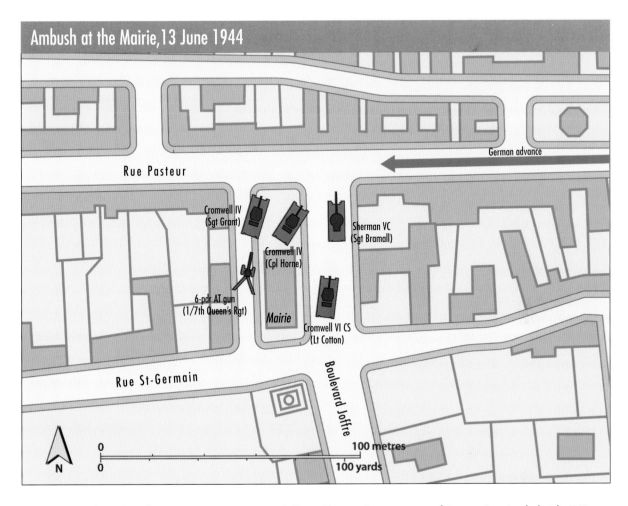

Ambush at the Mairie, 13 June 1944

German advance

Rue Pasteur

Cromwell IV
(Sgt Grant)

Sherman VC
(Sgt Bramall)

Cromwell IV
(Cpl Horne)

6-pdr AT gun
(1/7th Queen's Rgt)

Mairie

Cromwell VI CS
(Lt Cotton)

Rue St-Germain

Boulevard Joffre

0   100 metres
N   0   100 yards

The approximate arrangement of Lieutenant Cotton's ambush at the *Mairie*. Interestingly, he positioned his Cromwell CS well to the rear and dismounted to direct the fire of his remaining tanks. This would seem to indicate that his tank was not carrying any 95mm (3.7in) hollow-charge (HEAT) ammunition as this would actually have been more effective against Tigers than the 'standard' Cromwell's 75mm (2.9in) AP rounds.

While Ritgen's force was unsuccessfully attacking Villers-Bocage, *Panzer Lehr*'s Intelligence Officer, *Oberstleutnant* Kauffmann, was hastily assembling forces for a further attempt. The Divisional HQ was stripped of all non-essential personnel, who were formed into an improvised *Kampfgruppe* and sent forward to cordon off the outskirts of Villers-Bocage to prevent a British breakout. At the same time, maintenance crews scoured the division's workshops at Parfouru-sur-Odon for any AFVs that could be quickly patched up, and a force of 10 more-or-less serviceable Panzer IVs was readied for action.

At around 13:00 *Panzer Lehr*'s tanks advanced into Villers-Bocage, but almost immediately began to take losses due to a lack of adequate infantry support. A group of four Panzer IVs attempted to push into the town's southern outskirts, where they passed a previously disabled Panzer IV, but as they

moved up a further two tanks were knocked out by a 6-pdr anti-tank gun firing from a side street. Two Tigers were brought up and although one was hit, they succeeded in silencing the anti-tank position.

TIGER SUPPORT

After the 101st's 1st Company had helped to force the surrender of the British troops trapped on Point 213, *SS-Hauptsturmführer* Möbius sent his Tigers to support *Panzer Lehr*'s assault on Villers-Bocage. It seems likely that three were detached to hold the eastern end of the town, while two further detachments were sent in to make the main assault; the first comprising four Tigers commanded by *SS-Obersturmführer* Hannes Philipsen attacking down the Rue Pasteur, while the second advanced more or less parallel to the first through the southern part of the town. The Tigers on the Rue Pasteur advanced slowly, their commanders confident that they could intimidate the British into withdrawing.

However, as they reached the square by the *Mairie*, they ran into Cotton's ambush. The Firefly commanded by Sergeant Bramall opened fire on the lead tank and missed, but it was knocked out by the 6-pdr anti-tank gun supporting the position. The 'southern group' of three Tigers had followed

The artist Bryan de Grineau produced this highly imaginative illustration of Sergeant Bramall's Firefly in action at Villers-Bocage for the *Illustrated London News*. While the Tiger is reasonably accurately portrayed, the Firefly more closely resembles the obsolete Covenanter – this may have been a deliberate security measure. (If so, it was totally ineffective, as at least one Firefly was captured intact at Point 213.) The Tiger also seems to be approaching from the west along the Rue Pasteur, when it fact the Germans had advanced from the east.

the line of the railway before moving into the town along the Evrecy road and regrouping in the Place du Marché. They were now alerted to the ambush and split up in an attempt to outflank Cotton's force. Arguably, this was a fatal mistake – splitting up robbed them of mutual support that might have partly compensated for the lack of infantry support to deal with anti-tank guns and infantry anti-tank teams.

Picking their way through the back streets, one was destroyed by a 6-pdr anti-tank gun concealed in an alley. The second was knocked out by a Projector, Infantry, Anti-Tank (PIAT) in the Rue Emile Sampson and the third was immobilized by another PIAT as it advanced along the Rue St-Germain towards the war memorial in an effort to get behind Cotton's force.

In these conditions, the much-maligned PIAT had a distinct advantage over contemporary recoilless infantry anti-tank weapons such as the bazooka and *Panzerfaust*, all of which had dangerous back-blast that prevented their use in buildings and other enclosed spaces. The spigot-

The Tiger numbered 121, which was knocked out by a British 6-pdr anti-tank gun on the Rue Pasteur in the centre of Villers-Bocage during the afternoon battle.

fired PIAT had no back-blast and could be fired from rooms, attics and just about anywhere that an infantryman could go.

Contemporary accounts also refer to some German tanks being disabled or destroyed by 'sticky bombs'. These had been rushed into production as emergency anti-tank grenades in 1940, but were almost as dangerous to the user as the enemy. The vast majority of those produced were only issued to Home Guard units and it is very unlikely that any were used in Normandy. The most probable explanation is that the term was loosely applied to Gammon bombs – perhaps due to the 'stickiness' of the plastic explosive used in these grenades.

URBAN SHOOT-OUT

Another Tiger halted on the Rue Pasteur just short of the ambush site, apparently waiting for the British to emerge from cover. This was spotted by

Bramall through the side and front windows of a shop on the corner of the square. He decided that the only way to safely engage would be to reverse his Firefly and shoot diagonally through the windows. He fired twice, damaging the Tiger's mantlet; it pulled back slightly and then raced past the square before Bramall could respond. However, Corporal Horne's Cromwell quickly pulled out onto the Rue Pasteur and knocked out the Tiger with a close-range shot into its rear, before reversing back into cover. The next victim of the ambush was a Panzer IV, accounted for by Bramall's Firefly.

In this type of close-range tank action, perhaps the most significant British advantage lay in turret traverse speeds. In the immediate pre-war period

Britain developed a hydraulic turret traverse system based on the power-operated turrets fitted to RAF bombers. This was later supplemented by an electrical system, both of which were designed to meet a specification demanding 360° traverse in 20 seconds. (The hydraulic system was first tested on an A9 Cruiser in 1938 but the War Office specification of a full rotation in only eight seconds proved to be overambitious and a slower speed had to be accepted.)

These systems gave a range of creep speeds, so that power could actually be used for the fine laying of the gun, which speeded up the firing process in situations where a split second could mean the difference between life and death. In comparison, German, Soviet and early US systems were less effective, the former being dismissed in a British post-war report as 'exceedingly cumbersome and inefficient. Training by power was never attempted, possibly because German turrets were usually wildly out of balance.' Hydraulic traverse systems in British tanks were gradually replaced by electric gear to avoid problems with leaking hydraulic fluid, and to lessen the fire risk if a vehicle was penetrated.

German hydraulic systems were directly dependent on engine speed, while the Panzer IV used a crude electrical system. (The simplified Panzer IV Ausf. J, which entered service in 1944, lacked any form of power traverse.) Another German disadvantage was that their better but more complicated sighting equipment took a little longer to operate, and this could give Allied vehicles an edge in a close-range gun duel.

ASSAULT REPULSED

Lieutenant Cotton was only too aware of the efficiency of the German recovery and repair teams and was determined to completely destroy as many of the knocked-out enemy tanks as possible. During a lull in the action, he and Sergeant Bramall gathered some blankets and a jerrycan full of petrol. They then went from tank to tank, stuffing a petrol-soaked blanket into each and throwing in a lighted match to complete the destruction. (This was possibly inspired by some of the tank destruction techniques taught to the Home Guard during the invasion scare of 1940, but in any event it was highly effective – it seems that all the tanks that received this treatment were completely 'written off'.)

Away to the south, an ad hoc force of German infantry was attacking 'A' Company 1/7th QRR, which was defending the area around the railway station. Similar German infantry detachments were gradually infiltrating the rest of the town, exploiting gaps that opened up as 'A' Company was slowly forced back by a series of attacks. By 18:00, QRR's Battalion HQ was pinned down and it seemed likely that German infantry would soon be in position to threaten the British armour in the town. The situation was further confused by both sides' attempts to support their forward troops with

Turret Traverse Speeds

The general superiority of British systems can be seen in the following table:

VEHICLE	FASTEST TRAVERSE TIME (SECONDS) 360°	CONTROL QUALITY (AND TYPE)
Tiger I	60	Poor (H)
Panzer IV	25.07	Poor (E)
Cromwell	14–15	Good (H)
Stuart M3A3	15.4 left / 15.92 right	Poor (H)
Sherman	15 (Oilgear type)	Good (H)
Sherman	15 (Loganport type)	Poor (H)
Sherman	15 (Westinghouse type)	Poor (E)

(H) = hydraulic mechanism, (E) = electric motor.

artillery bombardments. German efforts were not solely directed against Villers-Bocage – the British forces in the town were at the end of a long and tenuous supply route. If this could be cut, there was every chance of destroying almost all of 22nd Armoured Brigade. The village of Amayé-sur-Seulles formed a critical link in this route, housing Brigade HQ, 1/5th QRR and three batteries of 5th RHA. The position had been subjected to a number of German attacks that were only beaten off by the Sexton self-propelled 25-pdrs firing over open sights, supported by small arms fire from the batteries' 'cooks and bottle washers'.

WITHDRAWAL

German pressure on Villers-Bocage increased steadily throughout the afternoon, convincing a still-shaken Brigadier Hinde that the town could not be held. These German attacks, coupled with the (somewhat exaggerated) threat posed by 2nd Panzer Division's advance from the south, led Brigadier Hinde to conclude that Villers-Bocage would have to be abandoned. He decided to pull his entire force back to Amayé-sur-Seulles that evening and review the situation the following day. (It was hoped that 50th [Northumbrian] Division would break through the German defences around Tilly-sur-Seulles and advance southwards to outflank *Panzer Lehr*'s forces in Villers-Bocage.) Despite some anxious moments, the phased withdrawal from Villers-Bocage began at 19:00 and went smoothly, with its final stages covered by an artillery bombardment.

The Germans seem to have made no real attempt to integrate their armour and infantry for the attacks on Villers-Bocage during the afternoon of 13 June. This may have been due to overconfidence in the aftermath of Wittmann's attack and the surrender of the British force at Point 213. If so, it was an expensive mistake, leading to unnecessary losses of valuable Tigers, which were never replaced during the remainder of the Normandy campaign.

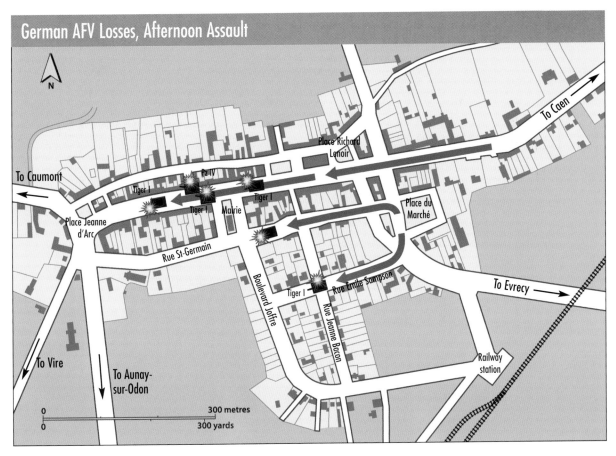

German AFV Losses, Afternoon Assault

Knocked-out tanks – a Panzer IV and a Tiger – both victims of Lieutenant Cotton's ambush, in the Rue Pasteur.

13 June – Winners and Losers

Both sides claimed victory following the encounter at Villers-Bocage. Many commentators agree that the British had let slip a good opportunity to encircle the German forces at Caen.

At first sight, it seems that the Germans were the clear winners of the day's actions – after all, they had destroyed a total of at least:

- 16 Cromwells
- 4 Fireflies
- 3 Stuarts
- 1 OP Sherman
- 9 halftracks
- 4 Loyd Carriers
- 3 6-pdr anti-tank guns

In addition, they had forced 22nd Armoured Brigade to retreat from Villers-Bocage, temporarily removing the threat to outflank the defences of Caen. However, British claims were not insignificant, totalling 10 Tigers and four Panzer IVs. German sources admitted the loss of five Tigers – the difference between the two figures for this type probably represents those knocked out or immobilized and which were subsequently recovered and repaired.

Unfortunately, it is impossible to confirm the number of Panzer IVs destroyed as *Panzer Lehr*'s records failed to separate the losses sustained in Villers-Bocage from those incurred at Tilly-sur-Seulles and other sectors of its front.

Despite the clear German 'lead' in terms of vehicles destroyed, it is worth noting that the Tigers lost were never replaced during the rest of the Normandy campaign – for all its formidable skill and expertise, the 101st SS Heavy Panzer Battalion was steadily wasting away under unremitting Allied pressure.

Superficially, the Germans seem to have had a clear edge in terms of tactical skill and combat capability, as they succeeded in defeating the British offensive with improvised and numerically inferior forces. However, once again, the situation is not entirely as it seems. While Wittmann's single-handed attack was almost certainly the best course of action in very difficult circumstances, subsequent German attacks into Villers-Bocage were often inept. The town was a relatively important communications hub for German forces and had to

be retaken, but its final recapture arguably owed as much to failings in the British command structure as to the German assaults.

The most notable failure in these German attacks was an almost complete lack of armour/infantry co-operation. It is fair to say that this would have been more difficult than usual, given the fact that small, ad hoc groups of Panzergrenadiers were already scattered through the town by the time that German tanks arrived; but it seems that no real effort was made to form tank/infantry teams at any stage. This failure left the tanks unnecessarily vulnerable to anti-tank guns and infantry anti-tank teams. General Bayerlein was right to call off 'his' column's attack, given the lack of infantry and artillery support, but there is no indication that he made any attempt to rectify the problem, as further forces were fed into the town later in the day.

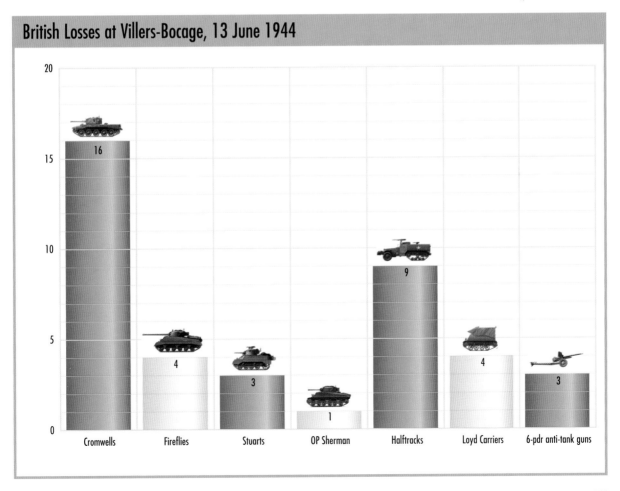

British Losses at Villers-Bocage, 13 June 1944

	Cromwells	Fireflies	Stuarts	OP Sherman	Halftracks	Loyd Carriers	6-pdr anti-tank guns
	16	4	3	1	9	4	3

British Armour in Normandy

British tank crews rapidly became aware of the technical superiority of Tigers and Panthers. As one tank commander noted: '... because of the pervading fear of 88s, Panthers, Tigers and Panzerfausts, initiative was lost and squadron commanders tended to go to ground at the first sign of any serious opposition and call up an artillery "stonk"'.

The action at Villers-Bocage had emphasized in dramatic fashion the problems posed by the Tiger, which could destroy any Allied tank at up to 1500m (1640 yards), but was almost invulnerable to the 75mm (2.9in) medium velocity (MV) guns which armed the vast majority of the Shermans and Cromwells in Normandy. In theory, these 75mm (2.9in) guns could penetrate about 70mm (2.76in) of armour at 500m (550 yards) – and possibly 85mm (3.35in) at up to 250m (275 yards).

However, this was not much help, unless they could take very close-range flank or rear shots against the Tiger which had:

- 120mm (4.7in)/100mm (3.9in) mantlet
- 100mm (3.9in) frontal hull armour
- 80mm (3.15in) turret side and rear
- 80mm (3.15in) upper hull sides and rear
- 60mm (2.36in) lower hull sides (partially covered by the overlapping road wheels)

There was also the major problem of surviving for long enough to get into position to take such shots – in the circumstances it isn't too surprising that German reports remarked on the tendency of Allied tanks to fire low – they were aiming at tracks and road wheels in an attempt to immobilize seemingly invulnerable Tigers and Panthers.

Approximately 900 Panzer IVs were deployed in Normandy, far more than any other German tank type. By this stage of the war, the type had reached the limits of its development potential, but was still at least the equal of most Allied tanks. Although the Panzer IV's 75mm (2.9in) L/48 had a rather better armour-piercing capability than the 75mm (2.9in) guns of the Cromwell and Sherman, both Allied tanks had thicker armour.

In practice, such differences had little real impact in the conditions of the Normandy campaign, where it was found that all three types were roughly equivalent in terms of combat effectiveness. However, the Panzer IV did have problems in dealing with the heavily armoured Churchills, which were only vulnerable to flank or rear shots at ranges below 500m (550 yards). It was also highly vulnerable to the 6-pdr at ranges up to 1000m (1100 yards) and could be penetrated by the 17-pdr deployed by the Sherman Firefly at ranges of up to 2000m (2200 yards).

Although no Panthers were reported to be in action at Villers-Bocage, it is possible that some of *Panzer Lehr's* vehicles were involved in the Battle of the Brigade Box on 14 June. In practical terms, the Panther's 75mm (2.9in) L/70 had a roughly equivalent armour-piercing performance to that of the Tiger I's 88mm (3.5in) L/56. However, the type required careful tactical handling as, although its frontal armour gave excellent protection against almost all Allied guns, its thin side armour was far more vulnerable.

BRITISH ANTI-TANK CAPABILITIES

The action at Villers-Bocage reinforced the tendency of Allied troops to identify every German tank as a Tiger. To some extent, this was understandable – the *Schürzen* (skirting armour) fitted to Panzer IVs gave their turrets a very similar appearance to those of Tiger Is, especially when briefly glimpsed in the heat of action. Second Army's intelligence summaries claimed that the Tiger was the most numerous enemy tank encountered in the opening stages of the campaign,

Cromwell Tank Deployment, June 1944

UNIT	IV, V, VII	OP	VI	ARV
7th Armoured Div	201	8	24	14
11th Armoured Div	62	–	6	3
Guards Armoured Div	59	3	6	3
Polish Armoured Div	53	–	6	3
Total	375	11	42	23

British Anti-Tank and Tank Gun Capabilities *

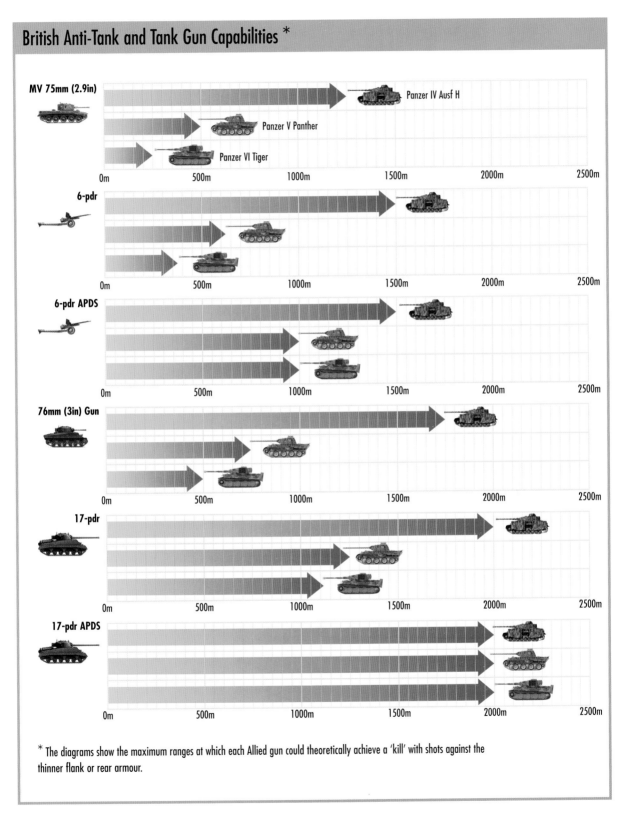

MV 75mm (2.9in)

Panzer IV Ausf H
Panzer V Panther
Panzer VI Tiger

0m   500m   1000m   1500m   2000m   2500m

6-pdr

0m   500m   1000m   1500m   2000m   2500m

6-pdr APDS

0m   500m   1000m   1500m   2000m   2500m

76mm (3in) Gun

0m   500m   1000m   1500m   2000m   2500m

17-pdr

0m   500m   1000m   1500m   2000m   2500m

17-pdr APDS

0m   500m   1000m   1500m   2000m   2500m

* The diagrams show the maximum ranges at which each Allied gun could theoretically achieve a 'kill' with shots against the thinner flank or rear armour.

despite the fact that, in reality, no more than 130 Tigers in all were deployed in Normandy throughout the entire campaign.

Events at Villers-Bocage showed that even at true point-blank range, the Cromwell's OQF 75mm (2.9in) could not be relied upon to penetrate the Tiger's side or rear armour. From the very beginning, the weapon was a 'stop-gap' – although the earliest Cromwells produced in 1942 were armed with the 6-pdr gun, its poor HE capability led to the decision to fit a new gun in later production vehicles. The preferred weapon was a high-velocity 75mm (2.9in) L/50 gun developed by Vickers, and everything went smoothly until May 1943 when it was realized that the Cromwell's turret ring was too small.

OQF 75MM GUN

The spin-off of that debacle was that the Vickers high-velocity 75mm (2.9in) developed into the OQF 77mm (3.03in; actually 76.2mm/3in) around which the Comet was later built. As there was now no gun for the Cromwell, priority was given to another Vickers design, which had been under development for some months. This was a 75mm (2.9in) weapon based on the 6-pdr, but firing US 75mm (2.9in) ammunition. Although its armour-piercing (AP) performance was mediocre, even by the standards of 1943 (and worse than that of the 6-pdr), it had the saving grace that it could be fitted to any AFV capable of mounting the 6-pdr. As a result, the type was adopted as the OQF 75mm (2.9in) and armed the majority of Cromwells and Churchills deployed in the Normandy campaign.

Although the 6-pdr was largely supplanted as an AFV weapon by 1944, it remained in service as the standard anti-tank gun of British infantry units. (British anti-tank regiments, then part of the Royal Artillery, were equipped with towed or self-propelled 17-pdrs.) In contrast to the woefully inadequate OQF 75mm (2.9in), the 6-pdr proved to be a highly effective weapon at Villers-Bocage, immobilizing Wittmann's Tiger and destroying more Tigers and Panzer IVs later in the action. Even with conventional AP ammunition, it was quite capable of penetrating the Tiger's side or rear armour at close range and with the newly issued tungsten-cored armour-piercing, discarding sabot (APDS) rounds, the Tiger was vulnerable at up to 1000m (1100 yards). (It is uncertain if any of the 6-pdrs at Villers-Bocage had received APDS ammunition.)

In 1944, the 17-pdr was the British Army's most potent 'tank-killer'. The towed gun was heavy and difficult to bring into action quickly, but self-propelled versions such as the M10 Achilles were in great demand.

However, the most effective such vehicle was the Sherman Firefly, a brilliant improvisation that managed to squeeze this high-velocity weapon into a slightly modified turret. The type's worst failing was that there were never enough of them – only 84 had been landed in Normandy by 11 June and even by the end of July, 21st Army Group had no more than 235 in all.

SHERMAN FIREFLIES IN NORMANDY

Fireflies entered service with 21st Army Group in 1944, just in time for the Normandy campaign in which they encountered a far greater concentration of the highest-quality German AFVs than had been expected. Tigers, Panthers and Jagdpanthers accounted for only 30 per cent of the 2300 German AFVs deployed in Normandy, with the remainder largely comprising the less formidable Panzer IVs, Sturmgeschütz IIIs and other vehicles that could be dealt with by the standard Shermans, Cromwells and Churchills.

However, Montgomery's series of offensives around Caen led to the majority of the elite Panzer

Stuart Tank Deployment, June 1944

UNIT	III	V	VI
7th Armoured Div	–	44	–
11th Armoured Div	–	44	–
Guards Armoured Div	–	–	44
4th Armoured Bde	33	–	–
8th Armoured Bde	33	–	–
27th Armoured Bde	33	–	–
6th Guards Tank Bde	–	12	4
31st Tank Bde	33	–	–
34th Tank Bde	33	–	–
15th/19th Hussars	–	–	4
4th Canadian Armoured Div	–	44	–
2nd Canadian Armoured Bde	–	33	–
Total	165	177	52

formations in Normandy being drawn into the defence of that sector.

Ultimately, over 70 per cent of all German AFVs in Normandy were facing 21st Army Group – a concentration of armoured firepower that was rarely equalled during the war. In these circumstances, Fireflies were highly prized as the only tank in British service capable of destroying Panthers and Tigers at normal combat ranges.

The Germans rapidly appreciated the threat posed by the Fireflies with their instantly recognizable long-barrelled main armament, and instructions were issued to treat all Fireflies as priority targets. Similarly, Firefly crews realized that the distinctive long barrel of the 17-pdr made the tank highly conspicuous and adopted a variety of camouflage measures. Some crews had the front half of the gun barrel painted white on the bottom and dark green or the original olive drab on the top to give the illusion of a shorter gun barrel. A few vehicles were also fitted with a false muzzle brake halfway along the barrel to enhance the effect of the painted camouflage.

Despite being a high priority target, Fireflies appear to have had a statistically lower chance of being knocked out than standard Shermans; this probably owed more to their tactical employment

than the actual effectiveness of camouflaging the gun's long barrel. Given the Fireflies' high value, it became common practice for commanders to carry out a preliminary terrain reconnaissance before each operation in order to identify good hull-down positions.

In action, Fireflies would attempt to remain in these 'overwatch' positions to cover the advance of the standard Shermans and Cromwells, only moving forward when the area had been secured, or when they could no longer provide cover from their current position. Similarly, when on the move, troop commanders tended to position Fireflies at the rear of the formation to reduce the chances of them being knocked out.

TANK-KILLER

Although such tactics could not always be employed in the confusion of combat, the Firefly quickly proved itself to be a highly effective 'tank-killer'. One of the earliest demonstrations of its firepower was given in the defence of Norrey-en-Bessin on 9 June when the village came under attack from 12 Panthers of *Hitlerjugend*'s 12th SS Panzer Regiment, which had outrun their supporting infantry. As the Panthers closed to within 1000m (1100 yards) of the village, nine

Sherman Tank Deployment, June 1944

UNIT	I	I OP	IC	II	II OP	II DD	III	III OP	III ARV	V	V DD	V OP	VC	V CRAB	V ARV
7th Armoured Div	–	–	–	–	–	–	–	–	–	–	–	–	36	–	–
11th Armoured Div	–	–	–	–	–	–	–	–	–	157	–	8	36	–	11
Guards Armoured Div	–	–	–	–	–	–	–	–	–	157	–	8	36	–	11
4th Armoured Bde	–	–	–	157	8	–	–	–	–	–	–	–	36	–	11
8th Armoured Bde	–	–	–	–	–	76	95	8	9	–	–	–	22	–	2
27th Armoured Bde	–	–	–	–	–	–	126	8	9	–	38	–	29	–	2
30th Armoured Bde	–	–	–	–	–	–	–	–	–	72	–	–	–	180	12
1st Tank Bde	50	8	–	27	–	–	–	–	–	–	–	–	–	–	6
6th Guards Tank Bde	–	–	–	–	–	–	–	–	–	4	–	–	–	–	–
31st Tank Bde	–	–	–	–	–	–	–	–	–	4	–	–	–	–	–
34th Tank Bde	–	–	–	–	–	–	–	–	–	4	–	–	–	–	–
15th/19th Hussars	–	–	–	–	–	–	–	–	–	–	75	–	–	–	–
4th Canadian Armoured Div	–	–	–	–	–	–	–	–	–	225	–	8	36	–	14
2nd Canadian Armoured Bde	–	–	–	–	–	–	95	8	9	–	76	–	22	–	2
Polish Armoured Div	–	–	2	–	–	–	–	–	–	139	–	5	23	–	11
Total	50	8	2	184	8	76	316	24	27	762	189	29	276	180	82

With its 17-pdr anti-tank gun, the Sherman VC Firefly proved the only effective Allied tank-killer in Normandy. Fireflies were distributed in small numbers across most British and Canadian armoured formations.

Shermans of the Canadian 1st Hussars (including Lieutenant Henry's Firefly) opened fire from flanking positions. Lieutenant Henry's gunner, Trooper A. Chapman, waited until the Panthers were 'lined up like ducks in a row' and quickly knocked out five with just six rounds. The German attack was repulsed with the loss of seven of the 12 Panthers.

A similar example occurred on 14 June, during Operation 'Perch'. Sergeant Harris' Firefly of the 4th/7th Dragoon Guards, along with three standard Shermans, took up defensive positions after successfully driving out the Germans in the village of Lingèvres, near Tilly-sur-Seulles. Looking

Miscellaneous Tank Deployment, June 1944

UNIT	VALENTINE B/L	CRUSADER AA	GRANT CDL
7th Armoured Div	3	28	–
11th Armoured Div	3	28	–
Guards Armoured Div	3	18	–
4th Armoured Bde	3	20	–
8th Armoured Bde	3	20	–
27th Armoured Bde	3	20	–
1st Tank Bde	3	–	162
6th Guards Tank Bde	–	11	–
31st Tank Bde	–	20	–
34th Tank Bde	–	20	–
4th Canadian Armoured Div	3	27	–
2nd Canadian Armoured Bde	3	20	–
Polish Armoured Div	3	–	–
Total	30	232	162

through his binoculars, Sergeant Harris spotted two Panthers advancing from the east. He opened fire at a range of 800m (880 yards), knocking out both Panthers with two shots. Moving to a new position on the other side of the village, he spotted another three Panthers approaching from the west. Firing from his well-concealed flanking position, he and his gunner, Trooper Mackillop, destroyed all three with just three rounds.

CHURCHILLS IN NORMANDY

The Churchills were some of the first Allied AFVs to land in Normandy, but these were the specialized AVREs of 79th Armoured Division rather than conventional gun tanks. The first such tanks to go into action in Normandy were those of 31st Tank Brigade (comprising 7th and 9th Battalions, Royal Tank Regiment), which landed at Juno Beach on 19 June.

Early combat experience showed that the heavily armoured Churchill VII had a high degree of immunity to the German 75mm (2.9in) Pak 40 and the 75mm (2.9in) L/48 guns of the Panzer IV, StuG III and Jagdpanzer IV, but was still vulnerable to all 88mm (3.5in) guns and the Panther's 75mm (2.9in) L/70. More worryingly, it soon became clear that the decision to fit the OQF 75mm (2.9in) in the Churchill left the type with a woefully inadequate performance against the heavier German AFVs.

This was all the more serious as the Infantry Tank Brigades were not issued with Sherman Fireflies and had to rely on ad hoc anti-tank support from M10 tank destroyers. Other measures included reissuing a limited number of earlier 6-pdr-armed Churchills with the new APDS ammunition to give the brigades some degree of integral anti-tank capability. These were generally issued on the scale of one per troop and were quite effective in the short-range actions common in Normandy, although they lacked the sheer power of the Firefly's 17-pdr.

These problems were, however, offset to some extent by the Churchill's extraordinary cross-country performance – it was one of the very few

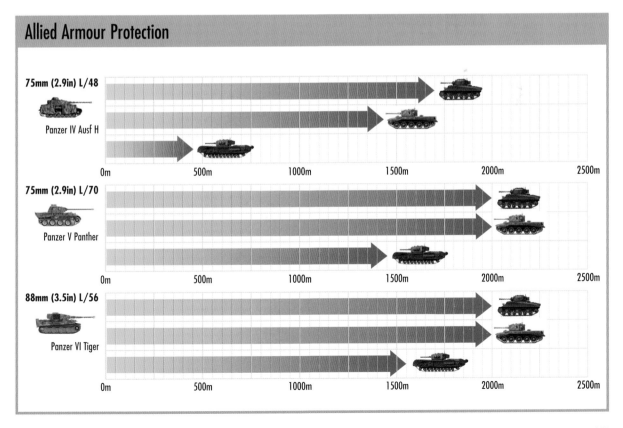

Allied Armour Protection

75mm (2.9in) L/48

Panzer IV Ausf H

0m   500m   1000m   1500m   2000m   2500m

75mm (2.9in) L/70

Panzer V Panther

0m   500m   1000m   1500m   2000m   2500m

88mm (3.5in) L/56

Panzer VI Tiger

0m   500m   1000m   1500m   2000m   2500m

Allied AFVs that could readily cope with the difficult close terrain of the bocage. (In Operation 'Bluecoat', the Churchills of 6th Guards Tank Brigade broke through terrain that the thoroughly surprised Germans had classified as '*panzerschier*' – tank-proof.)

A Churchill Mk VII tank halts in the bocage accompanied by infantry, late June 1944. The Churchill was a slow tank with thick armour with a design based very much on the pre-war notion of tanks providing close support for infantry operations. This made it unsuitable for mobile-manoeuvre warfare, but surprisingly good in the close fighting in the bocage, where its cross-country capabilities proved effective.

Churchill Tank Deployment, June 1944

UNIT	III	IV	IV OP	VI	VII	V, VIII	ARV	B/L	75 CONV.
6th Guards Tank Bde	–	156	8	–	–	18	11	3	164
31st Tank Bde	60	12	8	31	–	18	11	1	34
34th Tank Bde	90	18	8	24	24	18	11	2	59
141st Royal Armoured Corps	–	7	–	–	45	–	–	–	7
Assault Brigade RE	–	–	–	–	–	–	15	–	–
Total	150	193	24	55	69	54	48	6	264

Battle of the Brigade Box: 14 June

On 14 June, with the British withdrawal from Villers-Bocage complete, the force formed an all-round defensive position: a 'brigade box'. This was a tactic that had been successfully used in North Africa, to allow a position to be held by limited forces while making the fullest possible use of artillery and air support.

The precise location of this position is uncertain, but there is a strong case that it was established around the Brigade HQ on Hill 174, to the south of the village of Amayé-sur-Seulles. The fighting that followed on 14 June is known as the 'Battle of the Island', or 'Island Position', this name deriving from 22nd Armoured Brigade's after-action report. Other names given to the action include the 'Battle of the Brigade Box' and the 'Battle of Amayé-sur-Seulles'. It is generally agreed that the box was less than 2 km² (0.77 square miles) in area. The position was less than ideal

British infantry advance down a country lane somewhere in the Normandy bocage, summer 1944.

as it was overlooked by higher ground on three sides and the bocage imposed severe restrictions on fields of vision, making it difficult to spot enemy activity at ranges beyond 91m (100 yards).

The position was certainly crowded – crammed into its perimeter were the two remaining squadrons of 4th CLY, 8th Hussars, 11th Hussars, 5 RTR, 1/5th and 1/7th QRR, 1st RB and 5th RHA. The 'Box' was also supported by the divisional artillery, backed up by that of 50th (Northumbrian) Division to the north and a US artillery battalion to the west.

A vast concentration of other Allied artillery within the beachhead was also in range and could be called upon to fire defensive bombardments in a real emergency.

Panzer Lehr's staff were confident that there was still a real opportunity to destroy most of 22nd Armoured Brigade – bad weather during the afternoon and evening of 13 June had allowed the Germans to redeploy with unusual freedom from Allied air attacks. By the following morning, Bayerlein was assured that the division was capable of eliminating the Brigade Box, while simultaneously fending off any renewed assault by 50th (Northumbrian) Division.

German confidence received a further boost with the arrival of 2nd Panzer Division's reconnaissance battalion, although the bulk of the division was still en route to the front, as its approach march had been delayed by near constant Allied bombing and strafing. However, *Panzer Lehr*'s brief respite from Allied air attack was to end as the skies cleared during the early morning of 14 June, allowing rocket-firing Typhoons to attack German positions around the Box.

To the north of the Box, 'I' Company, 1st RB, spotted some enemy movement in a wood and called down an artillery bombardment from 50th (Northumbrian) Division, US V Corps and 5th Army Group Royal Artillery (AGRA), which virtually obliterated the wood and most of its occupants. At 09:00 hours 1/7th QRR reported German infantry to the east, which were engaged by 5th RHA and 1/7th QRR's mortars, as they were too close to the perimeter for the other artillery units to fire on safely. However, this failed to halt the German advance, so at 10:00 5 RTR sent out a patrol to provide close support for the defenders. As the German force was exclusively made up of infantry, the tanks were able to wreak havoc with machine-gun and HE fire, inflicting heavy casualties.

At about this time, the Germans managed to overrun a forward platoon of 1/5th QRR, but a counter-attack by the battalion's 'C' Company with artillery support recaptured the position in little more than half an hour. At about 14:00, the positions held by 1/7th QRR came under intense mortar fire, which forced one of their companies to withdraw slightly.

A Cromwell Mk IV kicks up dust somewhere in Normandy. Unusually, this tank has a Bren gun on the turret roof.

PROBING ACTIONS

Throughout the day there was intermittent enemy activity all around the Box, with constant sniping, interspersed with mortar fire and small-scale probing attacks. The bulk of these attacks were launched by *Panzer Lehr* with the support of the 101st's 1st Company and elements of 2nd Panzer Division. As had been apparent on 13 June, coordination of most of the German attacks was remarkably poor, especially as far as infantry/armour co-operation was concerned. Lieutenant Derrick Watson of 1/5th QRR recalled a typical action: '... enemy tanks were seen and heard to be forming up. Almost immediately the forward companies were attacked by two battalions of Panzer Grenadiers. Owing to the terrain it was a close range battle. I recall a battery of 5 RHA cheek by jowl with Bn HQ engaging the enemy over open sights with airburst and Bren guns ... I clearly remember Pte Baldwin, the company cook and a

crack shot standing on top of a 3 ton lorry bringing down a German sniper who had foolishly climbed a very tall tree. This brought forth a great cheer from the ranks.'

The Box provided a potential base for a renewed offensive and was relatively easy to defend. However, XXX Corps' commander, Lieutenant-General Bucknall, decided that the Brigade should withdraw to straighten the frontline, as 50th (Northumbrian) Division had been unable to make much progress in their attacks around Tilly-sur-Seulles. The withdrawal, code-named Operation 'Aniseed', was scheduled to begin at 23:15 that night.

GERMAN ATTACKS

Early in the evening the order for the withdrawal was being issued to all units when signs of preparations for renewed German attacks became apparent. A newly arrived force of two Panzergrenadier battalions from 2nd Panzer Division attacked the southern sector of the Box with armoured support. Diversionary attacks in company strength were made in other sectors to prevent the defenders reinforcing the threatened side of the perimeter. At about 20:00, the main assault was made against 1/5th QRR, accompanied for the first time that day by a sustained German artillery bombardment directed mainly against the positions held by 1/7th QRR. At the same time, another attack was made by *Panzer Lehr* on the northern perimeter held by 1st RB.

By now the calls for support from 5th RHA were so frequent that it was allocating separate targets to each of its component batteries – 'G' Battery fired over open sights at ranges down to 365m (400 yards) on Panzergrenadiers as they advanced on the southern side of the Box. 'K' Battery fired mainly on the plentiful targets to the east, while 'CC' Battery supported the southern perimeter. During the day, 'G' Battery alone fired 244 HE and 89 smoke shells.

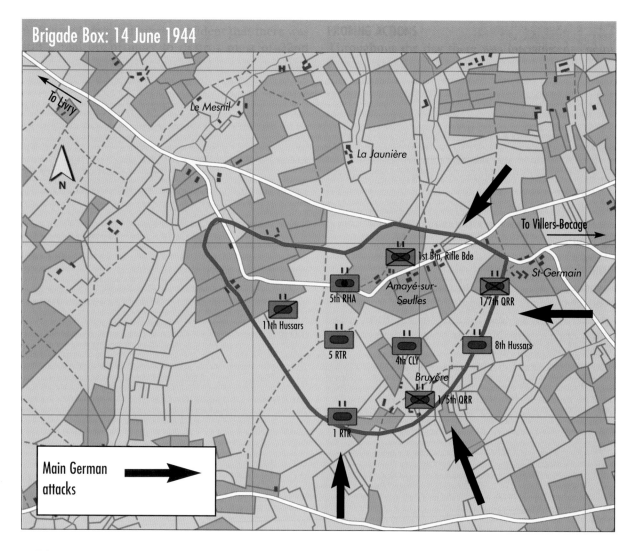

The map shows the approximate deployment of combat units within the Brigade Box. German attacks on the perimeter throughout 14 June encountered the same problems of terrain which bedevilled Allied attacks in the bocage. German units forming up for these attacks were particularly vulnerable to Allied artillery (including naval gunfire support) and suffered heavy casualties as a result.

This final series of attacks almost reached Brigade HQ before being repulsed and the fighting died down by 22:30. The withdrawal was postponed by an hour and a watch was kept for any further attempts to disrupt the operation. Despite the ferocity of the German attack, British tank losses were confined to 5 RTR, which had lost just three Cromwells. However, it was clear that the Germans had suffered badly, with up to 20 tanks and hundreds of dead or wounded Panzergrenadiers lying in or around the Box.

BRIGADE PULLED OUT

At 00:30 the exhausted brigade, which had been in almost constant action for 72 hours, began to pull out, covered by an RAF raid on Aunay-sur-Odon and an artillery barrage to drown out the noise of the vehicles. The last units to leave were an exhausted contingent of 1/7th QRR carried on 5 RTR's tanks. 7th Armoured Division was then moved to positions east of Caumont, where it remained until the end of June.

German losses for the day were estimated at 700–800 casualties, plus up to 20 tanks destroyed, but the immediate Allied threat to Villers-Bocage had been removed and the town remained in German hands until 4 August 1944.

164

Fighting in the Bocage: Tactics, Techniques, Hazards

'Life depended very often on … fast and accurate target identification, sighting, loading and firing. Truly it is said that there are the quick and the dead.' Norman Smith, 5 RTR.

The subject of fighting in the bocage is immense and worthy of a book in its own right. This section can do little more than scratch the surface of the topic, but it is hoped that the following quotations will at least give a feel for the setting and some key points of this particularly lethal and stressful form of combat.

TANKERS' VIEWS FROM THE TURRET

Captain John Sterling of 4th/7th Dragoon Guards wrote that: 'If ever a piece of country was ideal for defence by tanks and a nightmare for them to attack in, it was Normandy in summer. The countryside is so like England. Luxuriant green grass and foliage. Tall, thick hedges bounding small … fields, little sunken lanes with grassy banks, clumps of grey stone buildings forming a farm or a village. A delightful spot for a picnic, but a death-trap for an invading army. In this cover a tank or a gun could hide completely and bide its time. You only became aware of its existence when your leading tank went up in flames, and often several more went up before you had any exact idea of the position. It was difficult to see to shoot more than a few hundred yards. Instead of tanks picking a position on a flank and sitting there shooting while the infantry went forward, now they had to go forward side by side with the infantry and were duly picked off.'

Jack Geddes of 4th CLY reflected on the overwhelming exhaustion of prolonged combat, noting that: 'I have worn the same clothes for seven days running as have we all, but I know they must take us out of battle soon, for we are beginning to reach the limit of our endurance. We must come out of battle soon to lick our wounds and re-equip.'

THE INFANTRY'S WAR IN THE BOCAGE

Derrick Watson, Intelligence Officer 1/5th QRR: 'The 1/5th Queens in late June were positioned on the reverse slopes just north of the shattered village of Livry, in an area that was the bocage at its worst. The infantry, no longer lorried, living in slit trenches in the rain, suffered a steady drain in casualties from shell and mortar fire and occasionally from snipers. All the time enclosed in the damp prison of the bocage, the lines of sight bounded by a hedge 200 yards away. At night there was the constant anxiety of patrolling through close hedges which were often mined to pin down or identify an elusive enemy.'

Major 'Jack' Nangle, 1/5th QRR, on leading a fighting patrol ordered by Brigade Intelligence to bring back a prisoner for interrogation: 'I was leading the patrol along the hedgerow when I heard the click of a bolt being drawn back, so using my "Instinctive Pointing Sense" [IPS], I fired a burst from my Sten gun in the direction of the sound. There was a groan and a rush of feet. On

British infantry take cover during fighting in the Normandy bocage. A Sherman tank provides fire support in the background.

investigation we found a German lying dead behind a Spandau [MG42]. My burst had hit him between the eyes. This showed the value of the IPS!! ... so the patrol hoisted the corpse and I grasped his hands round my neck in front of me.'

Derrick Watson noted that Nangle was awarded the MC for his leadership of this patrol and how: 'It raised the morale of A Company and the battalion. Of particular comfort was the discomfiture of Brigade Intelligence when they received the gruesome remains. They were not amused.'

GUNNERS' CASUALTIES

Accidents were responsible for a surprisingly high proportion of casualties throughout the war. These were frequently caused by troops ignoring safety precautions and taking all manner of unofficial short-cuts to improve battlefield performance – the resulting accidents, especially those involving

artillery, could be devastating, as remembered by Leslie Gosling of 3rd RHA: 'M Battery was firing intensive scale; we thought we were pretty slick and could have 3 or 4 rounds per gun in flight at the same time. The 25-pounder gun breech was knocked open before full recoil and the next round slammed in. Unfortunately the No. 4 was poised to reload, but holding a round with a defective 117 fuse, the breech struck the cap and a premature detonation resulted. One man only of the six man detachment survived and he lost a leg at the thigh. The rest were splattered, and it was not until the next morning that the No. 1's head was seen suspended in the trees above.'

This photograph of two British Sherman M4A4 tanks advancing along a Norman back road shows the difficulty of operating in the closed-in terrain of the bocage. Tanks were often not able to see beyond the next hedgerow or clump of trees, making it ideal country for anti-tank and infantry ambushes.

British Camouflage & Markings

Officially, British tanks in Northwest Europe were simply to be painted overall olive drab, which replaced the earlier overall matt dark-earth paint scheme. No disruptive camouflage pattern was specified for tanks, although other AFVs and soft-skin vehicles were frequently partially overpainted with matt black, applied either in a rounded pattern (which was dubbed 'Mickey Mouse ear') or in more irregular bands.

Some Sherman Fireflies sported elaborate camouflage, including a false muzzle brake, made of painted papier mâché, fitted halfway up the barrel. Beyond that, the underside of the barrel was to be painted white, divided from the olive drab upper side by a wavy, disruptive dividing line. In practice, the false muzzle brake was rarely used and only the white paint was applied.

Allied white stars (see left) were ordered to be applied on the sides, rear and (circled) on the top of all vehicles. Soft-skin vehicles usually had the full array of stars left in place, but many tank crews felt that these were dangerously conspicuous and, in practice, the side and rear stars were frequently painted out, leaving only the circled upper star, which was painted on the engine deck or turret top. However, this increased the risk of mistaken identity and 2nd Household Cavalry Regiment and the Inns of Court Regiment even painted additional stars on the front of their armoured cars and scout cars following casualties suffered from friendly fire when returning from reconnaissance.

All formations up to brigade level were identified by a formation sign, usually a badge on a coloured background, 216mm (8.5in) wide and 241mm (9.5in) high. This was generally painted on the front and rear of all vehicles, most commonly on the left, although there was considerable variation, with the signs sometimes being applied on either side or even centrally. All vehicles also carried a similarly sized arm-of-service patch, often alongside the formation sign. These were colour coded:

HQ	*Black*
RASC	*Red over green, divided diagonally, top right to bottom left*
Signals	*White over blue, divided horizontally*
RE	*Light blue*
REME	*Blue/yellow/red, divided horizontally*
RAOC	*Blue/red/blue, divided vertically*
Royal Artillery	*Red over blue, divided horizontally*
Reconnaissance Regts	*Green over blue, divided horizontally*
Armoured Division's senior brigade	*Red*
Armoured Division's junior brigade	*Green*

AFVs within each armoured regiment were identified by the following tactical signs, which were usually painted on each side of the turret (or on the hull sides for vehicles without turrets):

HQ – Diamond
'A' Squadron – Triangle
'B' Squadron – Square
'C' Squadron – Circle
'D' Squadron – Vertical Rectangle

The colours of these signs were determined by the seniority of the regiment within its armoured brigade:

Senior Regiment	*Red*
Second	*Yellow*
Third	*Blue*
Fourth	*Green*

Aftermath – Propaganda

The Germans were determined to wring the maximum propaganda value from Villers-Bocage. Wittmann was awarded the Oak Leaves and Swords to his Knight's Cross, and embellished versions of his exploits appeared in a host of publications, including the official SS newspaper *Das Schwarze Korps* and the German forces' *Signal* magazine.

Goebbels' Propaganda Ministry was not to be outdone and so it swiftly dispatched camera teams to Villers-Bocage to film the jumble of wrecked British vehicles and equipment for newsreels to be shown in cinemas throughout the Reich.

From the British point of view it was clearly going to be far more difficult to put a 'positive spin' on the battle – indeed, recriminations flew thick and fast. Montgomery and Dempsey were initially restrained in their comments, but the operation undoubtedly marked the 'beginning of the end' for Bucknall, Erskine and Hinde, although they were not removed from their commands until August 1944 after their uninspired performances during Operations 'Goodwood' and 'Bluecoat'. (Dempsey was far less reticent in a post-war interview, remarking that: '… 7th Armoured was living on its reputation and the whole handling of that battle was a disgrace.')

FEARS AND RECRIMINATIONS

The impact of the battle was soon felt throughout the chain of command and beyond – Dempsey noted in a 21st Army Group report that: '… at the present time our armour is fighting under a considerable handicap'. However, the greatest source of the panic that began to filter out to Britain was XXX Corps HQ, undoubtedly still in shock in the aftermath of Villers-Bocage. On 16 June, a 7th Armoured Division report concluded that: '… recent operations have revealed that the Tiger and Panther tanks now form a high proportion of the equipment of German Armoured Regiments'.

By 24 June, Montgomery's Chief of Staff felt that the situation was serious enough to warn him that: 'If the sentiments expressed therein [XXX Corps' report] get down to the troops, they may have a very great effect upon their fighting. If we are not careful there will be a danger of our troops developing a

Tiger and Panther complex – when every tank becomes one of these types.

'P.J. Grigg [Sir James Grigg, Secretary of State for War] rang me up last night and said he thought there might be trouble in the Guards Armoured Division as regards the inadequacy of our tanks compared with the Germans. Naturally the reports are not being circulated.'

On 25 June, Montgomery wrote to Grigg as follows:

My Dear Secretary of State,

It has come to my notice that reports are circulating about the value of British equipment, tanks etc. compared to the Germans.

We cannot have anything of that sort at this time. We have got a good lodgement area, we have built up our strength and tomorrow we leap on the enemy. Anything that undermines confidence and morale must be stamped on ruthlessly. I have issued the enclosed letter.

Yours ever,
B.L. Montgomery

An extract of the open letter intended for public consumption to which Montgomery referred read: '… we have had no difficulty in dealing with German armour, once we had grasped the problem. In this connection British armour has played a notable part.

'We have nothing to fear from the Panther or Tiger tanks; they are unreliable mechanically, and the Panther is very vulnerable from the flanks. Our 17-pdr gun will go right through them. Provided our tactics are good, we can defeat them without difficulty.'

While Montgomery had to do something to counter the exaggerated and alarmist reports of

German forces in Normandy fielding swarms of virtually invulnerable Panthers and Tigers, he was being 'economical with the truth'. The 17-pdr would indeed 'go right through' a Tiger I or Panther with a flank or rear shot, but it needed APDS ammunition, which was rarely available until the latter stages of the Normandy campaign, to reliably defeat a Panther's frontal armour at normal combat ranges. Equally significant was his failure to mention the relatively small numbers of Sherman Fireflies deployed in Normandy, which left the vast majority of British tanks in theatre armed with 75mm (2.9in) guns, which were hopelessly inadequate to counter the heavier German AFVs. At the same time, Montgomery also wrote to Alan Brooke, the CIGS, to inform him that:

'I have had to stamp very heavily on reports that began to be circulated about the inadequate quality of our tanks as compared with the Germans. In cases where adverse comment is made on British equipment such reports are likely to cause a lowering of morale and a lack of confidence among the troops. It will generally be found that when the equipment at our disposal is used properly and the tactics are good, we have no difficulty in defeating the Germans.'

Lieutenant Bill Cotton: Citation for the award of the Military Cross

British propaganda had relatively little material to work with and tended to concentrate on relatively low-key 'personal gallantry' stories. Lieutenant Bill Cotton was swiftly awarded the Military Cross (MC) and promoted to captain for his part in repelling the German attacks on the afternoon of 13 June. The citation read:

'From 10th to 14th June the determination shown by this officer to hunt out and destroy enemy tanks has been remarkable. The following instance is given: Early in the morning on 13th June, the Regiment had advanced through the town of Villers-Bocage, and its leading elements were on the 213 feature east of the town. Enemy tanks counter-attacked and cut off the leading squadron and Regimental Headquarters. Capt. (then Lt.) Cotton pushed round the south flank of the town shooting up some MET [Mechanised Transport] on the way, and then, cutting back into the town, sited his troop so as to shoot across the main street. Making his reconnaissance on foot, he directed some anti-tank guns to protect his right flank and rear.

One Mk IV followed by three Mark VI then attacked down the street, and the Mk IV was knocked out. Capt. Cotton dismounted and peered round the corner, to find the leading Mk VI a yard away from him, with the other two close behind. Instantly appreciating that if he could block their rear he would have them trapped, he had an anti-tank gun manhandled to shoot across the main street behind the rear Mk VI.

While Capt. Cotton organised and controlled his tanks, the anti-tank guns and infantry with PIATs endeavoured to knock out the enemy tanks, the latter attempted to shoot down one of the buildings to escape. He personally attempted to stalk the rear tank from behind with a tank of petrol, intending to set fire to it. At intervals each in turn made an attempt to escape, and by the end of the day all four tanks were knocked out. The action was fought at ranges of 30 yards, and reconnaissance done round corners within touching distance of the enemy tanks.

The brilliant and determined handling of his troop prevented, for the whole day, the re-capture of the town, which was the junction point of the Panzer Division and enabled the Fence Bocage [sic] to be controlled. This feature remained as a threat to the 2nd Panzer Division and the rear of the Lehr Division for a further 24 hours.'

(Approved by Lieutenant-General G. Bucknall, 12 July 1944)

Chapter 5

Aftermath:
June–August 1944

Immediately after Operation 'Perch', the badly battered 7th Armoured Division was pulled out of the line, going into reserve near Caumont. Its infantry had taken the worst casualties during the fighting of 13 and 14 June – 1st Rifle Brigade (1st RB) lost 83 men, 1/5th Queen's Royal Regiment (QRR) 42, and 1/7th QRR 128. Although the division remained in reserve for the rest of June, a steady trickle of losses (mainly from artillery and mortar fire) brought its total infantry casualties for the month to 1000.

While losses in armoured regiments had been less serious, they still proved to be too much for the limited pool of replacement tank crews. This forced the amalgamation of 3rd and 4th County of London Yeomanry (CLY), which became 3rd/4th CLY on 31 July 1944. The new regiment served with 4th Armoured Brigade for the remainder of the war, its place in 22nd Armoured Brigade being taken by 5th Inniskilling Dragoon Guards.

OPPOSITE: A British Sherman tank drives along a road in Caen. Next to the commander's hatch is mounted a heavy 12.7mm (0.5in) Browning machine gun.

Caen to the Seine, June–August 1944

Montgomery had hoped to take Caen on D-Day, but it was not entirely cleared until 18 July, largely due to the exceptionally skilful defence by I SS Panzer Corps. Even after the capture of Caen, Hitler's insistence on holding ground at all costs prevented a rapid Allied breakout from the beachhead but committed elite Panzer formations to inevitable defeat in a prolonged battle of attrition

The erosion of 7th Armoured Division's strength during June was such that it was excluded from Operation 'Epsom' (26 June–1 July) – the next attempt to take Caen. In late June it was withdrawn to the area around Jerusalem to rest and refit, a lengthy process that kept it out of action until mid-July. During this period, Operations 'Epsom', 'Charnwood' and 'Jupiter' painfully edged the Allied lines forward and took the northern half of Caen, but all failed to achieve

the elusive breakthrough on Second Army's front. The delayed offensive, Operation 'Epsom', began on 26 June. Lieutenant-General Richard O'Connor's VIII Corps was assigned the primary objective of capturing the high ground south of

The Sherman Crab flail tank was a modified M4 Sherman equipped with a mine-clearing flail, which consisted of a rotating drum fitted with weighted chains that beat the ground to detonate mines. The Crab was designed to be used for beach clearing and against fixed defences.

Bretteville-sur-Laize, and cutting the Caen–Falaise road. A crushing preliminary bombardment by 736 guns plus naval gunfire support and air attacks was expected to allow VII Corps to break rapidly through badly battered German defences, but bad weather grounded much of the anticipated air support and the Germans showed their usual resilience in defence. Nonetheless, despite inflicting heavy losses on the attacking forces (Allied casualties exceeded 4000 men), I SS Panzer Corps was steadily worn down.

OPERATION 'GOODWOOD'

Operation 'Goodwood' was intended to make maximum use of Second Army's impressive armoured strength to break the deadlock around Caen. Three armoured divisions – 7th, 11th and Guards – were to cross the River Orne and enlarge the bridgehead on the far bank, destroying as much of the German armour as possible in the process before spearheading an advance on Falaise. The terrain was far from ideal, with deployment being badly restricted by the few Orne bridges capable of taking tanks.

The division moved up from Jerusalem to positions north and northwest of Caen on 17 July, crossing the Orne the following day. Shortly afterwards 5th Royal Tank Regiment (5 RTR) encountered German armour at Cuvervilles, losing six tanks, while 11th Armoured

Division lost over 10 tanks. On 19 July, 5 RTR engaged Tigers and Panthers at Bourguébus. Despite heavy shelling and congested roads, it took the town the next day and at the same time 4th CLY reached the Caen–Falaise road near Bras. The weather then broke and torrential rain turned the ground to virtually impassable mud, forcing 7th Armoured to concentrate near Demouville, where it remained for eight days, under constant artillery fire.

Although Operation 'Goodwood' ground to a halt in the mud in front of the defences of Bourguébus Ridge, it had pinned down the vast bulk of the Panzers on Second Army's front, allowing US forces to achieve an overwhelming armoured superiority in preparation for their own offensive.

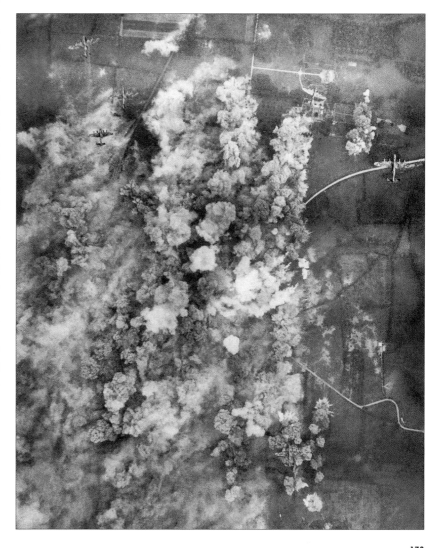

On 30 June, a force of 266 RAF Lancasters and Halifaxes dropped 1117 tonnes (1100 tons) of bombs on Villers-Bocage, virtually flattening the centre of the town. The raid was ordered to prevent 2nd and 9th Panzer Divisions using routes through the town for a counter-attack against the junction of the British and US sectors of the front.

OPERATION 'BLUECOAT'

The objectives of Operation 'Bluecoat' were to secure the key road junction at Vire and the high ground of Mont Pinçon in support of Operation 'Cobra', the US breakout from the western sector of the Normandy beachhead. On the morning of 1 August, in thick mist, 7th Armoured Division advanced towards Aunay-sur-Odon, but became entangled with the traffic of 50th Division, which was also using the same roads. A network of fortified villages imposed constant delays and two days later the division was still 8km (5 miles) short of Aunay-sur-Odon, although 11th Armoured Division was making good progress towards Vire. During the afternoon of 3 August the German 326th Division counter-attacked, inflicting heavy casualties on both the QRR's infantry and 5 RTR, which lost most of 'A' and 'B' Squadrons. On the

same day, 1/6th QRR suffered 150 casualties, 1/7th QRR 35 casualties and the Norfolk Yeomanry lost three guns, with 35 casualties.

On 4 August, 8th Hussars relieved 5 RTR, but progress was still slow, due to minefields protected by anti-tank guns, but 11th Hussars finally linked up with 50th Division's 69th Brigade south of Villers-Bocage. The main armoured thrust was then redirected to La Poste, a few kilometres to the west. The plan was to move south and then outflank Aunay, which fell to 50th Division the next day.

The assault on Mont Pinçon during the night of 6–7 August by 1/7th QRR and 43rd Wessex Division, supported by 13th/18th Hussars, was successful, despite strong defences that included over 40 88mm (3.5in) and 75mm (2.9in) guns. A counter-attack the following morning was beaten off with the support of the Royal Horse Artillery (RHA), which fired 600 rounds per gun in a 12-hour period.

By the evening of 9 August, the ridge from Aunay, via Mont Pinçon, to La Vallée was in British hands. At this point, it was decided to leave the Inniskilling Dragoon Guards and 3rd and 5th RHA to support 43rd Division, while the remainder of 7th Armoured Division pulled back to Aunay. The division had suffered a further 523 casualties, in

The wreckage of Michael Wittmann's Tiger near the village of Gaumesnil. On 8 August, Wittmann led the 101st Battalion's 3rd Company in a pre-emptive attack against a mass of Allied armour near the village of Cintheaux, to the west of the Caen–Falaise road (RN 158). Wittmann and his entire crew were killed when a shot from a Firefly of the 1st Northamptonshire Yeomanry penetrated the Tiger's side armour, detonating the ammunition. The force of the explosion blew off the turret, which landed upside down several metres behind the hull.

addition to the 1000 incurred since the end of 'Goodwood', leaving many units well below strength. Rifle companies of 1/6th QRR, each nominally with 127 men, could field only 8, 15, 40 and 55. Reinforcements soon arrived from 59th Infantry Division, which was being broken up, but, in common with many other infantry units, 1/6th QRR remained well under strength.

Normandy: the Breakout Plan

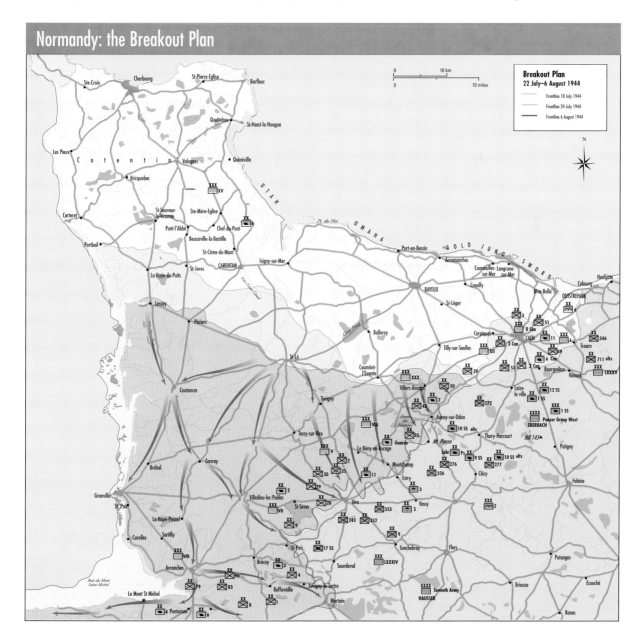

Breakout Plan
22 July–6 August 1944
Frontline 18 July 1944
Frontline 24 July 1944
Frontline 6 August 1944

22 JULY–6 AUGUST 1944

The continuous attacks by British and Canadian forces around Caen had sucked in German reinforcements intended for the western sector of the front. By 25 July, there were only 190 German AFVs facing the First US Army compared to 610 opposing Montgomery's 21st Army Group. On 25 July, US forces launched their breakout, Operation 'Cobra', after a preliminary bombardment by 1500 heavy bombers. Despite this, it took two days to penetrate the German defences, but once the breakthrough had been achieved, there was little left to oppose Patton's VIII Corps – by the evening of 30 July, its leading units had liberated Avranches.

Breakout to the Seine

On 15 August, while the Falaise Pocket was still being closed, 7th Armoured Division joined First Canadian Army, for a 120km (75-mile) advance to the Seine. With the German front collapsing, 7th Armoured Division was on the move again, sweeping through the countryside to Picardy.

The division moved off on 17 August, with 11th Hussars in the lead, supported by the Queen's Brigade and 8th Hussars. The *Luftwaffe* was still active at night, but on the 18th the River Vie was crossed near Livarot, with the town being captured on the 20th.

The bridge over the Vie was strengthened to allow 22nd Armoured Brigade to cross that

Canadian armour advances across open country during Operation 'Totalize'. The force appears to be equipped with at least one Churchill Crocodile Flamethrower tank, an M10 tank destroyer and a number of Stuart light tanks.

afternoon and advance towards the River Touques, where a bridge was found intact.

The town of Lisieux was strongly held, but eventually surrendered on the morning of 23 August, after an attack by 1/5th QRR and the Inniskilling Dragoon Guards supported by 51st Highland Division. Meanwhile 1/7th QRR had skirted the town to reach the River Orbiquet. The next day, 11th Hussars made their way through the town, followed by 22nd Armoured Brigade and moved up to the line of the River Risle. On reaching the river, it was found that the bridges had been

Allied Advance through Northern France

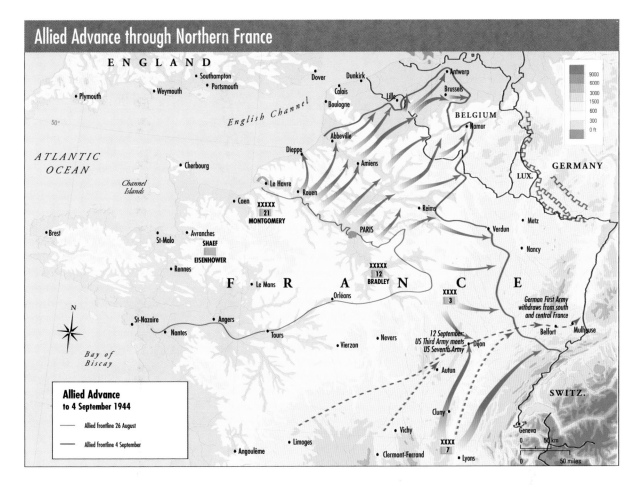

**Allied Advance
to 4 September 1944**

—— Allied frontline 26 August

—— Allied frontline 4 September

destroyed, but after a search, the Inniskillings found an intact bridge near Montfort, and the Scout Troop captured another in good repair at Pont Authou, which allowed the rest of 22nd Armoured Brigade to cross the Risle that afternoon. For the next three days the division advanced through rolling wooded country between the Risle and the Seine, taking many prisoners in a series of actions against small pockets of German troops. By the evening of 28 August, it had reached the Seine by the Forêt de Brotonne.

Of the original 14 German infantry and 10 Panzer divisions that had been deployed in Normandy, only about 65,000 men and 115 AFVs escaped across the Seine. This sudden German collapse allowed the rapid liberation of almost all French territory – by 25 August, General Leclerc's Free French *2e Division Blindée* and 4th US Infantry Division had captured Paris, and by the 30th Patton's Third Army had taken Sedan and Verdun.

For a few heady weeks after the victory at Falaise, it seemed that the war was almost over – Paris was liberated on 25 August and 21st Army Group raced towards the Belgian frontier, taking Amiens on 31 August where General Eberbach was captured, together with the HQ of the re-forming Seventh Army. On 3 September, the Guards Armoured Division liberated Brussels, but this marked the point at which German resistance began to harden, as the Allied armies outran their supplies. Despite the spectacular Allied advances of late August and early September, it would not 'all be over by Christmas'.

However, 7th Armoured Division's war was far from over, as it took part in the rapid Allied advance through Belgium and the Netherlands, liberating Ghent on 5 September, before advancing to the River Maas, where the front stabilized until the new year. In January 1945, the division was committed to Operation 'Blackcock' to clear the Roer Triangle, followed by the assault crossing of the Rhine (Operation 'Plunder'), finally taking Hamburg and Kiel in the last days of the war.

Allied Air Power

On 24 June 1944, the newly commissioned Lieutenant John Eisenhower was in Normandy with his father, General Eisenhower, observing the aftermath of the invasion. He recalled that: 'The roads we traversed were dusty and crowded. Vehicles moved slowly, bumper to bumper. Fresh out of West Point, with all its courses in conventional procedures, I was offended at this jamming up of traffic. It wasn't according to the book. Leaning over Dad's shoulder, I remarked, "You'd never get away with this if you didn't have air supremacy." I received an impatient snort: "If I didn't have air supremacy, I wouldn't be here."'

As preparations for Operation 'Overlord' intensified, Allied tactical air power became increasingly important. Two great tactical air forces supported the ground forces in the invasion – the RAF's Second Tactical Air Force and the USAAF's Ninth Air Force. Both were under the overall command of Air Chief Marshal Sir Trafford Leigh-Mallory. In addition, Eisenhower and his ground commanders could call upon strategic aviation as required, in the form of RAF Bomber Command and the USAAF's Eighth Air Force.

In June 1944, the Ninth Air Force consisted of several commands, including IX Fighter Command, which in turn spawned two Tactical Air Commands (TACs), the IX TAC with three fighter wings, and the XIX TAC with two. Each of these fighter wings contained at least three and usually four fighter groups, with each group typically comprising three fighter squadrons (each with an average strength of 16 aircraft). Of the two, IX TAC was the 'heavy', with 11 fighter groups, while XIX TAC had seven. From late 1943 to early 1944, IX Fighter Command had served primarily as a

This Hawker Typhoon Mk IB carries a typical warload of eight rocket projectiles alongside its four 20mm (0.8in) cannon.

Hawker Typhoon

The Typhoon was designed as a medium-altitude interceptor and was intended to be the successor to the Hawker Hurricane. However, its performance in this role was disappointing and it was developed into a very potent fighter-bomber that equipped 26 operational squadrons by mid-1944. The aircraft proved itself to be the most effective RAF tactical strike aircraft, both on interdiction raids against communications and transport targets deep in Northwestern Europe prior to the invasion, and in direct support of the Allied ground forces after D-Day. In the Normandy campaign, highly effective close air support was provided by an airborne reserve of Typhoons operating in what became known as a 'Cab Rank', called in to attack targets identified by RAF liaison teams attached to frontline Army units.

■ CREW

■ SPECIFICATIONS

Type: Single-seat fighter-bomber
Length: 9.73m (31ft 11in)
Wingspan: 12.67m (41ft 7in)
Height: 4.66m (15ft 3.5in)
Wing Area: 25.92m^2 (279sq ft)
Weight (Empty): 3993kg (8800lb)

Weight (Maximum Take-Off): 6341kg (13,980lb)
Powerplant: 1 x 1626kW (2180hp) Napier Sabre II H-24
Maximum Speed: 652km/h (405mph)
Range: 820km (510 miles)

Service Ceiling: 10,365m (34,000ft)
Armament: 4 x 20mm (0.79in) Hispano cannon, plus 2 x 454kg (1000lb) bombs or 8 x 27.2kg (60lb) rockets.

training HQ, under the command of Brigadier-General Elwood Quesada. Eventually, Quesada assumed command of IX TAC, and Brigadier-General Otto P. 'Opie' Weyland took over XIX TAC. The Ninth and its subordinate commands were not directly linked to specific US Army formations, although there was a general understanding that IX TAC would support the First Army, and XIX TAC would support Patton's Third Army once the Third became operational in France. This arrangement was eventually formalized on 1 August 1944, when both Patton's Third Army and Bradley's 12th Army Group became operational.

TACTICAL AIR SUPPORT

The RAF's 2nd Tactical Air Force (2nd TAF) had grown out of proposals in mid-1943 to create a 'Composite Group' to support the invasion of

Europe. It had replaced the moribund and unsatisfactory Army Co-operation Command. In January 1944, Air Marshal Sir Arthur Coningham took command of 2nd TAF, and two months later he assumed additional duties as commander of the Advanced Allied Expeditionary Air Force (AAEAF). Ironically, at this critical point, two serious command problems arose. Relationships among the RAF commanders, particularly Coningham, Leigh-Mallory and Arthur Tedder (Deputy Supreme Commander of Operation 'Overlord') were strained at best. Much more serious was the breakdown in trust between the RAF's senior officers and Montgomery in his dual role as commander of both Allied ground forces and 21st Army Group.

During the Desert War, Montgomery had been an enthusiastic supporter of the air campaign in the

Mediterranean and accepted wholeheartedly Coningham's thoughts on air support. Ironically, Montgomery and the RAF now came to disagree over the relationship between the air and the land commanders. Montgomery paid lip service to the concept of independent air action, but he increasingly came to regard his equals in the RAF as merely advisers. For their part, Coningham and Tedder nursed grudges dating back to what they saw as the Eighth Army's plodding advance after second El Alamein, which they attributed to Montgomery's excessive caution in the pursuit of Rommel's retreating forces.

For the airmen, the critical question in 'Overlord' was how rapidly Montgomery's 21st Army Group would seize sufficient airfields so that Allied tactical air forces could operate from Normandy rather than from bases in England. In fact, this issue turned out to be far less important than had been

Flying Officer, Royal Air Force

This RAF pilot wears the standard RAF battle dress under a US-made flak vest. The flak vests were designed to limit wounds from shrapnel and anti-aircraft shell splinters. He wears a British C Type flying helmet and British 1943-pattern flying boots. The shafts of the boots were designed to be easily removed so that the pilot would have a pair of comfortable walking shoes, which could be worn on the ground if shot down over enemy territory. He wears standard-issue leather gloves and carries his parachute in his right hand.

originally thought. Forward operating bases were quickly established in Normandy, sometimes only a few thousand metres behind the frontlines. In practice, Montgomery's planned rate of advance from the beachhead (which the airmen considered too slow) turned out to be overoptimistic. RAF resentment at this, coupled with Montgomery's fury over Leigh-Mallory's de facto veto of Operation 'Wild Oats' by refusing to fly 1st Airborne Division into Normandy, soured Army–RAF relations for the rest of the war.

The RAF's 2nd TAF consisted of four groups: Nos. 2, 83, 84 and 85. Of these, only the first three were really available for the air–land battle in Normandy; 85 Group was under the temporary operational control of No. 11 Group for home defence duties. No. 2 Group consisted of four wings of Boston, Mitchell and Mosquito bombers. No. 83 Group, apart from a reconnaissance wing and some light aircraft used for artillery spotting, comprised one Mustang wing, four Spitfire wings, and four Typhoon wings. No. 84 Group, again apart from reconnaissance and artillery observation aircraft, consisted of one Mustang wing, five Spitfire wings, and three Typhoon wings. As the campaign progressed, 2nd TAF's subordinate units tended to work with specific formations within 21st Army Group – No. 83 Group usually supported the Second Army, while No. 84 Group supported the First Canadian Army.

Another important relationship was that which evolved between the Ninth Air Force's IX TAC and 2nd TAF's 83 Group. IX TAC's Elwood Quesada and 83 Group's commander, Harry Broadhurst, worked well together. This became especially important once the Allied beachheads were firmly established and control of tactical aircraft passed from shipboard teams to two land-based control centres – one for IX TAC in the American sector and one operated by 83 Group in the British sector. Coningham later praised the 'excellent teamwork' between the two control centres, which would be refined even further in the weeks ahead.

In all, the tactical air forces had 2434 fighters and fighter-bombers, together with approximately 700 light and medium bombers available for operations over Normandy. Their aircraft were heavily committed to the pre-D-Day bombing campaign,

Typhoon Rocket Attack Technique

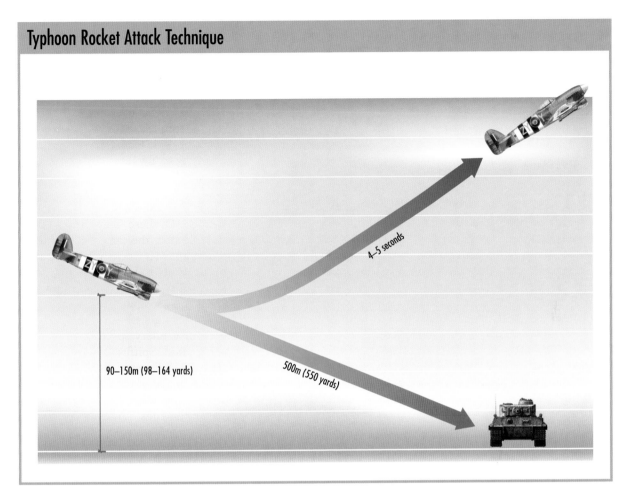

4–5 seconds

90–150m (98–164 yards)

500m (550 yards)

which really got under way on D-60, when Allied air forces began interdiction attacks against rail centres. These attacks increased in ferocity and tempo up to the eve of the invasion itself and were supplemented by strategic bomber raids against the same targets. The bridge campaign, intended to isolate the battlefield by cutting Seine bridges below Paris and Loire bridges below Orléans, began on D-46.

Fighter-bombers proved more effective in attacks against bridges than medium or heavy bombers, largely because their agility enabled them to make precision attacks in a way that the larger bombers, limited to horizontal bombing runs, could not. The fighter-bombers also had the speed, firepower and manoeuvrability to evade or fight the increasingly overstretched *Luftwaffe* interceptors. Though ground fire and (rarely) fighters did claim some fighter-bombers, the loss rate was considerably less than it would have been with conventional bombers.

By D-21, Allied air forces were attacking German airfields within striking distance of Normandy and these operations continued up to D-Day itself.

AIR POWER IN SUPPORT OF ARMOUR

With the elimination of the *Luftwaffe* as a serious threat to the invasion, Allied air forces gave increased priority to close air support and interdiction operations. Close air support always posed the greatest challenges in terms of target identification and the need to minimize the risks of friendly fire. One of the most effective solutions to these problems had been pioneered by British forces in Italy who fielded 'contact cars' – AFVs serving as mobile air–ground control posts with armoured units. In Normandy, Broadhurst's No. 83 Group operated contact cars with leading British armoured forces, so that tactical air units were constantly updated on the precise location of friendly and enemy forces. These contact cars worked closely with tactical reconnaissance aircraft, reducing the time necessary to set up impromptu air strikes. The USAAF (primarily IX TAC) developed a very similar system under the designation 'armored column cover'.

FALAISE – A CASE STUDY OF AIR POWER VERSUS ARMOUR

The Falaise Pocket, formed by the collapse of the German forces in Normandy, was a near ideal target for Allied air power – the remnants of Fifth Panzer Army and Seventh Army, totalling possibly 80,000 men, were steadily compressed into a salient that by 16 August ran from Falaise, through Flers and on to Argentan. This was truly a 'target-rich environment' and air attacks certainly inflicted heavy losses, but subsequent investigations indicated that they were relatively ineffective against all but light AFVs.

After the action, the operational research sections (ORS) of 21st Army Group searched the area between the Falaise Pocket and the German crossing points at the Seine to compile a detailed analysis of the effectiveness of the air attacks on the pocket. A total of 667 German AFVs were recorded, although it is likely that many were missed in the maze of narrow lanes, orchards, farmyards and woods that covered much of the area. Of the total found, 385 vehicles, or just under 60 per cent, were examined to determine the reason for their abandonment or destruction. The size of the sample was sufficient to give a reasonable assessment of the effectiveness of the weapons used by the Allied air forces: 385 AFVs represented roughly the complement of two full-strength Panzer divisions. By that stage of the campaign, many German divisions were down to nearly 60 per cent of their establishment of armoured vehicles, so the 385 came closer to the complement of three Panzer divisions rather than two.

The causes of the abandonment of the 385 AFVs, with the causes of their destruction where applicable, are listed in Table 1 (see above right).

The two largest categories in the table are significant: those armoured vehicles destroyed by their crews to avoid capture, and those that were abandoned undamaged. Together these amounted to 269 vehicles, or 71 per cent of the total. The great majority of those vehicles had been immobilized due to lack of fuel.

Table 1: Abandoned AFVs

NUMBER	PERCENTAGE	CAUSE
14	3.6	Rockets
4	1.1	Bombs
21	5.3	Aircraft machine-gun or cannon fire
148	38.5	Destroyed by crew
121	31.5	Abandoned undamaged
77	20	Other causes
385		

Table 2: Abandoned Trucks and Cars

NUMBER	PERCENTAGE	CAUSE
6	0.4	Rockets
52	3.8	Bombs
377	27.85	Aircraft machine-gun or cannon fire
27	2.05	Destroyed by crew
502	37.05	Abandoned undamaged
397	29	Other causes
1361		

The 21 vehicles knocked out by machine-gun or cannon fire were thinly armoured reconnaissance vehicles and halftracks; 87 of these were examined. As expected, no heavier AFVs were recorded as having been knocked out by aircraft machine-gun or cannon fire. As Anthony Williams and Emmanuel Gustin noted in their study *Flying Guns: World War II*: 'The ineffectiveness of air attack against tanks should have caused no surprise because the weapons available to the fighter-bombers were not suitable for destroying them.

'Put simply, the heavy machine guns and 20mm cannon were capable of hitting the tanks easily enough, but insufficiently powerful to damage them, except occasionally by chance.

'The RPs and bombs used were certainly capable of destroying the tanks but were too inaccurate to hit them, except occasionally by chance.'

The survey results certainly vindicate this – the RP-3 rocket accounted for only 14 AFVs, 3.6 per cent, of those examined.

During the 21st Army Group ORS count, a total of 6656 German trucks and cars were found abandoned. Of these 1361 were examined and categorized as listed in Table 2 (see above).

Rules and Notes for Typhoon Rocket Attacks

The following notes were devised by Lieutenant-Colonel Raymond Lallemont, a Belgian Air Force officer, when he was commanding 609 Squadron RAF.

1. *The rocket apparatus was heavy and disturbed the aerodynamics of the aircraft. At first we fighter pilots did not like this 'Christmas tree', so we chose to get rid of the rockets first.*

2. *We soon learned that there was nothing more disagreeable than firing all our rockets at 'soft-skinned' vehicles, with the result that we then had to attack tanks with 20mm shells (useless!).*

3. *So I introduced a rule that we went down first only to find the tanks, so that we could use our rockets on those. On most occasions in such a low approach we could also see other tanks. Pilots as a rule would then attack individually.*

4. *We had to make up our minds swiftly which tank to choose – usually the one trying to get away to cover under the trees!*

5. *Those standing still may already have been destroyed – one should never believe one was the first to deliver an attack!*

6. *When these rules had been observed, the target was selected and was preferably the easiest in sight – i.e. away from obstructions, in the open, on a concrete road, etc.*

7. *Attack low down and as close as possible. It was necessary, however, to avoid shrapnel from the exploding rockets, and when low, the idea was to start climbing as soon as the rockets left the rails – and like Hell!*

8. *Many direct hits in such attacks were the result of a last check on aim, the time taken for this bringing you closer to the target. This was the main problem with inexperienced young pilots – fear of the ground or flak prevented them making this last check on their aim.*

9. *As for the flak, this was always very accurate and usually opened up at point blank range. I firmly believe that I avoided many hits by flying at treetop height, and always attempted to achieve an element of surprise. This made a straight approach difficult, for a camouflaged tank was not easy to spot at such low level and one could only make small last-minute corrections if the rockets were to slide well on their rails (sudden sharp movements would cause the runners to 'bind' on the rails due to the gravity drag). This was one of the reasons why the Typhoon was so good, because it was so manoeuvrable and so steady.*

10. *We usually delivered vertical attacks when a lot of aircraft were attacking a concentration of tanks, or tanks forming up for a counter-attack, and it was necessary for all to attack in a limited time. In such cases we often released our rockets in such a way as to saturate the area and after this type of attack the pilots never made any personal claims. Such was the case at Montain and Ponteaubault, where considerable success was achieved. (In a vertical dive an experienced pilot could achieve great accuracy with rockets.)*

Whilst air-launched weapons were relatively ineffective in direct attacks on AFVs, they were supremely effective in crippling Panzer formations by destroying their unarmoured supply and support vehicles. The survey indicated that cannon and machine-gun fire was the most effective means of attacking these targets.

The figures shown are, however, most likely to be an underestimate, as it was common for fighter-bombers to concentrate on the vehicles at each

Typhoon Operations in Normandy – Logistics

'The more I see of war, the more I realize how much it all depends on administration and transportation … It takes little skill or imagination to see where you would like your forces to be and when; it takes much knowledge and hard work to know where you can place your forces and whether you can maintain them there.' Field Marshal 1st Earl Wavell.

It required a substantial logistics organization to support a single six-squadron wing of Typhoons in Normandy. The figures below give the planning requirement for a single day's operations in terms of fuel, oil and munitions.

The planning assumptions:
- *Each squadron held 18 aircraft, of which 12 were available for operations*
- *The daily sortie rate was 24 sorties per squadron*
- *Aircraft fuel capacity was 682 litres (150 Imp gal), 77% used per sortie*
- *Oil requirement: 3.3% by volume of the quantity of petrol*
- *Ammunition expenditure was 25% per sortie*
- *Bomb expenditure was 100% on 75% of sorties*
- *Bomb types used: 40% 454kg (1000lb) bombs, 60% 227kg (500lb) bombs*
- *Drop tanks not carried*

The logistics requirement:
- *6 squadrons flying 24 sorties per squadron per day equalled 144 sorties per day*
- *Fuel requirement: 144 sorties at 527 litres (116 gallons) of petrol per sortie equalled 75,938 litres (16,704 gallons). Allowing an extra 5% for wastage, the total daily fuel requirement was 79,725 litres (17,537 gallons), which equalled 77.2 tonnes (76 tons) packed*
- *Oil requirement: 3.3% by volume of the quantity of petrol, 2632 litres (579 gallons), which equalled 2.34 tonnes (2.3 tons) packed*

Ammunition requirement:
- *Typhoon capacity was 576 rounds of 20mm (0.79in) ammunition. So 144 sorties per day at 25% expenditure per sortie totalled 20,736 rounds, which equalled 9.45 tonnes (9.3 tons)*
- *Bomb requirement: 144 sorties per day of which 75% were bombing sorties*
  454kg (1000lb) bombs: 86 – 38.6 tonnes (38 tons)
  227kg (500lb) bombs: 130 – 28.45 tonnes (28 tons)
  Total bomb requirement: 67.05 tonnes (66 tons)

- *Total daily fuel, oil and munitions requirement: 156.04 tonnes (153.6 tons)*

- *For Typhoons flying the same sortie rate in the rocket-firing role on the same planning assumptions, the daily requirement was 137.17 tonnes (135 tons)*

end of a convoy, boxing in those in the middle. Vehicles stuck in traffic jams would have been listed under the 'abandoned undamaged' or 'destroyed by crew' headings.

The 78th Fighter Group was one of the earliest operators of the P-47 in the European theatre. This P-47D includes the invasion stripes painted on all Allied aircraft involved in the Normandy campaign.

Republic P-47D-25 Thunderbolt

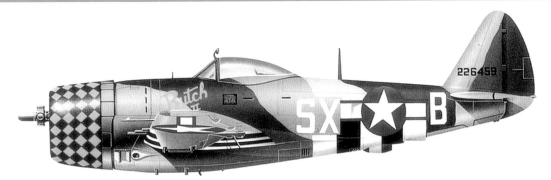

The big P-47 had been designed as a high-altitude interceptor, but its good range led to it being used primarily as an escort fighter in Europe throughout 1943. While it was quite effective in protecting the Eighth Air Force's Fortresses and Liberators on deep penetration raids, it could not match the range or performance of the Mustang, which began to supersede it as an escort fighter from late 1943. Most P-47s were then deployed as fighter-bombers carrying various combinations of 227kg (500lb) bombs and M8 114mm (4.5in) rockets. Between D-Day and the end of the war, Thunderbolt units claimed the destruction of 86,000 railway wagons, 9000 locomotives, 6000 AFVs and 68,000 trucks – and while these claims are greatly exaggerated, significant losses were certainly inflicted.

■ CREW

■ SPECIFICATIONS

Type: Single-seat fighter-bomber
Length: 11m (36ft 1in)
Wingspan: 12.42m (40ft 9in)
Height: 4.32m (14ft 2in)
Wing Area: 27.87m^2 (300sq ft)
Weight (Empty): 4536kg (10,000lb)

Weight (Maximum Take-Off): 8808kg (19,400lb)
Powerplant: 1 x 1492kW (2000hp) Pratt & Whitney R-2800-59 radial
Maximum Speed: 689km/h (428mph)
Range: 765km (475 miles)

Service Ceiling: 12,800m (42,000ft)
Armament: 8 x 12.7mm (0.5in) Browning machine guns, plus up to 1134kg (2500lb) of bombs or 6 x 114mm (4.5in) M8 rockets.

Bibliography

BOOKS

Agte, Patrick. *Michael Wittmann and the Waffen SS Tiger Commanders of the Leibstandarte in WWII.* Stackpole Books, 2006.

Bellamy, Bill. *Troop Leader: A Tank Commander's Story.* Sutton Publishing, 2007.

Bull, Stephen. *World War II Street-Fighting Tactics.* Osprey Publishing, 2008.

Delaforce, Patrick. *Churchill's Desert Rats, from Normandy to the Baltic with the 7th Armoured Division.* Sutton Publishing, 2003.

Fletcher, David & Harley, Richard C. *Cromwell Cruiser Tank 1942–50.* Osprey Publishing Ltd., 2006.

Fletcher, David. *The Great Tank Scandal: British Armour in the Second World War, Part 1.* HMSO Books, 1989.

Fletcher, David. *The Great Tank Scandal: British Armour in the Second World War, Part 2.* HMSO Books, 1993.

Hart, Stephen A. *Sherman Firefly vs Tiger, Normandy 1944.* Osprey Publishing, 2007.

Hastings, Max. *Overlord: D-Day and the Battle for Normandy, 1944.* Pan Books, 2010.

Hughes-Wilson, Colonel John. *Military Intelligence Blunders.* Robinson Publishing Ltd, 1999.

Keegan, John. *Six Armies in Normandy from D-Day to the Liberation of Paris.* Pimlico, 2004.

Kershaw, Robert. *Tank Men: The Human Story of Tanks at War.* Hodder & Stoughton, 2009.

Man, John. *The Penguin Atlas of D-Day and the Normandy Campaign.* Viking, 1994.

Porter, David. *Western Allied Tanks, 1939–45.* Amber Books Ltd., 2009.

Rottman, Gordon L. *World War II Infantry Anti-Tank Tactics.* Osprey Publishing, 2005.

Steinhardt, Dr Frederick P. *Panzer Lehr Division 1944–45.* Helion & Company Limited, 2010.

Taylor, Daniel. *Villers-Bocage through the Lens of the German War Photographer.* Battle of Britain International Limited, 2009.

Taylor, Daniel. 'Villers-Bocage Revisited', *After the Battle Magazine*, Number 132, 2006.

Zaloga, Steven J. *D-Day Fortifications in Normandy.* Osprey Publishing, 2010.

WEBSITES

Achtung Panzer! – *www.achtungpanzer.com/introduction-to-achtung-panzer*
A great introduction to the development of German AFVs from 1917 to 1945.

Battalion Level Organisations in World War II – *www.bayonetstrength.150m.com/General/Overview.htm*
An excellent source of information on a wide variety of Allied and Axis battalion level ORBATs.

Battlefield Normandy – *www.strijdbewijs.nl/uitbraak/bocage2eng.htm*
Text and photos of the battle of Villers-Bocage.

Brief History of the British 7th Armoured Division 'The Desert Rats' – *www.btinternet.com/~ian.a.paterson/history.htm*
A good introduction to all aspects of the wartime history of 7th Armoured Division.

British Equipment of the Second World War
– *www.wwiiequipment.com*
A useful source of information on British and US-supplied Lend-Lease equipment.

Engines of the Wehrmacht in WWII
– *www.german.o5m6.de/*
Oliver Missing's excellent website covers a steadily growing range of German trucks and AFVs.

The Life and Times of Germany's Tiger Tanks: Pz.Kpfw. Tiger Ausf. E
– *www.fprado.com/armorsite/tiger1.htm*
An excellent website on the Tiger I.

The Tiger I Information Center
– *www.alanhamby.com/tiger.html*
Another highly detailed website on all aspects of the Tiger I.

Guide to Symbols

UNITS

XXXX	ARMY
XXX	CORPS
XX	DIVISION
X	BRIGADE
I I I	REGIMENT
I I	BATTALION
I	COMPANY
●●●	PLATOON
●●	SECTION
●	SQUAD/TEAM

TYPE

CAVALRY	
INFANTRY	
MOTORIZED INFANTRY	
RECONNAISSANCE	
ARMOUR/TANK	
SELF-PROPELLED ARTILLERY	
ARTILLERY	
ANTI-TANK	
AIR DEFENCE	
MORTAR	

MEDICAL	
ENGINEERS	
SIGNALS	
TRANSPORT	
SUPPLY	
MAINTENANCE	

Index

Page numbers in *italics* refer to illustrations.

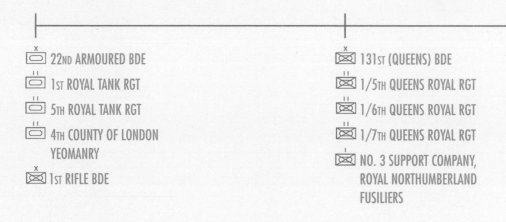

☐ 22ND ARMOURED BDE
☐ 1ST ROYAL TANK RGT
☐ 5TH ROYAL TANK RGT
☐ 4TH COUNTY OF LONDON
   YEOMANRY
☒ 1ST RIFLE BDE

☒ 131ST (QUEENS) BDE
☒ 1/5TH QUEENS ROYAL RGT
☒ 1/6TH QUEENS ROYAL RGT
☒ 1/7TH QUEENS ROYAL RGT
☒ NO. 3 SUPPORT COMPANY,
   ROYAL NORTHUMBERLAND
   FUSILIERS

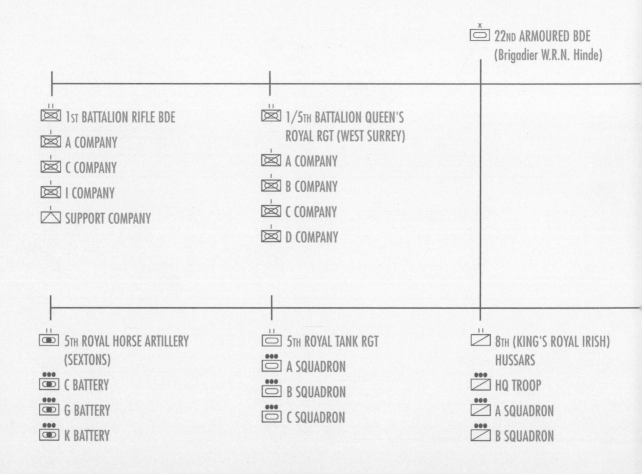

☐ 22ND ARMOURED BDE
(Brigadier W.R.N. Hinde)

☒ 1ST BATTALION RIFLE BDE
☒ A COMPANY
☒ C COMPANY
☒ I COMPANY
◿ SUPPORT COMPANY

☒ 1/5TH BATTALION QUEEN'S
   ROYAL RGT (WEST SURREY)
☒ A COMPANY
☒ B COMPANY
☒ C COMPANY
☒ D COMPANY

☐ 5TH ROYAL HORSE ARTILLERY
   (SEXTONS)
☐ C BATTERY
☐ G BATTERY
☐ K BATTERY

☐ 5TH ROYAL TANK RGT
☐ A SQUADRON
☐ B SQUADRON
☐ C SQUADRON

◿ 8TH (KING'S ROYAL IRISH)
   HUSSARS
◿ HQ TROOP
◿ A SQUADRON
◿ B SQUADRON